Would I

LIE

to You?

Would I
LIE
to You?

The Amazing Power of Being Honest in a World That Lies

JUDI KETTELER

CITADEL PRESS
Kensington Publishing Corp.
www.kensingtonbooks.com

CITADEL PRESS BOOKS are published by

Kensington Publishing Corp.
119 West 40th Street
New York, NY 10018

All Kensington titles, imprints, and distributed lines are available at special quantity discounts for bulk purchases for sales promotions, premiums, fund-raising, educational, or institutional use.

Special book excerpts or customized printings can also be created to fit specific needs. For details, write or phone the office of the Kensington sales manager: Kensington Publishing Corp., 119 West 40th Street, New York, NY 10018, attn: Sales Department; phone 1-800-221-2647.

CITADEL PRESS and the Citadel logo are Reg. U.S. Pat. & TM Off.

ISBN-13: 978-0-8065-4008-5
ISBN-10: 0-8065-4008-7

First Citadel hardcover printing: January 2020

10 9 8 7 6 5 4 3 2 1

Printed in the United States of America

Library of Congress Control Number: 2019944530

Electronic edition:
ISBN-13: 978-0-8065-4010-8 (e-book)
ISBN-10: 0-8065-4010-9 (e-book)

*To my parents, who set me up for success,
and to my children, who are a daily reminder not to squander it.*

Contents

Would I
LIE
to You?

Paying Attention to Honesty

Everybody wants the truth, but nobody wants to be honest.
—Anonymous

IN THE SAME MONTH I STARTED WORKING on this book, I had to stop wearing my contacts for two weeks in preparation for a Lasik surgery consult. My distance eyesight is very impaired, and I can't see much without contacts. For working, driving, watching television, and general functioning in life, I simply switched to wearing my glasses. Running, however, was another story. The sweat made it impossible to keep my glasses on, and the way they bounced slightly with each foot strike made me feel dizzy. Without them, I could glean a few feet in front of me, see cars, and distinguish if a traffic signal was red or green. I decided it would have to do for running. I stuck to main roads with sidewalks, versus the winding, wooded roads I often ran, and muddled through.

Still, running without being able to see properly was slightly terrifying. It's not an exaggeration to say that I couldn't see shit, because I actually stepped on dog poop at least once. The world around me was so fuzzy. I couldn't see the faces of people I passed on the sidewalk. I couldn't see houses or trees or flowers. I had run these routes hundreds of times before, so it wasn't that I was missing anything exciting. I just felt unmoored that I couldn't see the familiar. Obviously, the experience made me think about people who have vision impairments that can't simply be corrected with glasses or contacts, and how much I took my own sight for granted. It was a lesson in gratitude, to be sure.

Each time, when I got back from running, I would head inside my house, wipe the sweat off my face, and put my glasses right back on. It was such a startling sensory experience—to go from trying to navigate a world of hazy shapes to a world where everything was suddenly in focus. What felt even more startling was knowing that I had the power to decide if I would walk through the world only seeing the vague outline of the landscape, or if I would grab the lens I needed to truly be able to see.

I'm telling you this because I realized something else during those strange few contact-free weeks that coincided with me settling down to start writing this book: Focusing on honesty is a bit like putting on glasses after you've been out running familiar paths, but only being able to partially see them. Suddenly, you can see so much more, and absorb texture and nuance that was unavailable before. I could get by running without my glasses, but only *just enough*. I couldn't participate in the world in a very real way. For that, I needed corrective lenses. Paying attention to honesty is a kind of corrective lens that helps you engage with the world in a much fuller, much richer way. When you start to notice the choices you're making to lie or truthtell, life comes into focus in a new way. And if you commit to paying attention—I mean *really* paying attention—you will inevitably bump up against the great irony of human beings' relationship with honesty, which is this: We want honesty from others so badly, yet we struggle so mightily with our own honesty. In fact, "want" is probably an understatement. We don't merely want honesty. We *demand* it. We protest when we don't get it. We divorce spouses who withhold it. We send people to jail who fail to exercise it. We give our children stern looks when they don't practice it. Yet when it comes to our own behavior, well, um . . . can we change the topic?

On one hand, we know that dishonesty is a big societal problem, often leaving victims in its wake. We can quickly tick off the multiple public arenas where dishonesty lives: Politicians routinely lie; tabloid-like fakery gets passed off as news and spread around on social media; corporations break the rules and their top executives willingly deceive the public. Dishonesty affects us in very personal ways, too. For example, if our significant others, friends, family members, or children lie to us, we may feel betrayed, embarrassed—shattered even. When we find out someone we love has done something suspect or hurtful and tried to cover it up, it's not uncommon to say, "It's not so much that I'm mad that you [fill in the blank], it's that I'm mad because you *lied* about it."

It's very clear that lying is hurtful, harmful, and often criminal.

On the other hand, when it comes to the decisions we make about our own honesty, the waters quickly muddy. I want to be honest because I want to be a good person. I don't want to be hurtful, harmful, or criminally negligent. Yet I still struggle to be forthcoming with people in all different kinds of situations. The struggle may be that I don't want to hurt someone else's feelings. Or I might be struggling against my own self-interest. Other times, it's a struggle to simply be honest with *myself*. I've talked to enough people about their experiences with honesty to realize this phenomenon: Demanding honesty in others, yet so painfully grappling with our own truth and lies, is part of the human experience. I think it's accurate to label it *cognitive dissonance*, a term that simply means that you are holding two or more contradictory values or beliefs in your brain. This is why you can hold up honesty as utterly non-negotiable in one hand, while letting it slip quietly away in the other.

Like . . . when your kid asks you about Santa Claus.

Or when revealing a secret will do more harm than good to people you love.

Or when you wake up thinking about having sex with someone who isn't your spouse.

Or when you avoid giving difficult feedback to someone who is vulnerable.

Or when you live a life of one-second happy-face snapshots on Facebook and cry yourself to sleep a few nights a week.

Would I Lie to You? The Amazing Power of Being Honest in a World That Lies is about those moments and many more: the big and the small; the obvious and the not-so-obvious; the shameful and the redemptive; and, in the words of the serenity prayer, the wisdom to know the difference. Given our current political climate and the speed with which lies are spread, honesty is one of the hottest topics of the day. We're bombarded with dishonesty, and have learned that we can't take the information we see at face value, but instead, must constantly be evaluating at every moment for lies and fakery. It's incredibly stressful and demoralizing. And yet, it does no good to lament all of this dishonesty in the world if we don't also look within ourselves to identify our own patterns around lying. Our own choices. Our own fakery. Our own falsities. That's what I'm daring myself to do by writing this book, and it's what I hope you dare yourself to do, too. Though it can be difficult, this self-exploration is also incredibly empowering. Not only can this work help you strengthen your relationships and improve your communication skills, it can also help you feel less like a victim of a dishonest world and more like a fully engaged human being. If you are feeling powerless in today's climate of lies, focusing on your own is a way to find your power again.

THE QUESTIONS I AIM TO INVESTIGATE in this book include the following: Is there any such thing as a truly honest life? What does it feel like to work toward living a more honest life—at home, at work, and in the world at large? When is deception better than honesty? Why do we lie out of habit? Why is the conversation around honesty so fraught and full of truisms that aren't, in fact, true? How did we evolve to value honesty so highly, yet act so deceitfully ourselves? What are the consequences of repeatedly lying to ourselves? And finally, what is the power of honesty in a world so full of lies? My intent is not to cast myself as the person who has all the answers about honesty. Rather, I am simply the person who is willing to ask the uncomfortable questions, and this book is my attempt to write my way through them, with as much transparency as possible. It is only *my* attempt, though, and I don't claim universality in my experience. You can read my story and apply whatever labels and qualifiers seem relevant (she was raised Catholic;

she's white and middle class; she grew up sheltered; she's too liberal, too American, too Midwestern, or too provincial; she and her husband have an unconventional marriage; she hasn't faced real adversity), and you wouldn't be wrong. I've obsessed about who this book is for and who it applies to. Like, does it apply to refugees, who are barely holding on to life? Does it apply to people who have to lie or parse truth for a living, like clandestine intelligence officers? Is it equally relevant for people on the political left and people on the political right? For college students and retired people? For husbands and wives? (Or for husbands and husbands, or wives and wives?) What about for people who have faced terrible trauma and the truth feels too dangerous? Or constitutionally shy people or people with social anxiety disorder? From the beginning, I worried about who I might offend, who I might anger, who I might leave out, or who I might lose credibility with. I wondered if I should avoid mentioning politics, and mute my feelings about charged social issues, lest I get cast as some kind of pundit. I wondered what was my story and what was someone else's story, and how I would know the difference. I wondered if I was being self-indulgent and naïve in writing from a place of privilege, compared to the way the majority of people in the world live. I wondered if I was being irresponsible by focusing mostly on the psychology of honesty and people's inner lives, versus addressing the complicated social and economic factors that shape our behavior. But through all the ruminating and hand-wringing, I kept writing. And the best I can say now is that the book is for anyone who decides they want it to be for them. I wrote it for mostly selfish reasons—to help me figure out this business of honesty so I could be a better person. I encourage anyone who reads it to be equally selfish in your motives and how you apply it to your life, because I believe those around us can greatly benefit from our selfish desire to keep try-ing. There is a Buddhist saying I particularly like: *You heal the world by healing yourself.* What starts inside has a ripple effect. If my ripple reaches you, that is something. But how far yours may reach is the real power. The inner work of honesty can never take the place of values like civic responsibility, fighting for justice via legislation and reform, and holding people accountable—but I would suggest these things are rather hollow without a personal understanding of honesty.

How This Book Is Structured

We've all developed patterns related to honesty, guilt, and shame. Because of all the conflicting messages we get about honesty, we often can't see our way through these patterns unless we take the time to trace them and commit to some deep excavating. That's what I set out to do in the first chapter of this book, beginning with my earliest memory of lying. I trace my relationship with honesty through my teen years, young adulthood, and early motherhood, until I arrive at the point in time a few years ago when I had an honesty crisis. The next two chapters define the key terms and explain some underlying theories about deception. Chapters 4 through 9 explore honesty in the various areas of life, including social honesty, workplace honesty, honesty in friendship, honesty in marriage, honesty in family and raising kids, and self-honesty. In each of these areas, I reflect on my own struggles and share stories from my life, as well as stories others have shared with me. I address some common conundrums and dilemmas, and then offer suggestions gleaned from different places, including philosophy, behavioral economics, etiquette, organizational psychology, evolutionary biology, spirituality, and personal development.

In essence, the structure of the book follows my own internal process of working my way through honesty in the different areas of my life, which I envision as three concentric circles. The outermost circle is social honesty, the middle one is intimate honesty, and the innermost one is self-honesty. The outermost circle of social honesty is basically honesty "outside of the house" and outside of your closest relationships. How honest do you need to be with the person working in the cubicle next to yours? With the supplier on the phone? In the stands of your kid's football game? At that once-a-year-lunch with people you have less and less in common with every passing year? It's not that these social connections are all low quality. In fact, our social connections are extremely important, and we couldn't have developed as a society without being able to trust each other. Our honesty struggles in this outer tier of relationships have to do with conflicting motivations involving group cooperation, social empathy, fear of being judged, and how we identify as individuals or members of a group. In general, they are the day-to-day concerns of life—if not short-term, then very much the present tense. They can matter a lot in the moment, but they often don't have the same weight as the concerns we face in our more intimate relationships.

Intimate honesty—the next circle—is concerned with honesty in our more intimate, loving relationships. I don't simply mean romantically intimate, though honesty in marriage/long-term relationships is definitely an area we'll explore. I also mean in friendship, within families, and in the space of raising children. Some of the conflicting motivations that intensify the honesty struggles in this area include fear of disappointing or hurting loved ones, personal vulnerability, and high expectations of relationships. The honesty questions we face in our intimate relationships tend to focus more on the long term. The dilemmas can feel every bit as "of the moment" as the social dilemmas, but they are more future focused. What you say to your spouse or your child doesn't just affect that day or week, it may affect your whole (or their whole) future.

Finally, the last circle is less a circle than a dense core. "Self-honesty" is about the questions we wrestle with in our most interior lives. This includes the beliefs we have about ourselves, how we shape our personal history, and the stories we tell—both publicly and privately. Shame, specifically avoiding shame, is one of the biggest motivations for lying to ourselves. Self-honesty is a concern in all tenses—past, present, and future. There is an element of self-honesty that's more past focused than the other circles of honesty, because trying to be more honest with yourself almost always involves going *back* in time to be able to correct the story.

The circles are interrelated, of course. They are separate, too. I'll walk through a lot of research in the book, but here is one piece to chew on as we get started: A 2018 paper found that if you engage in one type of dishonest behavior in a specific area of life, you are more likely to engage in some other type of dishonest behavior in that area. For example, if you lie to your boss at work, you are more likely to also pad an expense report at work. But here is what else the researchers found: People seem to behave differently in *different areas* of their lives, and how you behave in one "life domain" doesn't necessarily predict how you will behave in another. In other words, the way you are at the office may not reflect the way you are at home, or the choices you make about honesty with your kids may be different from the choices you make about honesty with your spouse. I think the findings on behaving differently in different life domains are sound (the data is from more than a thousand people across five different countries, and the research was conducted by smart researchers with deep expertise in human behavior), but I don't know if I buy it or not. Some days it sounds right and other days it doesn't. Some days, I am certain we are who we are all the time, and other days, I think we are experts at compartmentalizing. I don't have the answer—I don't think there *is* a definitive answer—but working through it piece by piece, life domain by life domain, circle by circle, seems like the only way forward, no matter what you discover.

I'VE ALWAYS KNOWN HONESTY WAS A STRANGE BEAST. What I understand now, and why I'm writing this book now, is that I finally understand that the complexities that surround honesty aren't just my personal struggle, but a human struggle—yet one that most humans don't want to talk about.

When I tell people my stories, either casually during a conversation or in the pieces I write, over and over again, they say, "Judi, you are so honest. You talk about these things I think, too, but don't want to say." I understand that we all have different degrees of privacy, and that my tolerance for sharing intimate details of my life is far higher than someone else's may be. It's not vanity or the desire to hear myself talk that compels me to tell you about my flirtation with infidelity, or how

I screamed and cursed at my dead brother, or any of the other stories I will tell you in this book. It's that one of my gifts is the ability to see and hear the pain that's lodged within people because of their shame and fear. I can't prescribe them medication or teach them meditation or give them the right cognitive behavioral tools to ease their pain. I can only tell my stories from an honest place, and hope these stories land like a hand that reaches out to them. *This is life. This is how it goes. This is who we are. Let's just be honest about it. Life will be better if we are.*

CHAPTER 1

My Strange Relationship with Honesty

Tell all the truth but tell it slant.
—Emily Dickinson

WHEN I WAS SEVEN YEARS OLD, I had my "first confession"—a terrifying experience involving confessing my sins to an old man behind a screen. I said all my lines, just like a play, and then . . . well, I made stuff up. After all, why would I tell this priest the sins I was least proud of, like wanting terrible things to befall the girls who teased me, or touching myself "down there"? (This was listed as an official sin in our second-grade religion book.) Surely, it was not his business. I didn't like the way lying made me feel, since it was Wrong, with a capital "W," but the thought of being honest in that moment didn't feel right, either. So I made a calculated choice about what to share, and made up generic sins to confess, like fighting with my brother or taking an extra cookie when my mom wasn't looking. These things may have had some kernel of truth—I'm sure I had snuck a cookie at some point in my young life or screeched at my brother—but they were not real in my mind.

The priest gave me a penance of saying ten "Hail Marys." (If you're not familiar with how Catholic confession works, the priest who hears your confession essentially gives you an "assignment"— your penance—to say some prayers. And if you say them—either there in the confessional, or later, on your own time—you are absolved.) That reciting words could make sins go away was absurd, but I *really* wanted to be absolved. In fact, I hoped they would absolve me from both the sins I didn't utter, and the lie I told to create the "stand-in" sins. As I left the confessional to rejoin my parents in the church pew, I vowed to myself to say the prayers before bed that night, and planted a fake smile on my face. This was my first time receiving a sacrament, after all. I was supposed to be joyous. But I didn't feel happy. I definitely didn't feel pure. Instead, I felt confused, guilty, ashamed, angry, and worried over the state of my soul.

I look at my own kids, who are now ten and eight, and I think, *Yep, what a weird little time of life they're in.* Remember that space of childhood, between being a kindergartner and a tween? You're starting to have concrete thoughts and memories that hang together. You know that the world is the world and that magic *probably* isn't real. A lot is expected of you, but you're not actually in charge of anything. Grown-ups are supposedly the sole reliable source for what is right and what is wrong, but so many of the things they say contradict each other. And yet, when you point out a contradiction to them—like how they tell you that you should always respect what your school principal says, yet you heard them calling him bad names the other night when they thought you were asleep—they only get angry. So you stop pointing it out, and eventually take on the contradictions as reality. It is such a flawed system that even the most well-adjusted among us gets miserably tangled up in knots around this idea of honesty. We wind up utterly confused and spending a lot of time feeling terrible about various honesty transgressions.

Or at least that was my experience.

In my case, I assign a chunk of the blame to Catholicism—at least the particular breed of it I was surrounded by in ultra-conservative Northern Kentucky—and its predilection toward making children feel as guilty and shitty as possible. Who tells a seven-year-old their soul is in trouble unless they reveal their most embarrassing thoughts and actions to a cranky old man they are told has a direct connection to God? Still, I know that even without the nuns and their stern looks or the priests and their shady screens in back rooms of churches, I would have been a shy, sensitive kid who broke toward earnestness. I can thank my DNA, my upbringing, and whatever X factor creates our personality for that. I'm the youngest of seven kids. In order: Herb Paul Claire Laura Nancy Tony (say it in one breath for the full effect) . . . and four years after my mother must have thought she was done . . . there I was. My oldest brothers were so much older than me (my oldest brother got married when I was seven), and mostly absent from the day-to-day of my childhood. But my sisters doted on me exactly as you would expect. I admit, being the youngest of seven kids is a pretty good gig, if you can get it. But it also meant that I had a lot of people to charm, please, and prove myself to. As the youngest and the one people seemed to have their eyes on, I couldn't just do things halfway. I sought to do them to their fullest, whether it was perfecting my gymnastics routines or being a good Catholic.

My parents, Bert and Mary Ketteler, were raised during the Great Depression, which I heard about *constantly*. They came of age in the years around World War II, and told us kids stories of rationing, air raid sirens, and Harry Truman. Though they came from intact and loving homes, each lost their father at a young age. My mom was seventeen when her father died, and my dad was only eleven when his passed away. Both deaths were sudden (from diseases now easily controlled with medications), and both were financially devastating for their families. My parents' childhoods were imprinted with a national crisis of poverty, a second world war, and unexpected death. This led them to imbue in me a sense of humbleness and civic responsibility. Watching their behavior, I had clear and explicit examples about gratitude, decency, and doing the right thing. After all, they were the tail end of the Greatest Generation and they held those values closely.

There was something else, though. Something that I didn't piece together then, but see looking back now. Though they each had emotionally and economically challenging childhoods, as young adults, they also each had tiny strokes of luck. My dad was drafted in 1952 into the Army's Fourth Infantry Division. But instead of getting sent to Korea, the Fourth Infantry was sent to Frankfurt, Germany, as part of NATO. My dad would talk about how the other GIs spent their leaves getting drunk. Not Bert Ketteler. He sent most of his money home to his mother, and used the rest to sightsee. He visited old castles and World War II battle sites, and took hundreds of photographs—which he learned to develop himself. He was so grateful to not be at the Korean front where his contemporaries were dying, that there was no way he was going to waste the opportunity. He used to talk about how he assumed when he was drafted that he was going to die in Korea. He got a deferment to finish college (he paid his way through the local Catholic college by working constantly), but then, it was time to go. He didn't want to go, but he had to do what he was told. When my dad didn't get sent to battle, it was a piece of luck that seemed to instill in him the idea that you should find the good in whatever opportunity you're offered.

On my mom's side, the piece of luck was an inheritance from her grandmother, who died in 1956. That this chunk of money—about $5,000—was somehow left to her seemed almost impossible. Her mother advised her to buy a winter coat and save the rest for her future. That money was how she and my dad were able to afford to build a house in the suburb of Ft. Wright, Kentucky, in the same year they got married. Like the majority of other houses in the neighborhood, it was a modest ranch with an unfinished basement to accommodate the large family that all new homeowners in the highly Catholic neighborhood were sure to have. My parents were told by both their government and their church to go forth and multiply, and the miracle that they were here at all, not dead on a battlefield and not forced to live in a cramped apartment in the poorer neighborhood to the south, made them only too happy to comply.

I say all of this because I think perhaps one of my earliest lessons was that good things happened to good people who were earnest and worked hard. There are so many fundamental flaws in this thinking. It's a dangerous and simplistic narrative, with the potential to be used for the worst kinds of violence and justification of inequality. I realized this as an adult, when I came to understand the unfairness of the world.

But as a kid, you see what you see. You Etch-A-Sketch your reality, and it takes years of education and experiences (and writing books about honesty) to fully clear away some of those early sketches that keep your thinking too small. I know now that being born in the time and place I was born and getting these two particular people as parents was my own tremendous stroke of good fortune. I did nothing in particular to deserve it, but I have tried to make the most of every opportunity it's provided. I've thanked the universe in every way I know how, but I am open to more suggestions because the luck of the whole thing can't be overstated. I will say, though, between their strong moral presence and my six older siblings, I had *a lot* to live up to. When I failed to be as true as I should be, I felt the collective weight of all of them. This is no one's fault (well, it's a *little* bit the Catholic Church's fault), and I wouldn't change anything about my upbringing. It just set the course for a rocky relationship with things like honesty and shame.

FIRST CONFESSION IS MY EARLIEST MEMORY of having a run-in with honesty, but these incidents outline my childhood like fence posts.

There was fourth grade, when a girl named Christy stole my Easter stickers. I held in my tears long enough to make it to my house a few blocks away, but I broke into pieces the minute I got back home. The stickers were right there in her room, the day after she swore she didn't take them. How could she lie to my face? Then I remembered how I lied, not just to the priest behind the screen or to the nuns who asked me if I loved Jesus (how could I love some guy I never even met?), but also to my cousin who was rich and got way more than me for Christmas. Whenever we compared our Christmas morning loot, I always went second, because I needed to know how many gifts to invent to feel equal to her. I also lied to the girl in my gymnastics class who was always bragging about her parents, telling her that my sister might be going to the Olympics. Many nights while falling asleep, I thought about these and other instances with deep shame.

Then there was sixth grade, when a girl who was made fun of

mercilessly for her stringy hair asked me if I had heard kids making fun of her. She was so sad, so defeated, in how she asked. How could I tell her yes? Instead, I deflected and talked about how stupid the popular kids were. I recall trying to make some kind of joke about it. Maybe a better friend would have been straight with her, and said, without judgment or teasing, "Wash your hair more." I don't know. It wasn't in me to do that, and I felt both guilty about it and, also, good about it. I never wanted to hurt anyone's feelings, having been on the receiving end of a lot of taunts about being weird, especially after I had a spell in fifth grade when I cried in school almost every day for the first half of the school year. I could never articulate the reasons why I was crying; I just knew that once I felt the tears coming, I couldn't stop them, and it was deeply shaming. I knew that other kids thought I was strange. My solution had been to withdraw into myself and create my own little fantasy world, where it was safe and I was in charge. I would never have told anyone this. Speaking the truth of it was frightening.

Then there was high school. I went to Notre Dame Academy, an all-girls Catholic school. I did not enjoy it. I do believe these kinds of spaces have the potential to be progressive and empowering. That was not the case in Northern Kentucky, which I would describe as neither progressive nor empowering. Notre Dame certainly produced many brilliant young women (I'm fairly certain the no-nonsense nun who taught physics was a genius), and every one of us was encouraged to live up to our academic potential. The problem wasn't the education. It was the culture. You could say all high school culture is messed up and damaging. But there is something especially toxic about a group of girls behaving badly and thinking they have God on their side. There was a righteousness and sense of entitlement that wafted through every corridor of Notre Dame. It was always the most popular girls who loved to talk about things like peace and following Jesus's example in religion class. But right after, in the hallway, that was all forgotten, because it was time to solidify their status and place in the pecking order. Shy and awkward girls like me were the easiest target. My hair bow was stupid and obviously procured cheaply, my shoes were wrong, I didn't have a boyfriend, I was a weirdo who was too quiet. The list changed every day. I hated them. They were a bunch of liars and hypocrites, and I could never reconcile their behavior with the idea that we were supposed to be loving our neighbor as ourselves. And yet, another emotion always waited for me like prey on the other end of that hate and confusion: *guilt*. Big scary deadly guilt. It was Christy and the stickers all over again. Was *I* truly loving my neighbor as myself? Wasn't I dishonest, too? Didn't I make things up to avoid embarrassment, like telling the girls on my gymnastics team that I had a boyfriend? Didn't I hide my true feelings about things? Pretend to laugh when I didn't get the joke? Go to church every week and say the words that I either didn't comprehend or didn't believe? These were all small things. But together, they had the weight of shame—one of the heaviest substances in the universe—so they piled on. And as they did, my frustration with others' dishonesty and my guilt over my own became locked even tighter in a vicious tug-of-war.

I could see the path of what I should do. *Be true. Be honest. Stop being afraid.* And yet, so often, I couldn't do it. I couldn't speak the words, own up to my failings, or even be real with myself. It felt like there was so much more to hide than there was to show. That I wasn't being the best and truest I could was a constant source of discontentment, so I poured my desire for perfection into gymnastics. I couldn't master social situations, but I could master the balance beam. I loved how gymnastics felt in my body and how I could use it to express myself. I didn't have the drive of a champion—already too independent, I never could have submitted to some egomaniac coach's will—but I was motivated and dedicated, and trained extremely hard. I loved the transparency of gymnastics, too. If you fell or screwed up, you got a low score; if you hit your routine and stuck your landing, you got a high score. It was all there for people to see, and while bad performances were disappointing, they were at least honest.

My family was of modest means, but we weren't poor. However, I heard the stories about how we had been close-to-poor in the decades before me. My mom was a traditional homemaker and my dad was the breadwinner. For forty years, he worked as a scientist—a pharmacologist—in a lab at a small pharmaceutical company in Cincinnati (those were the days when there were still small pharmaceutical companies). Because he didn't have a PhD, he didn't advance much—but he loved his job. Toward retirement, he was promoted and made more money than he ever thought he would make, but for most of the sixties, seventies, and eighties, budgets were tight. Even after they loosened, my parents told us we had to work for the things we wanted. I did work, but my siblings would surely tell you how I got far more than they did. They are right: I benefited greatly from my birth order. And yet, being surrounded by wealth at my high school was still a daily reminder that I was out of my league. Catholic education was making its transition from affordable to outrageous in the early 1990s. The school—which is now around $10,000 a year—was already starting to feel elite during my time there, when it was probably half that amount.

I think this is why, around junior year in high school, I developed an interest in social justice. I started listening to Harry Chapin songs and reading activist poetry, from John Lennon to Audre Lorde. Unlike the vast majority of people at my school, my parents were Democrats. I'm not entirely sure how this came to be, because Northern Kentucky was—and still is—such a conservative area. Though the church was a huge influence in their lives, they never went along with the church's conservative political agenda. My dad used to scream things like, "Deregulation doesn't work!" at the television whenever Ronald Reagan was talking. I would have lengthy arguments with my oldest brother, Herb, about liberalism versus conservatism (Herb was, and still is, extremely conservative: Picture *Family Ties* character Alex P. Keaton giving lectures). I loved this sparring (I still do), and it helped me start to crystallize some of my politics. I was still frightfully naïve, though. As a senior, I took a new independent study elective at Notre Dame called Social Concerns. It involved a service project, and I chose to volunteer at a homeless shelter in Covington, Kentucky, which served the large urban community living in poverty just four miles from my middle-class suburb. I talked a good game with my protest poetry, but it was the first time I spent any time in the inner city. The first time I was around groups of African Americans. The first time I understood that poverty and homelessness affected children. I was, of course, merely a kind of "tourist" in this community. Nonetheless, the experience was jarring and profound. I was embarrassed by how little I understood about the world and ashamed at how shielded my upbringing had been. I didn't yet know terms like *white privilege, white fragility*, and *white savior complex*—mostly because they hadn't been coined yet. I knew things weren't equal, but my own role in it was confusing. When I tried to talk to my friends about this, I didn't have the right words. I already felt disconnected from them, so I faked smiles and nodded along at the lunch table when everyone was talking about who was dating whom. I was a mass of internal contradiction, feeling sorry for myself for not belonging socially while simultaneously feeling guilty for not being poor—and then, in the next breath, feeling resentful that we weren't nearly as well off as most of the other families at my high school.

Above all, I wanted to be a good person who made a difference. I no longer connected this with religion—or at least not with Catholicism. While I saw that some cultures did use religion as a positive tool, my view of it by then was too jaded, too connected with shame and guilt. I didn't know the words or theory yet, but I was already starting to develop my feminist beliefs. I didn't like that men were in charge of everything in the church, and throughout history, had made seemingly arbitrary rules that mostly served them. I could have voiced this dissent. But it was easier to stay silent with my opinions, write bad poetry in the solitude of my bedroom, and bide my time until high school was over. That's exactly what I did, opting out of Catholicism (and all organized religion) as soon as I graduated on that glorious evening in May 1992.

Leaving all that behind as I started college definitely helped me shed one layer of the cognitive dissonance about who I was, but I still lacked social confidence. I didn't have a typical college experience, since I lived at home and paid for college myself. I coached a gymnastics team, worked at a fabric store, tutored at the campus writing center, and babysat on the weekends. Working hard helped me see myself as the upstanding, independent person I wanted to be. By then, my honesty tug-of-war was related less to sin and guilt than it was to crystallizing what I believed and who I wanted to be.

WHEN I WAS ABOUT TWENTY, I had two realizations around the same time. The first was that I was a feminist. The second was that I didn't like my body. I had been a gymnast all my childhood. I was strong and flexible, but also curvy. The curves, which had stayed lean throughout my competitive years, began to unfurl when I quit gymnastics right before college. I gained weight, first just a few pounds, but within a year, it was twenty pounds, pushing hard on twenty-five. So I decided to go on a strict diet and exercise *a lot*. I became obsessed with losing weight and developed what I would classify as a moderate eating disorder. I did eat, but I was completely consumed by food, calories, exercise, and weight. I lost the twenty-five pounds I had gained. And then about fifteen more just because. I read the canon of feminist authors, my ire at the patriarchy steadily growing—all the while I tried to ignore my stomach rumbling. I simultaneously starved myself of food and fed myself empowering theory that told me what I was doing was twenty-nine kinds of wrong, and not at all feminist. The contradiction was so intense, so shaming, so fucking confusing that I didn't know what to do. I felt trapped in my own web of lies about who I was.

But that wasn't the only contradiction I was living. I was writing passionate papers about women's liberation, the male gaze, and sexual freedom, yet my sense of how I might go about expressing my own sexuality was still repressed. It's not that anything terrible, like rape or abuse, had happened to me. It's that I was wholly inexperienced. Still painfully shy about the opposite sex, I was sure that I was unattractive and sexually unappealing. I had a series of unrequited crushes, and fixated on the question of whether or not I would ever lose my virginity. I was simultaneously ashamed by these things, and angry with myself that I cared so much about these things. As I read female slave narratives and feminist treatises about how women had been mistreated and disenfranchised throughout history, and fought back in both overt and subversive ways, I would think: *Damn the whole system!* And in the next breath, I would wonder if a boy could *please just kiss me*.

As I edged closer to senior year of college, I started to come out of my shell a little, and even had a few dates with a sweet boy. He liked me, but I wasn't into him. I said yes to going out with him because I didn't want to hurt his feelings. My ultimate solution when I didn't want to have any more dates was to make sure I wasn't home when he called and to never return his calls. I felt horrible about it, but I couldn't bring myself to be honest with him. I knew I handled it completely wrong, and I felt enormous guilt about that—how could I have been so awful? However, I didn't judge myself for not wanting to date him. I wasn't willing to be with someone I didn't connect with just to have a boyfriend. But would I ever find anyone? I wondered the same question nightly as I drifted off to sleep. I tried to push down whatever desire I might feel toward men and focus on creating the future I wanted— which was graduate school. I would get a PhD in English. Somehow a fairy tale would happen, and I'd marry another professor and we'd have this terrific life. As conflicted as I was about all of these areas of my life, I had a sense that I would somehow figure it out. After all, I was Bert and Mary Ketteler's youngest daughter! I was resourceful and clever! Graduate school would make everything clear.

It did. But not in the way I thought.

I GOT ACCEPTED WITH A FULL RIDE and a teaching stipend to the graduate program in English at Miami University of Ohio, which was about an hour away from home. But before I left for graduate school in August, I went to London. I had saved up my money to be able to afford a summer study abroad program that was a partnership between NKU and Kings College in London. When I boarded the flight to London on July 4, 1996, it was my first time flying. Though I was officially a college graduate by this point, my level of inexperience with the world was vast, and slightly shameful. I knew how to work hard, how to study, how to do gymnastics and coach gymnasts, how to sew and cut fabric, how to be the youngest of a big family and make everyone be amused by me, and how to try to be perfect at everything I did. But I didn't know romantic love or have sexual experience. I didn't know cultures different from my own. That summer, living in London on my own—well, not quite on my own, because I was part of a study abroad program and living in dorms—was the first step in my physical independence. I mastered the subway system, learned London's parks (I ran several times a week), and took day trips to places like Bath, Stonehenge, and Brighton. I made a small group of friends and we took a weekend trip to Wales, where I walked the old city wall of Conwy and hung out with the mountain goats. I understood for the first time that America was an infant in the world. The buildings in Europe were like a thousand years old. The history there was startling. I walked and gawked and took it all in. I sat in Bloomsbury Square and wrote a letter in my diary to the writer Virginia Woolf, whose "A Room of One's Own" essay about female independence had made such an impact on me. I told her that I felt so naïve and embarrassed in the ways I struggled to be forthcoming with people, but I believed that big things were ahead for me if I could just fucking speak up. I had graduate school waiting and I had faith that I would figure everything out.

Because the study abroad program overlapped with the start of graduate school, I missed the first three days of the two-week summer class all new graduate students in English with teaching assistantships took to teach them how to teach. By the time I got there, the new crop of master's students had already started to gel, and I felt like the odd one out. I had been determined to talk more in class and be more assertive among my peers, but I found myself sitting and listening silently as my peers spoke with confidence about their ideas about whatever pedagogical theory we were studying that day. The longer I was quiet, the more awkward I felt about talking. I was angry at myself, and would ask myself during my runs: *What the fuck is the matter with you, Judi? Why can't you just talk? Why can't you just speak up? What are you so afraid of?*

I scoffed at my stupid letter to Virginia Woolf. How would I ever do big things if I couldn't open my mouth?

After a few weeks of feeling lonely and cut off, I decided to force myself to be social. It wasn't difficult. My fellow graduate students were generally friendly. Unlike high school, it wasn't cliquish. We were all adults, all smart, all here because we wanted to be here, all interested in engaging with the world in a serious way and talking about books. Something about being on my own, away from the small (and small-minded) suburb where I grew up, freed me at last. I started going out more and joining in the fun. Even flirting. Once I got over the initial nervousness of speaking up and introducing myself, it was surprisingly easy to find my way. I discovered that my social skills were actually quite good. I liked people. I liked conversation. I liked being part of it all—I just needed to do things on my own terms. I developed a crush on another student in the program named Tim, and after talking at a party one night about our mutual addiction to ChapStick, he asked me out. The first time we kissed, every part of me tingled. I was desperate to not be a virgin anymore, and later that week, I happily fell into bed with him. I pretended it was fantastic, but the whole thing was disappointing, as first experiences so often are. I figured there was just something wrong with me. I had smidges of honesty with Tim (he knew I was a virgin and did everything he could to make me comfortable), but mostly, I pretended. As I lost some of my awkwardness, the sex got better. But I still lacked confidence. Looking back, I realize that I couldn't have asked for a better first boyfriend. Tim was kind and funny and respectful. These are all the reasons we're still friends today. Back then, though, I was so gaga over him, I couldn't see straight most of the time. Although I was fiercely independent and quite capable of taking care of myself, I was immature in ways I didn't even know. Mostly, it's that I was negotiating experiences in my early twenties that were usually the territory of sixteen- and seventeen-year-olds, feelings like jealousy, insecurity, and infatuation. I was so in love with him, but so unfamiliar with what to do with that.

Tim and I dated for about a year, and then . . . he broke my heart. Not on purpose or out of cruelty, but because we were young and he recognized that the timing wasn't there. He had wrapped up his MA program (he was a year ahead of me) and was moving back east to a PhD program. He didn't want to commit, and he didn't want anything long-distance. It was excruciating, the way your first heartbreak is. I actually thought something was physically wrong with me, I was so broken about it. I listened daily to The Cure and The Smiths, and thought I might die.

But after a few months, it started to dissipate. I developed solid female friendships with other grad students, and finally had some perspective. I met another guy and dated him for a while. That didn't work out, but it was no big deal. So I dated someone else. Ditto. This repeated itself, and soon I realized that this was how dating and sex worked, and it was all kind of fun. All in all, I had a much more solid sense of myself by my mid-twenties than I did in my early twenties. Those few years of independence had made all the difference, and the decade I had spent being so frightened of boys and having a tortured self-esteem seemed like such a waste of time. My high school insecurities were fading (though, of course, they never actually go away completely). I had come out the other side of my eating disorder (which never reached a dangerous pitch—it was mostly emotional torment). I also finally admitted something to myself that I had been trying to ignore from the moment I got to grad school: I didn't actually like teaching. I loved my graduate work and writing papers and discussing books in seminar classes with my fellow grad students, but I did not like being responsible for teaching others. After I completed my MA, I opted to find a job instead of going on for a PhD. I eventually found a job as a proofreader and copywriter at an agency that designed packages, brochures, and a strange new thing called "web sites." I freelanced for newspapers on the side and started to build up connections. I was a professional. I had friends. I had cats. I ran marathons. I saved money. I traveled a bit. I volunteered at the local women's crisis center.

I always had a sense that I would like being an adult more than being a kid, and once I was an adult, I realized that I was absolutely right! It was far superior. I bloomed later than most, but I bloomed nonetheless. At last, it was confirmation that I wasn't a total weirdo. I had done what I wanted to do for so long: I had figured it out.

THOUGH I HAD COME INTO MY OWN, I was still playing at emotional dishonesty. For one, I routinely faked orgasms because I was too embarrassed that I couldn't figure out how to have one. I also pretended not to feel certain things, because I definitely didn't want to get my heart broken again. When I was about twenty-six, I had a boyfriend tell me that I was the most emotionally guarded girl he had ever dated. I took this as a compliment. It meant that I was doing a good job hiding my struggles, so that I didn't appear too needy. I showed men a curated version of myself: an independent, smart, fun girl who didn't really need anyone. The version of me I kept secret had vastly more needs, was still trying to figure out sex, and sometimes had the disgustingly un-feminist longing to weep openly and just be rescued.

In April 2002, I got laid off for the second time in six months (remember the 2001 recession?). That same week, I started corresponding with a guy on Match.com. His screen name, AngelClare34, caught my eye, because I knew Angel Clare was a character from *Tess of the d'Urbervilles* by Thomas Hardy. I was intrigued, and then slightly horrified as I read his profile. "I don't want to date a woman more than ten pounds overweight," he wrote. "And no dog owners. If a cat, not more than one." It went on in a similar fashion for another paragraph. I pinged or winked, or did whatever you did in 2002, with a lengthy response, most of which I don't remember. I'm pretty sure it started: "So . . . your character is a total jerk, which is fitting, since you seem like a total jerk, too." It definitely ended with me saying that I didn't intend to end up arrested at Stonehenge like Tess. He emailed back: "Well, at least we both like books."

His name was Allen, and reluctantly, I agreed to go out with him. But I was purposely ambivalent about the whole thing. I had been getting ready to sign a contract to buy a house when my layoff had come, so I was deeply disappointed and skeptical about anything ever working out. And then his ridiculous Match post? It felt like there was literally nothing to lose by being exactly who I was. To my surprise, this *eh, whatever* approach somehow let me be more myself than I had ever been. I wasn't concerned with what I should or shouldn't feel, or holding on to any expectations. I said what I thought. I called him out on shit. I never faked orgasms. Instead, I admitted it was an issue for me, and he was only too happy to help me figure it out.

This tell-it-like-it-is version of me was someone I hadn't seen before. I liked her. *A lot.* She was so honest! Allen and I had a steady banter and lightness about us. Nothing was forced and nothing was really expected. It settled me, in the best way possible. That job layoff is also what led me to start working for myself as a freelance writer in 2002. No more feigning company loyalty or pretending to care about contrived company cultures. I was on my own and loving it, setting my own agenda every day and making good money (far more than I ever made working for someone else). I worked my way from writing for the local paper to nabbing bylines in dozens of national publications and working with big companies to help them tell stories.

Allen and I dated solidly for about two years, and then started an on-again, off-again pattern for another two years—mostly because he never wanted to get married and never wanted kids. I knew that I did, but I wasn't in a hurry. It wasn't a problem, and then eventually . . . it was. By early 2006, I was feeling done with the looseness of where we were going. I told him what I wanted and that it was okay if he wasn't able to do it, but that I had to move on. I loved him and hoped he would come around, but I didn't plead with him. I let it be and started thinking again about buying a house. That spring, he decided that he wanted us to be together, and reluctantly agreed that he would do the whole shebang: house, marriage, and kids. At the time, I saw his reluctance as romantic—he would give up his childless bachelorhood for me!

I didn't need him financially, so the first part—getting a house—seemed low risk. I figured we'd just live together and see if it worked out. Buying a house together in the summer of 2006 seemed to go well. So we got married the following year, when Allen was forty and I was thirty-three. I got pregnant immediately, and wound up having two babies in two years—our son, Maxwell (or Maxx, as he likes to spell it, for short), was born in July 2008 and our daughter, Georgia, in September 2010. Allen became a stay-at-home dad within weeks of Maxx's birth. That had been an incentive that sweetened the pot for him. He didn't like his job and it wasn't particularly lucrative (he had never found a true career calling and just took various low-stress, low-paying jobs to get by). I loved being a freelance writer and made enough to support the family. In fact, I took great pride in it. We had a novel division of labor, but it worked well for us. I was happy. Actually, I was smug that other women hadn't figured out how capable men were with children and taking care of the house. When they would complain that their husbands didn't do housework or know what to feed the kids for lunch, I secretly judged them.

My tug-of-war seemed to fall away. Finally, I had arrived at the best version of myself! The feeling of being two different people? Gone. The feeling of having to keep myself guarded? Gone. Pretending? Gone. The guilt and shame surrounding Catholicism? Long gone.

With a thriving writing career and a family to support, I was too busy to obsess about truth.

For a while.

And then, as I edged closer to forty, I found myself becoming obsessed with honesty again—for some of the same reasons as always, but also, for new reasons altogether.

THE FIRST THING THAT HAPPENED is that my brother died. I was working at home one Tuesday in November 2009 when my sister Laura called and said, "I think Paul is dead." Paul, the second oldest in the family (fourteen years older than me), was the one we could never figure out. Looking back, I've made the unofficial postmortem diagnosis of oppositional defiant disorder—which is characterized by having a defiant attitude and being hostile and difficult to get along with. It's also linked with developing an addiction, which he did in his teenage years. He started drinking early, and added pain pills to the mix after a back injury when he was nineteen (he fell off a billboard while working for a sign company). Ultimately, the combination of smoking, drinking, taking pain pills, and generally beating up his body is what killed him at the age of forty-nine. Every step and every phase of Paul's life felt tumultuous. I know he caused my parents a lot of sleepless nights, but I was oblivious to it for a long time because I was so much younger, and a good bit of the drama had already come to pass by the time I was even aware. He moved out when I was about nine. He would go through years of being involved with the family and years of being somewhat estranged (even though he always lived within a few miles of my parents' house). When he died, in a way, I barely knew him. I felt intensely sad, but mostly I felt regret that he had slipped through the cracks. His death had the effect of drawing my siblings and me closer together. Our unit had sustained a blow, and we realized the importance of sticking together. I always knew who I was inside my family—the youngest kid, the one eager to prove herself and please everyone. Now, I understood that I was also the family storyteller, and that while we all had our experience of who our family was, I had the job of synthesizing all of it. I say job, but in reality, telling stories was instinctual, and the only way I knew how to work through grief and make sense of anything. It wasn't just within my family—I started looking at the world-at-large more through the eyes of a storyteller, too. Being a freelance writer, I was certainly in the right business.

Except the economy collapsed. The recession of 2001 had launched me, but the 2008 recession gutted my business. It didn't happen right away. In fact, things were going really well right up until the time I had Georgia in September 2010. When I took a few weeks off for maternity leave, it felt like everything had shifted when I came back. In reality, it had been happening slowly, but I didn't notice until suddenly, I saw that the majority of my editors had been laid off. Publications where shutting down day by day, and the ones still around were barely assigning.

One of my main magazine journalism beats—home and garden—had been hit especially hard. By late 2010, our savings was nearly gone, especially after spending $10,000 to have Georgia, since self-employed health insurance plans didn't cover maternity at the time. (Georgia was a wonderful addition to our family, and of course, we didn't regret spending the money to bring her into the world. We just thought we'd be able to build the savings back up.)

I started working with a business coach named Darla. I couldn't afford Darla, but I made a leap of faith that the money would work out. It did. She helped me move away from magazine writing. I didn't even realize how beaten down I was feeling until we started working together. Darla worked with me to rebuild my business and taught me how to market myself as a writer in a different way. She also helped me see all the ways I'd been holding back saying what I really felt about things. I started to let go of some shame around showing emotions I had been holding on to since I was a kid. I had never forgotten the shame of crying uncontrollably in fifth grade, but I didn't see how much it had scarred me and made me fearful of expressing emotion. I had thought of myself like an emotional Swiss Army knife—capable of tending to myself in any situation. Working with Darla, and then reading books about vulnerability from Brené Brown, clued me in on how much I had let shame rule my life. What I called "independence" was, in part, just fear of speaking up.

My coach told me I should start a blog. This seemed like a dumb idea. What was I going to write about? Semicolons? Catchy headlines? I was a storyteller, she reminded me. So I should tell stories, starting with stories about my own life. She also told me that I needed to start public speaking, as a means of marketing myself. This seemed like an even worse idea than the blog! I was shy, I reminded her. I told other people's stories, not my own. I wasn't good at that. Darla's response was some-thing like, "Tough shit and oh, by the way, stop lying to yourself." She helped me see that these were all stories I had been telling myself about who I was. I was paying her a lot of money, so I followed her advice. That was the beginning of finding a new voice. Of writing essays about my life and telling personal stories. Of sharing truths and speaking in front of people with confidence (which took practice, but I got there).

Not only did I realize I was good at this public honesty thing, I also realized I wasn't too keen on being an emotional Swiss Army knife anymore. Lots of women talk about how having children causes them to lose parts of themselves, to compromise their independence. But for me, it was quite the opposite: I found parts I didn't know about that I wanted to explore. Also, my dad was getting sicker. By 2012, Alzheimer's had invaded his mind to the degree that he couldn't really hold a conversation anymore, or do any of the things he loved. He was still living at home with my mom, but it was unsustainable. My brothers and sisters and I started growing closer after Paul's death, and that only intensified as my dad became less and less of himself. We talked about him a lot, communicating openly with each other about our fears and frustrations.

I found that I didn't want to be emotionally self-contained anymore. I wanted to cry in front of people and admit when I needed emotional support. In reality, I had always wanted this, but I had shoved it aside. Working with my coach helped me realize that I was tired of ignoring that part of me. The relationship I had with Allen wasn't quite built for exploring this other side of myself. It just wasn't what we *did*. This didn't seem like that big of a problem at first, because I had other means to do it. I had my writing. I had my siblings. And I had friends.

One of those friends was a colleague from my freelance work. Like me, he was married with two kids and was going through some shifts in his life. We had much in common, and because we found ourselves working on the same projects, we spent a lot of time together. One project involved making several driving trips to meet with a client about two hours away. For two summers in a row, we made the trek a dozen or so times. The first summer I worked with him, Georgia was still a baby, and there was so much going on in my life—including rebuilding my career—that I didn't think much about the time we spent together, other than simply enjoying it. By the following summer, I found myself looking forward to those two-hour trips like I hadn't looked forward to anything in quite a while. Still, it felt like nothing more than a working relationship, with a friendship on top of it. He was so easy to talk to, and I could talk to him about the things I had a hard time talking to Allen about, like how stressful it was to support a family or what the nature of a soul was. Talking to him started to feel like an escape. I felt like he saw right through to some essence of who I was. Plus, he was cute. Boyishly handsome, with clear eyes and a warm smile. I tried very hard not to notice this. But every time he would look at me, I would feel the familiar rumblings of attraction.

Allen and I were in the trenches with our two kids. They were little. They were needy. They sucked all the emotional resources Allen had. Plus, Allen had grown up with a very emotionally needy mother (who was most likely bipolar), and he confused providing emotional support with being emotionally manipulated. He had a much different childhood than mine—far less stable, and parents who routinely screamed at each other. He was an anxious person, conditioned to always be anticipating the worst, and parenting seemed to elevate his anxiety and negativity even more. His reluctance to have kids—which once seemed so romantic—was now a growing chasm between us. Though he loved our children fiercely, he resented me for wanting it all and for pulling him out of his simple bachelorhood existence. Over and over, I told him how childish this was. He agreed, but couldn't seem to let go of it. Getting a job was always an option, I would remind him condescendingly, at which point he would accuse me of thinking he was a failure. I was constantly trying to "fix" him, and he was constantly defending himself. Our discussions were circular and unproductive, and ultimately, only created more disconnection.

Watching my dad decline made everything worse. By 2013, he was in a nursing home, and I would cry every time I came back from visiting him there. Allen's answer would be that I was visiting too often. I didn't understand why he would regard me almost with disdain when I was upset, or when I wanted to talk about if there was a God or not. It's as if I was shedding these layers of protection around myself just as Allen was building up his own. The ambivalence that had been so instrumental in shaping our relationship now felt very limiting inside our marriage. Though I loved him and I knew he loved me, *eh, whatever* no longer worked as a comprehensive relationship philosophy.

I needed more. I needed *connection*. But Allen seemed locked into seeing me a certain way, which felt like he wasn't seeing me at all. He had always relied on my fierce independence and self-sufficiency—and while I valued those things in myself, too, I wanted us to explore vulnerability together. My fresh need to feel connected to him in a more emotionally mature way only wound up causing disconnection. I felt lost and frustrated.

This is how the relationship with the other man tipped toward more than friendship. (Note that I am only going to refer to him as "the other man" throughout the book, because I care about his privacy. But know that he has read and approved every word I've written about him.) In the spring of 2013, he and I started a new client project that had us traveling on longer trips, involving planes and overnight stays. I knew my feelings for him were deepening. At first, I thought of it as a crush, and figured it was one-sided—the way all of those old teenage crushes had been. But as our conversations became more intimate, I sensed he had feelings for me, too. I didn't shut it down. If anything, I encouraged it and probed. I *had* to know how he felt. One night in May 2013, when we were out of town on one of the client trips, we drank a bit too much, and I told him how I felt about him. The truth came out that we were both attracted to each other—but more than that, we felt connected to each other in ways that we didn't feel connected to our spouses. With him, I could be vulnerable and it felt safe. It was such a sweet relief! He had an amazing way of making me feel taken care of. Like me, he felt emotionally abandoned by his spouse, and he feared they were headed for divorce.

Though we didn't do anything physical (we worked extremely hard not to touch each other, and only gave in to some stolen hugs) something fundamental shifted after that night. We texted and emailed much more fervently, and since we continued to travel together for the project, we had time away from our "real" lives to be together.

Essentially, we were having an *emotional affair*. By July, we were trying to figure out if there was a way for us to really be together. I knew this was both wrong and impossible. He did, too. We were tormented. Once the project wrapped up at the end of July, we decided to back off from each other for a bit.

And then my dad died at the end of August. When I texted Allen from the nursing home the morning my dad passed to tell him it was over, his only response was, "Okay." He simply didn't know how to deal with situations like this—but in that moment, his reaction felt like disinterest, which hurt very badly. Naturally, I turned to the other man again. We wound up meeting for drinks one evening, and at the end of the evening, we kissed for the first time. It was electrifying and wonderful. It was also terrible, and I felt intensely guilty.

I confided in my sister Laura about what was going on. She was always the voice of reason, and I knew she was right when she told me that I wasn't seeing clearly, and that whatever issues I was having with Allen, I couldn't involve someone else in. Logically, I knew it was all too cliché—the same way I knew in college that developing an eating disorder was all too cliché. It didn't make it go away, though.

Hiding my feelings from Allen felt awful. While I loved him and didn't want to break up our family, I was angry with him for being emotionally unavailable and resentful of me. I was also angry with myself for . . . what exactly? Being dishonest? Being a shitty wife? Letting myself fall for someone else? Breaking a marriage vow? It was all of the above. I tossed it over in my mind day after day. Sometimes, after the kids were in preschool and my husband left for the gym, I would lie on the bed and sob. I thought back to childhood, to all those dilemmas and crises of conscience. I knew that I had to be honest with my husband, especially after all the work I had done on myself to be this person who spoke the truth. I had started seeing a therapist earlier in the summer, and she helped me work through how I would tell him.

A few weeks after my dad passed away, I finally told Allen the truth about the emotional affair. His reaction was interesting and probably not very typical of how spouses usually react. He was caught off guard (he knew the other man and I were friends, but he didn't suspect anything else was going on). But he wasn't angry. He actually showed incredible empathy in understanding why it happened. He had been seeing a therapist for a while, too, and had been trying to make some changes in his life because he wasn't happy with how he was being as a father and a husband. He knew he was holding on to resentment related to parenthood. He saw my emotional infidelity as a by-product of that. I did, too, but I also knew I had responsibility in it. Ultimately, it launched a series of conversations about the future of our marriage, and what we each needed to do to strengthen it.

Things initially improved in our marriage. We were kinder to each other, and I worked on being more patient and less judgmental of him. Yet my feelings for the other man didn't really go away. We cut off contact for about six months as we each focused on strengthening our respective marriages. But . . . work is work, and the following summer, it was time for the project to start again. I said yes, because this project represented a significant chunk of my income, and also, I wanted to see him again. He brought something to my life I wasn't willing to give up—I just didn't want it to destroy my marriage (or his, for that matter). We put boundaries in place, and we stuck to them. When we talked about our spouses with each other, we only said positive things. Neither one of us wanted to be people who had affairs. This motivation was strong enough to keep things in check. I'd like to say that I completely left the emotional affair behind, but it lingered in the background. My marriage still had so many ups and downs as Allen worked to make the changes he wanted to make and let go of his resentment over parenthood. I compartmentalized my feelings as best as I could, and tried to focus on my family. So did the other man.

I continued to tell stories about my life on my blog and in my published essays. There was so much to mine in my big crazy family, after all! I had a treasure trove of memories, but also the painful moments, like my dad's death and Paul's death. Writing about these things opened up a whole new territory for me. It felt good to be vulnerable. To be *real*. Readers started responding, telling me how much they appreciated my honesty.

While I was certainly writing from an authentic place, I couldn't shake the idea that I was living these separate lives—my interior life (which contained my judgments of others, feelings of shame, and my marriage discord) and my life that faced the world. These two lives seemed almost independent of one another, though I was continually looking for ways to bridge them. For example, I wrote a blog post in October 2013 about how the experience of almost making a mistake—but then catching yourself and making a better decision—winds up saying a lot about you and your character. I told a story from childhood to make the point, but I was really thinking about how I almost made the mistake of having a full-on affair, but caught myself. No one knew this was the real impetus behind this blog post, of course. I wanted to share the sentiment, because it was genuine. But I was disguising its true origin. This wasn't lying, but it didn't seem wholly honest, either, not when I was on this journey toward vulnerability and shedding layers. How could I be simultaneously unpeeling layers of myself and adding more on?

An avid runner, I thought about this misalignment of my inner and outer lives for miles and miles and *miles*. I sorted through it as I ran up and down the same hills day after day, month after month, year after year. Answers were always elusive, but I came to realize one thing for sure: A whole lot more was at stake in this honesty game than before. It wasn't just about boyfriends or high school bullies. Now, it was about my marriage, my children, and the essence of who I was.

Time passed—days that were long by the hour and short by the year. I stayed busy, wrote essays, and watched my children grow into grade school kids. I continued to work with the other man. And I kept trying to figure out if my husband and I would ever find peace and ease in our relationship.

And then, of course, the presidential election of 2016 happened.

If my obsession with honesty was at yellow-alert during the presidential campaign, it moved to full-on red alert when Donald Trump actually became president. Sure, we had been-there-done-that with the whole lying president thing, but Trump's clear and unchecked self-interest, dangerous narcissism, and attacks on the media elevated questions of truth to new heights. (Interesting fact: As of this writing, when you do an internet search for the most recent polls on lying, the top results are all polls about Donald Trump.) His victory terrified and angered the half of the country who hadn't voted for him and never saw his candidacy as legitimate. As a progressive and firm believer that pussy-grabbing was, you know, *assault*, I shared the pain, and considered myself part of "the resistance." At some point, though, there was so much screaming, unchecked name-calling, haughty preaching, and shocking twinges of unexamined racism, anti-Semitism, and classism among my fellow resisters, I had to step back. It seemed counterproductive. And something else: a little bit dishonest.

I noticed that people were lashing out, calling Trump out for all kinds of dishonest and generally disgraceful behavior and practices—and rightfully so. Yet, I also noticed that some of those same people seemed to lack self-awareness about their own actions. I don't know how many times I heard my fellow liberals talk about all the "hillbillies" who voted for Trump, or how many times I witnessed my fellow feminists who positively exploded when people picked apart Hillary's physical appearance insult every aspect of Trump's appearance. It's easy to hold a villain to standards you just assume you meet, without really looking to see if you do. After some psychological sleuthing, I came to realize that this is called the *actor-observer bias*. It means that we think our own behavior is justified, caused by extenuating circumstances that feel almost beyond our control. But if we observe someone else taking part in that behavior, we judge that person harshly and assume they lack personal integrity. In other words, we cut ourselves slack while demonizing others who do a version of what we're doing.

Did this describe me, too?

I didn't want it to. I wanted to behave differently. To be true. To avoid hypocrisy. To examine the unexamined. But I had built up so many defense mechanisms and justifications and compartments of feelings that I wasn't sure I could even trust myself to know when I was being honest and when I wasn't. I started to make a list of my questions:

Was there any such thing as living a more honest life?

What would it look like and feel like to work toward that life?

When was dishonesty a true kindness, and when was it merely self-serving or self-delusive?

What was the cost of not paying attention to our own dishonesty?

In mid-November 2016, I gave a talk to my son's third grade class about being a writer. The week after, I wrote a blog post about how standing in front of those young people made me realize that no matter what, my voice still mattered. Everything I said in that blog post was true. It was just *half the story*. Everything in my life felt like *half the story*.

I was a citizen of a country I deeply believed in, yet we had a crazy, narcissistic president and a cadre of strange people who invented terms like *alternative facts*.

I was the mother of two wonderful kids who were the most important thing in the world to me, yet I often paid little attention to how I answered their heaps of questions.

I was a writer sharing brutal truths, yet I was hiding some of my most painful ones.

I was a wife who loved my husband, yet I couldn't shake the feeling that I might be in love with someone else.

I was a daughter, sister, friend, and neighbor who believed in generosity of spirit and open communication, yet continually held on to judgment.

I was a privileged, white, middle-class person who publicly railed against institutional racism, yet other than giving my kids speeches about Rosa Parks, did very little in my private life to actually counteract racism.

I was an active user of Facebook and Instagram, with a smiling profile and carefully curated bank of mobile uploads and pithy posts, yet I often didn't recognize myself in them.

I was a generally content, healthy, well-adjusted, non–clinically depressed person, yet I felt like a mad woman every time I laced up my running shoes looking for answers to my questions about honesty.

While this push and pull all seemed intensely personal, as if this struggle belonged only to me, I had a sense that I probably wasn't alone, that other people were navigating their own contradictions regarding honesty. Those contradictions might involve infidelity, a toxic friendship, an untenable situation at work, a family secret gnawing at them, a truth about themselves they were trying to admit, or any number of other shit storms brewing in that place where lies, shame, and guilt converged, with the ability to cause great pain.

I couldn't accept that *pain* was the last word in all of this. I couldn't accept the notion that we just live in a dishonest world and we all "do our best."

There was no fucking way I was doing my best.

I wanted to, though. I wanted to *do* better, so that the world—my corner of it and maybe a lot of other corners of it—could *be* better. Honesty seemed like the way. It *had* to be the way. Didn't I intuitively know this when I was seven? Why was it so hard now? How did it all get so complicated?

More than anything, the question was this: *What was I going to do?*

I pondered this as 2016 turned into 2017. I kept turning it over as I took down the holiday decorations, watched the snowflakes fall, cut out Valentine's Day hearts with my kids, and saw the first daffodils poking through the soil. Around the time I started sneezing from pollen, I finally had a real idea.

If everyone else was yelling and freaking out, I would go quiet. I would do one simple thing: I would start paying attention to when I was being honest and when I wasn't. I would make a practice of noticing, and I wouldn't hold back.

On April 1, 2017, I opened a Google document and wrote "Honesty Journal" at the top. I didn't know where it would lead, but I knew I would have to follow it.

CHAPTER 2

What Is Honesty, Anyway?

ON THE MORNING I STARTED my honesty journal, I woke up thinking about having sex with the other man. I felt bad about this, of course, and redirected my thoughts. It was a Saturday, so the kids were home from school. Georgia (then six years old) had made a mess of necklaces and tape in her room, and Maxx (then eight years old) was in and out of the house, bringing a trail of mud with him each time, since it had rained the night before and the yard was a swampy mess. Allen—a neat freak when it came to the house—was already in yelling mode before I had even finished my coffee. I wrote all of this down in my journal, because it all led to one thought: *I should be with someone else, like the other man.*

I reminded myself that my project was one of noticing without always judging, so I let the thought be.

Coffee in hand, I went into my office, curled up on my couch, and read a few articles from *The New York Times* on my phone. Trump was peddling a theory that Obama spied on him. Sean Spicer (remember him?) was trying to sell it for him. "I'll always be more honest than Trump," I wrote in my journal. It was a depressingly low barometer.

Later that day, I worked on a personal essay about the seven lessons I had learned on the seven hills of Cincinnati. It was the first published piece in which I was going to mention the emotional affair. I was only going to give it a few lines in one of the lesson vignettes. I knew nothing I would write would be the complete truth yet, and I reflected in my journal about the power of what we leave out of stories. *Aren't I always consciously leaving out the hard parts?* I asked myself.

That night while I was giving her a bath, Georgia randomly asked me if putting the cat to sleep last year meant that I had killed him. My first instinct was to redirect and talk about how he was in kitty heaven chasing a ball of yarn. Then I remembered the journal. I told her yes (with some explanation about how we don't want the animals we love to suffer) but skipped the part about kitty heaven, because, well, it was a lie, wasn't it? Was the entire idea of heaven a lie? It was a lot to think about while rinsing shampoo out of her hair.

By the time I went to bed that night, I was sure my journal was a terrible idea. I was only going to wind up feeling (1) confused, (2) guilty, and (3) like a fraud—writing one thing in my journal, but then writing essays full of half-truths. *So what*, I told myself. *Let the shit come. Don't hide the truth from yourself. Just stick with the journal.*

By the end of the first week, I realized the extent to which questions of honesty touched every aspect of my life. Yes, my husband and I were having issues—I knew that one already. But there was also a whole aspect of parenting that I realized I had been phoning in rather than truly exploring. Had my kids always asked so many questions? Did I just not hear them before, when I wasn't as focused on thinking about honest answers for their questions? When my son had hard questions about things like sex, suicide, divorce, racism, and school shootings, why was my first response always the defense mechanism of "Why do you want to know that?" versus really listening to him and figuring out how to answer as honestly and age-appropriately as possible?

It came up in my work life, too. I had always considered myself transparent in my business dealings. An issue arose that first week—not a big issue, just a discussion with a potential client. I had to make a decision about how to talk about an existing client I worked with that was a direct competitor for this client. I didn't lie, but I softened the language and downplayed the extent of my involvement with the other client. Was that just the way it worked? If it was merely "the way it worked," was that acceptable?

I found myself noticing the range of conversations I had with lots of different people. Over and over, I caught myself making statements that were not exactly false, but not altogether true. It was usually quite trivial. For example, I mentioned to a colleague (another freelance writer) that I wrote "all the time" for *The New York Times*. In fact, I had written three articles for them at that point. I also paid more attention to my conversations with my mom and my sisters—the people I'm closest to in the world and arguably feel most comfortable with. I noticed how I would sometimes backpedal in conversations to avoid . . . what exactly? Arguments? Having to explain too much? It was all silly stuff. I didn't even know if it mattered. But I found it curious that I hadn't noticed it before.

There were other strange things, too. I noticed in my running log my tendency to round up mileage. Was that loop around Drake Road really 4.5 miles, or more like 4.42? Recording it as 4.5 would get me to my weekly mileage goal. What could possibly be at stake in that? Why would I delude myself, *in my own running log app*, which zero other people in the world cared about or would ever see? I wondered a similar thing when I went to yoga and accidentally wound up sitting next to the leggy blonde who must moonlight as a model for *Yoga Journal*. Let me just say: I used to be a gymnast, I'm crazy flexible, and I can hold a perfect handstand with locked-out legs and pointed toes with no problem. But she was *better* than me, which is why I tried never to sit by her, because I would start to feel competitive. That morning I wound up beside her, I wondered if I was being honest with myself about why I was even going to yoga. Was it to show off? I always told other people it was all about things like "finding the balance between work and surrender" and "being mindful about movement and breathing." Was that just a crock of shit? Was it actually about trying to impress a room full of strangers with my perfect handstands and 180-degree-split dancer's pose? What kind of egomaniac was I?

That Friday evening was the father-daughter dance. Naturally, I took pictures of my daughter and my husband together and posted them on Facebook. I didn't include a gushing commentary (that's never been my social media style), but it was important to me to show this slice of my life. *Look, see how normal we are? See what good parents we are? See how much love we must have floating around in this family? See see see?* My daughter was excited, but then it turned out that she absolutely hated the dance (it wasn't what she expected). She started crying about an hour in, was inconsolable, and they had to leave early. My husband and I didn't have a fight about it, but I remember thinking that if I had been there, it would have been different. I would have known what to do.

None of that made it into the Facebook post.

Those questions of self-honesty came back to me over and over again that week. At one point, I wrote in the journal: "Am I telling myself stories that aren't true?" When I wrote it, I was initially thinking about my marriage, wondering if I was fixated on this narrative that something in my marriage was lacking, without really examining it. But as I thought more about it, I realized that I was most likely telling myself untrue stories in *every* area of my life.

If just one week revealed this much, I knew there was far more ahead. I also knew that I couldn't tackle every area of my life at once. While I would keep noticing and jotting down everything that came to me regarding honesty, ultimately, I would need to find a way to work through it systematically.

Start with the Truth

The business coach I worked with back in 2011 still sends me weekly newsletters, which I sometimes read. I happened to open one just a few days into keeping my honesty journal. In the newsletter, she was telling stories from the retreat she had just hosted, which Elizabeth Gilbert had spoken at. This caught my attention because I've read Gilbert's books and have interviewed her a couple of times, and I'm generally a fan. The retreat focused a lot on "speaking your truth." This is a fairly ubiquitous theme in coaching, and even though I'm a supporter of truth speaking (hence, this book), the rhetoric around it can get stale and the clichés tiresome to the point of being offensive and tone deaf, as if inspirational quotes about love and truth can replace real action or change. But my former coach included a quote from Liz Gilbert that caught my attention:

"The truth will always be the last thing standing, so you might as well start there."

After I read that quote, I pondered in my journal what it meant to start with the truth. I intuitively loved this idea, but the problem was *getting* to the truth. We were in the middle of a national debate about truth—fake news versus real news—just as I was in the middle of an internal debate about truth—how did I know what was true and what I was making up? Also, what was the relationship between truth and honesty? Was it about starting with truth and journeying toward honesty, with truth being a concrete thing and honesty a way of being? Did it make sense to slice them out like that? My questions were dizzying and highly abstract. These ideas were like gossamer. I was trying to knit their delicate strands together into a loose weave, but it felt like it kept unraveling. As soon as I would think I knew something concrete about honesty, I would consider some other aspect I had missed before and the thread would work its way free again. I saw this happening each day in the different scenarios I observed and conversations I had.

For example, a few weeks into keeping the journal, I had a conversation with Georgia, and she asked, "What if the teacher asks me what I'm thinking and I don't want to tell her the truth? Is it a lie if I tell her I'm thinking something else?" I responded that she never had to tell anyone what she was thinking, and that it was her right to hold secret thoughts and not share them. It seemed accurate when I told her this. "Aren't the secrets and things you hold in your mind deliciously yours?" I wrote in my journal.

Except . . . secrets could also be dishonest and hurtful. Were those deliciously yours, too? What was the difference between private thoughts no one else had a right to know and purposely keeping information secret from other people? Was it simply about context? What about intention? For example, what about holding back saying what you really thought because the truth was harsh? I noticed more than one time in those first weeks of keeping my journal that I moderated my thoughts on many things when talking to my kids, my husband, my family, and my clients. I noticed my husband doing it, too, especially when he talked to his father on the phone. Lies could hurt and lies could be kind. Not all lies seemed equal. Although . . . that seemed like something Trump might say (alternative lies!?). Was this a potentially dangerous idea, or a loving idea? My barometer was having trouble telling whether it was the political climate I was living in, or the experience of middle age and its unexpected challenges.

My project was one of noticing, so throwing my hands up in frustration was not an option. Instead, I started thinking about all the words bound up in this notion of honesty. I made a working list in my journal of the different words and phrases that came to mind:

- Honesty
- Selective honesty/leaving things out
- Real truth
- Convenient truth
- Secrets
- Hypothesis versus theory versus fact
- Belief/opinion
- Integrity
- Lying
- Cheating
- Guilt
- Fear of speaking up
- Uncertainty

I knew it wasn't a complete list. I also knew it would be really handy to have some definitions.

A Better Word Than Honesty

I thought back to the philosophy class I had taken in college. Wasn't there a whole part of philosophy dedicated to defining truth? Surely, philosophers had written about this. As I started researching, I found something even better: YouTube videos! The "Three Minute Philosophy" series of videos was particularly helpful in understanding what philosophers had said about lying. For example, I learned that eighteenth-century German philosopher Immanuel Kant put forth a "categorical imperative" about lying, saying it's *always* wrong to lie—no matter what, end of story. That seemed utter nonsense to me. I was hardly the only one who thought that was a nutty idea; lots of philosophers had revised Kant in the few hundred years since. Grounding myself in the historical philosophical debates was definitely helpful, but what I really needed was a big ole' book of definitions.

I found precisely that when I discovered Thomas Carson, a professor of philosophy at Loyola University, and author of the book, *Lying and Deception: Theory and Practice.* Starting to read his book confirmed that I was correct when I intuited that I had only scratched the surface of all of the concepts around honesty. Dense and detailed, Carson's book dedicates two hundred pages to discerning the minutia of meaning between various terms related to honesty and dishonesty. "We philosophers like to fight about fairly narrow things," Carson joked when I talked to him on the phone (philosophers do actually joke). Talking to Carson helped me understand that the word *honesty* is fundamentally in our way, because it means so much, and yet also, nothing. It's loaded, but ineffectual. In other words, I wasn't crazy. I just needed more precise vocabulary.

Understanding the following concepts took my journal—and my project in general—to a new level. So, I'm going to spend the next few pages laying out the range of terms, and offering some basic definitions.

Let's start broadly by defining two key terms: *lies of self-interest* and *prosocial lying.*

To be self-interested is, well, human. There's nothing inherently unethical about self-interest. The problem is when we prioritize our own self-interest over being ethical, truthful, forthcoming, or some other important value that helps society function. This is the basis for *lies of self-interest.* If I cheat on a test or don't return the extra change a cashier gives me, I'm acting in my own self-interest. We tend to define self-interest as having to do with money, but it can also be about preserving or enhancing our own ego.

By contrast, to operate with prosocial interest is to operate with others' interests in mind. *Prosocial lying* then, is lying to benefit others. There are extreme examples of prosocial lying (Germans who hid Jewish people during the Holocaust) and smaller examples that we do every day without much thought, from thanking someone for a gift you didn't want to agreeing with a co-worker that her dog is cute when you really think pugs are one of the ugliest creatures on earth (I'm a cat person, but I assure you this is a random example). Without these lies, we're just a bunch of jerks. (Though of course, saying nothing is always an option.)

Carson defines *lying* as "a deliberate false statement that the speaker warrants to be true." A mom asks her teenage daughter if she caused the dent on the passenger side of the family car, and the teen driver—who knows that she did, in fact, cause the dent—says, "No, I didn't cause the dent!" Or, you write a wedding thank-you note to your grandmother, telling her that you can't wait to use the beautiful tablecloth she gave you (which wasn't on your registry), when in fact, you've already donated it to Goodwill.

Purposefully causing someone to believe something false is *deception*. If lying is the attempt, deception is the successful outcome. If the mom believes the teenage daughter, the mom is deceived and the daughter has orchestrated deception. If your grandmother folds up the note with a smile and believes she's made your day with her tablecloth purchase, she is deceived. These are *lies of commission*, which means to lie by saying purposefully false statements.

However, deception doesn't necessarily require someone to make a false statement. A statement can be true, but misleading in a way that causes deception. This is sometimes called *paltering*. Carson gives the example of a buyer asking a seller if a car has a problem with overheating, and the seller says that last year, he drove the car across the desert without it overheating. The statement is true, but it doesn't include the fact that the car overheated the next month, and four times after that—but not in the desert. You could also deceive your grandmother by simply saying, "Thank you for the tablecloth! It will go to a very good use!" The statement is technically true—it just won't be you who uses it. As

I started to keep my journal, I found that I paltered as a technique to avoid answering questions truthfully. A client asked me if I enjoyed the work I was doing for them. I mostly hated the work, but I liked the money. That was hardly a truth I was willing to admit. So I said that I enjoyed being challenged—a true statement (just not the true answer to their question). Bill Clinton is perhaps the most famous palterer of our time. Believe it or not, there is an entire philosophy book written, in large part, all about his paltering, called *Lying, Misleading, and What Is Said*, by Jennifer Mather Saul.

A *half-truth* is similar to paltering in that it's a true statement. It emphasizes only the facts that support your case and minimizes facts that would support the other side. We can also think of this as *spin*. Politicians do this all the time. It's not exclusive to political office, though. Consider two friends talking, and the one friend lists all the things her husband has done to wrong her, but leaves out the similar things she has done. These are *lies of omission*.

Withholding information is failing to give information that would help someone "acquire true beliefs or correct false beliefs" (that's Carson's definition). Related to that is *concealing information*, which means you purposefully hide the information. We can also think of this as *keeping secrets*. We all keep secrets, of course, and plenty of secrets are thoroughly mundane and unrelated to deception. I love to belt out Air Supply in the car and I don't particularly want anyone to know, but there's no effort involved in keeping it secret, and let's face it, nobody actually cares. The secrets that *are* related to deception—like if you kissed your best friend's boyfriend way back when and never told her—could be either prosocial or related to self-interest (or a little of both).

Failing to speak up can also be a form of deception. It's very often motivated by fear of reprisal—like the fear that you'll be fired if your boss finds out that you knew something was going on and never spoke up. We also fail to speak up for prosocial reasons, to protect people who need protecting, for example.

Conflicts of interest arise when people are pulled in two conflicting directions, and have to weigh their self-interest against someone else's. Dan Ariely, author of *The (Honest) Truth About Dishonesty*, cites the example of a dentist making a big investment in a new, high-tech device for her dental practice. She wants to use the device so she can charge for it, thus making a return on her investment, so she begins suggesting various treatments to patients, which they may or may not need. People have varying degrees of awareness about their conflicts, especially because of our "return the favor" culture (If you give me a good review, I'll give you a good review). I'd like to say that most conflicts of interest you can simply feel in your gut, but in my experience, they are sometimes easier to spot on paper, and by someone who isn't you. Seeing as how we all need to make a living somehow, conflicts of interest can get very thorny indeed.

To lie by *exaggeration* is to manipulate the basic facts in a way that makes you look better—round up, round down, shave a few hundred or a few years off, or turn that BA degree into an MA degree. Exaggerations range from minor to blatantly false. I'm not talking about the exaggeration involved in comedy or when we all know someone is exaggerating just for hyperbolic effect. I'm talking about exaggerations with the intent to deceive. If we're talking about marathons, and you ask me my best marathon time and I say "oh, a little over four hours," I'm exaggerating, because my best time is actually 4:41:55— but "a little over four hours" sounds a lot better than "almost five," and I want you to think I'm an amazing marathon runner! That same thing was at work when I told my colleague that I wrote for *The New York Times* "all the time," when in fact, I had just written three pieces. We frequently practice exaggeration on social media (less of the blatant nature and more of the half-truth nature).

There is also the phenomenon of *unexamined statements*. Here's one: Let's say I am interviewing parents about the good driving practices they want to pass on to their teenage drivers (maybe even the mom who was deceived by her dent-hiding daughter!). I ask you, the parent: When you're driving, do you always look right before you turn right? I'm going to guess you would answer, "Yes, I always look right before I turn right!" automatically. I'm 95 percent certain that you actually don't, because I have twenty-five years of running experience and have had numerous instances of nearly being hit at intersections by people hitting the accelerator to turn right while only looking left. I know, therefore, that the majority of drivers get a vague sense of what's to the right as they approach an intersection from several yards back, but they do not actually look right before they turn right once they are at the intersection. But I don't think you intend to deceive when you say you look right. You simply haven't examined it. (If you take nothing else from this book other than to start looking right before you turn right, I will feel that I have accomplished something!)

So much of what we say on any given day could fall under the umbrella of unexamined statements—most of small talk, for example. "Hey Gina, how's it going?" says Fred . . . to which Gina responds, "Ugh, why does it have to rain every Monday?" Does it really rain every Monday? But . . . who cares? Life is too short to examine Every. Single. Blasted. Word. However, we would do better to examine a few more of them—or at least the ones that could matter. Like this potentially unexamined statement: "I'm not a racist." We often say these kinds of sweeping statements for a mix of prosocial reasons and self-interested reasons. I do not want to ever be a racist. I hate racism. There is a slightly prosocial motivation to make the statement that I'm not a racist—I want to promote equality, which is something I believe deeply in. The larger share of it is self-interest, though, because, if you're a white person, admitting that you've ever struggled with racist ideas or thoughts (ideas and thoughts that you hate) or that you benefit greatly from a racist system (which you do), opens you up to judgment, and nobody wants to be judged (yes, it's sadly ironic that judgment is the root of racism). Unlike the unexamined turning right statement—which is about making an automatic assumption of something that seems obvious—the unexamined racism statement is about avoiding pain and shame. The point is, we fail to examine things we say for a variety of reasons, some more complex than others.

Finally, we should think about the difference between lying and *not being candid*—or put another way, honesty versus candor. We can find a great example of this in Abraham Lincoln. "Lincoln's reputation as honest was earned—he rarely lied. But he was not at all candid," says Carson, who is author of the book, *Lincoln's Ethics*. Carson tells the story of when Lincoln was thinking of running for Senate in the late 1850s. An abolitionist speaker was coming to town to speak to an abolitionist group, and Lincoln knew the group would ask him to speak. Though Lincoln was an abolitionist, the abolitionists were still small in numbers in Illinois. Lincoln was afraid it would cost him votes if he spoke. He was also afraid it would cost him votes if he refused to speak. A friend heard his dilemma and advised him to simply get out of town for the day. Lincoln took his son to the country and was gone all day. Party politics were as confusing back then as they are now, with alliances that straddled viewpoints. He played the game by not being candid, though. I like the Lincoln example, since Abe is our go-to guy for honesty. But I also like this one: A few years after Lincoln's Senate run, Harriet Ann Jacobs published her slave narrative, *Incidents in the Life of a Slave Girl*, under the pseudonym Linda Brent. Jacobs gave a painfully honest account of her life as an enslaved person—including her escape to the North. But she felt she couldn't possibly be candid about her true identity, for her own safety as well as the safety of her family. While we value candor—just like we value honesty—the ability to be candid is often laden with hidden privilege. Being candid can get certain people killed, while others get rewarded for it. Sometimes not being candid is about holding on to privilege, whereas other times, it's about basic safety.

Learning these definitions did several things for me. First, parsing out their meanings gave me more precise vocabulary to use in any given situation that involved honesty in some way. Second, it was an exercise in nuance, and nothing gets done in honesty work without an appreciation for nuance. And third, it created a bunch more questions to think about, the first of which was, "Why would anyone ever think honesty wasn't complicated?" But as I was about to find out, a lot of people apparently think exactly that.

CHAPTER 3

Is Honesty Really the Best Policy?

Honesty is the best policy.
—Benjamin Franklin

HOW MANY TIMES HAVE YOU HEARD someone wisely declare that honesty is the best policy? How many times have you said it yourself? We say it *constantly*. I think we mean well. There is something that feels fundamentally right about this idea that honesty is best. And the idea of having a personal policy feels good, too. After all, personal policies simplify things and remove difficult decision-making. For example, I have a personal policy that I do not buy things from people at my door, unless they are children. It makes it very easy to say to the people on my porch peddling gutter guards, lawn care services, or roof inspections, "Thank you for your efforts, but my personal policy is that I never buy from someone at my door, unless they are a child. Thanks, and have a nice day." I then gently shut the door with a pleasant expression on my face. Done. Yay for policies! If refusing to buy tree-trimming services from the interloper at my door is a good policy, surely *honesty* as a policy makes sense. It should be a no-brainer, especially given that dishonesty is a big problem in the world today, causing everything from economic disaster to personal betrayal. And yet, as with nearly everything, there's a rub. The honesty-is-the-best-policy rub is this: The balance of scientific evidence tells us that, as individual people, we actually step outside of the policy quite often—either because of self-interest or benevolence, or some complicated combination of both.

I didn't yet know what the research said when I started my journal. I just knew that the more I noticed and analyzed my behavior, the more I started to realize there was something funky going on, in that what I *said* about honesty often didn't match how I *acted* or what I *wanted* from others. This led me to the wondrous world of behavioral science, and to researchers who are attempting to explain the many peculiar things that go on around the notion that honesty is the best policy.

We Lie to Benefit Ourselves (A Lot)

Dan Ariely is a professor of psychology and behavioral economics at Duke University and author of *The (Honest) Truth About Dishonesty*, a book I started reading a few weeks into keeping my journal. Through running "cheating" experiments on more than forty thousand people, he and his colleagues found solid evidence that the great majority of us lie, but usually just a little bit. We lie mostly to benefit ourselves, but sometimes to benefit others. We lie less if you remind us that lying isn't good, and we lie more when we see our peers doing it and getting away with it. We have what Ariely calls a "fudge factor." It means we can lie fairly comfortably to a certain degree because we rationalize it, but we have a self-imposed cutoff, so that we don't gain too much from the lie.

His team has performed experiment after experiment, replicating their results over and over again. The scenario changes slightly with each experiment, testing for different control factors, but the basic setup is that participants are given a sheet with a grid of numbers—actually twenty different grids. Within each grid, they have to scan the numbers to find two numbers that add up to ten. These are unwieldy numbers with decimals, like 2.31 and 7.69. While it's a simple task to find the number pairs, it isn't a quick one. Experimenters didn't give participants much time. After just five minutes, they told participants to add up the number of grids they solved, go shred their tests, and tell the proctor how many they got right, because they would get paid one dollar per correct answer.

Now, Ariely and his team had already run non-cheating control groups through this same experiment, but instead of shredding their tests, the proctor counted up the number of grids they solved at the end of the five minutes and paid participants accordingly. People in the non-cheating group solved four of the grids, on average. People in the shredder group, on average, claimed to solve *six*. This isn't a one-time fluke. Ariely and his colleagues show this over and over and *over* again. (Plus, they had a special shredder that only shredded the sides of the test, so they could actually look and confirm that people were lying about how many they solved.) Most study participants only lied to receive an extra two dollars. What's two dollars, after all? It's fairly easy to justify. Well, two dollars multiplied by forty thousand people is a lot of money. The amount people cheated only went up when other factors were introduced—like an actor pretending to be a student who stood up after only a minute or so and claimed to have solved them all, so collected his money and left.

I knew I was having struggles with honesty, but not when it came to money or you know, stealing. Surely, I wouldn't lie about how many answers I got correct when no one was looking if it meant earning a few dollars more. Fudge factor? Please. You might be thinking this same thing about yourself. Then I started to pay more attention to some of his examples. What about going the speed limit? What about taxes? What about stealing office supplies? What about using my husband's pool membership pass to get a guest in instead of buying a guest pass? Keeping the journal didn't just help me record my decisions around honesty in the present, it also helped me reflect on past instances, too. I remembered how I used to use one company's postage meter to mail my own packages. How I snuck another employer's version of Microsoft Word on my computer before I bought my own. But that doesn't count, I rationalized! None of it counts! I had excuses for all of it . . . the speed limit was stupid . . . the government had enough of my money . . . that boss was kind of a jerk . . . I was poor and just out of college and could barely afford stamps . . . everyone pirates some piece of software . . . we paid a lot of money to that pool for membership and the person checking passes never paid attention . . .

That is the fudge factor. The little things that "don't count" because you justify them away. A few examples of this came my way during the first month I was keeping the journal. They so perfectly illustrated what Ariely was saying, I almost wondered if, in addition to being an incredibly brilliant behavioral economist, he also had some kind of voodoo power to make situations materialize in people's lives right when they needed to take a concept to heart.

SUNDAY AFTERNOONS ARE MY DAY to get a Diet Coke from McDonald's. I generally allow myself just one a week (just in case all those old cancer warnings about artificial sweetener were actually right), and I think McDonald's gets some special recipe direct from Coca-Cola to make their fountain drinks, because they are extra delicious. One particular Sunday, the drive-thru line was painfully slow and my kids were acting up in the backseat. Plus, I was in one of those woe-is-me moods where I was certain that no one cared about customer service anymore. I paid the cashier at the first window, and she gave me an extra dollar in change back. I realized it immediately, but paused for a beat. There was definitely a moment—maybe not even a full second, but a fleeting cloud of feeling—where I wasn't going to give the dollar back. Then I remembered I was focused on my honesty choices, and I gave it back. My behavior aligned exactly with what Ariely found: If people are reminded about the value of honesty just before "the act," there is a much greater likelihood they will be honest. Keeping my journal was my reminder.

Interestingly, though, when a client (a children's hospital) paid me twice for the same invoice, sending me a second check for $1,000 a week after they sent the first one, I sent the duplicate check back without even blinking. There was no internal debate. It was so clearly wrong to keep a $1,000 mistake, and from a *children's hospital*, that I didn't even entertain it. I wouldn't have entertained it even if I wasn't keeping an honesty journal. Nothing about a decision to keep an extra $1,000 from an organization I greatly admired was justifiable, whereas the decision to keep just one dollar from an organization I admired a bit less *could* have been justifiable.

And that, my friends, is the fudge factor.

Though fudge factor behavior is technically dishonest behavior, we are still able to think of ourselves as honest. Some people have a higher fudge factor than others, and later, we'll talk about moral character and other things that contribute to our behavior. However, in my experience, most of us have some degree of the fudge factor, and even the most upstanding and guilt-prone among us probably veers from the straight and narrow from time to time when it's easy to justify. But we still regard ourselves in a certain light, and in fact, do value honesty and good moral character. It's truly fascinating—at least to me, as someone who has recognized both her fudge factor and her deep desire to be good and true and honest. In fact, it makes me wonder . . . are there other places in our lives where this kind of cognitive dissonance is standard operating procedure? For this, I turned to the book *Everybody Lies: Big Data, New Data, and What the Internet Can Tell Us About Who We Really Are.* This book, by big data scientist Seth Stephens-Davidowitz, came out just about a month after I started my journal. Again, the serendipity was almost spooky. But not as spooky as the things Stephens-Davidowitz uncovers in his research.

We crop and filter our pictures just perfectly on Instagram, and post the highlights of our lives on Facebook. We know that we do this, and other people know that we do this . . . yet, we are hesitant to call it dishonesty. But Stephens-Davidowitz doesn't just call bullshit on our social media lives, he actually provides the data that conclusively shows the shape, size, and truly rank smell of our bullshit. One of the things Stephens-Davidowitz does is compare the words people use in Google searches to the words they use in Facebook posts. He finds that Google searches—which happen in private—are essentially "digital truth serum." For example, one of the most autocompleted phrases that starts with "my boyfriend . . ." is "my boyfriend won't have sex with me." Meanwhile, on Facebook, this same poor sexless soul likely posts image after image of a fulfilling relationship. A side-by-side comparison of the top words people use when describing husbands on social media versus in their Google searches makes this point even more clearly: *the best, my best friend, amazing, the greatest, so cute* (Facebook) versus *gay, a jerk, amazing, annoying, mean* (in searches).

It's pretty simple: We lie to appear in a more positive light. Stephens-Davidowitz has no shortage of data that shows this. We don't just lie on large public forums like social media; our deception is also rampant when we have to self-report in surveys. We consistently say we're donating more money, having more sex, reading more books, and getting better grades than we actually are. Stephens-Davidowitz points to a University of Maryland survey of graduates, where 44 percent of respondents said they'd donated money to the school in the last year. Only 28 percent actually had. We exaggerate, smooth over, round up or down, and just plain lie. We do it in everyday conversations, on paper, and on our screens. And—you guessed it—we still think we're honest. So, if honesty is the best policy, we're doing really lousy at actually following it. Sure, you could say that it's the policy we strive for, and that the notion of it is solid. We fail, but we try. And we want our children to try. We teach them not to cheat. These are essential lessons.

The only problem is that cheating is but one kind of dishonesty. There are multiple ways to deceive. As we've learned, in addition to lies of omission and commission—as well as secrets, exaggerations, and spin—there are also the lies we tell (or secrets we hold on to) for the benefit of others. And that's where the policy really starts to crumble.

We Lie to Benefit Others (a Lot)

Emma Levine, assistant professor of behavioral science at the University of Chicago Booth School of Business, studies prosocial lies, or the lies we tell to benefit others. She and her colleagues argue that prosocial lying isn't just seen as acceptable—it's seen as essential, as moral. It's also highly misunderstood. If you start to describe what a prosocial lie is, most people will automatically say, "Oh, you mean a white lie?" While I don't want to be the person going around correcting everyone's grammar (Truth: I don't like those people), it is actually important to correct this misnomer, and be clear that prosocial lies are not synonymous with white lies. Sure, some prosocial lies are white lies, but prosocial lies span a broader range of importance than the trivial nature we generally assign to a white lie. Also, a white lie can be a lie of self-interest, to gain something small or to avoid embarrassment. Let's say you're in a crowded elevator and you have wicked gas from the egg salad sandwich you had for lunch. You pass some gas that's silent but deadly. Sure enough, your brash co-worker starts waving his hand in front of his nose, saying, "Whoa." Lucky for you, Joe from marketing is visiting with his new baby that day and they happen to be in the elevator, too. Everyone looks at the adorable baby and giggles. It's a white lie of the *not speaking up* variety, but a white lie nonetheless. It's a lie of self-interest, though, not a lie told to benefit someone else.

Research has found that we lie about 20 to 30 percent of the time in our social interactions—some are the self-interested white lies, but about 25 percent are prosocial lies. These prosocial scenarios are so frequent, you may not think much about them. Imagine telling a co-worker who needs a confidence boost right before a presentation, "I know you'll do great!" when you actually know it's very likely she won't do so great. I've certainly been in a situation like this before, and keeping my honesty journal was making me even more aware of them. Having read through a bunch of Emma Levine's studies, I tell her about my frustration with the pervasive notion that "honesty is the best policy." As someone who researches our ideas about deception, Levine knows exactly what I'm talking about. "Despite being somewhat obvious, talking about these kinds of lies is still counter-intuitive. We think: *lying bad, honesty good,* painting the black and white picture. But in any specific case, we are far more comfortable with lying than we say we are," Levine tells me. I ask her why we continually resort to this black and white thinking. "It's so deeply engrained in us to think lying is always wrong," she says. Probably because we grow up hearing things like, "Honesty is the best policy."

If we can get past what we *say* about honesty, and focus on how we *feel*, we start to realize that we're likely relying on people to lie to us. "Lying is often welcomed from the target's perspective," Levine says—the target being the person who is on the receiving end of a prosocial lie. The real problem with trying to understand all of this is that deception always gets linked with the pursuit of self-serving lies. "By conflating self-interest with deception, we have sent conflicting and hypocritical messages to our employees, students, and children. We have exhorted them not to lie, while often modeling and even requiring them to engage in deception," Levine writes in her paper, "Why We Should Lie," published in the journal *Organization Dynamics*. Deception research has tended to focus only on the costs of deception. But there are costs to honesty, as well—like being cruel and hiding under the guise of "Hey, I'm just being honest." Levine advocates that more deception researchers start investigating the costs of honesty, more than just the costs of deception.

Fortunately, Levine *is* doing this research. I ask her more about what her research on prosocial lying has uncovered. First, she says, she's found that we perceive those who tell prosocial lies to be more ethical than those who tell hurtful truths, if we understand the intentions of the deceiver. In other words, we favor benevolence over honesty, when it's clear someone told a lie for benevolent reasons. "Most of our judgments about lying are actually driven by the person's intent, not whether they've told us the truth," she says. "It's rarely the case that people react negatively to lying on principle. If they see the good intentions, they see it was the right thing to do. But if they see the intentions were selfish, they will see lying as bad." Second, her team has found that prosocial lying can increase trust—which flies against the conventional wisdom that deception always destroys trust. In many situations, it's seen as far more ethical to lie than to deliver raw truth. Levine's research aims to tease apart prosocial lying from self-interested lying, so that we can better understand the benefits of prosocial deception and come up with clear and actionable guidelines around it.

One guideline we have for trust-building prosocial deception is around the notion of timing. Imagine that your best friend asks you how she looks as she's about to walk down the aisle of her wedding. You wish she had chosen a less bright lipstick, but you say, "You look beautiful!" She smiles and walks down the aisle and everyone is happy. You may think about the fact that you withheld a truth, but you also know that the truth wouldn't have done any good in that moment. She can't quickly change her lipstick. What she needed in that moment was to be happy and confident. If we back up to an hour before the wedding, and she asks you the same question as you're both looking in the mirror—then, you might be honest and say, "Let's try a different shade of lipstick." She can do something actionable with the truth.

The decision of whether or not to tell a prosocial lie also depends on how much insight you have into what the other person wants. For example, Levine and her team have worked with both patients and doctors, and found that patients are far more comfortable with false hope than doctors are. Some patients, for example, may want hope and optimism rather than the brutal truth. That's something a doctor should know ahead of time. If a doctor offers a terminal patient a watered-down more hopeful version of the truth when she doesn't know the patient's preference, it's called a "paternalistic" lie. The doctor merely *thinks* she knows what the patient wants. Paternalistic lies can be as destructive as self-interest lies. On the other hand, a doctor offering a patient a watered-down more hopeful version of the truth because she has discussed it with the patient and *she actually knows* their preferences—that's seen as a trust-building prosocial lie. "It's about whether you have true insight into what is best for the other person," Levine explains. These quandaries involving whether or not to disclose negative information or provide false optimism are not limited to the health care arena. Managers face these predicaments when providing feedback to employees. Government and law enforcement officials sometimes face Catch-22s surrounding national security and other threats. Parents routinely deal with tough dilemmas around how much to reveal to a child. Even friendships and romantic relationships get caught up in these dilemmas. In other words, we face these situations, like, *a lot*.

Clearly, a prosocial lie isn't always the right answer. Neither is honesty. Saying "Honesty is always the best policy" makes as much sense as saying, "Prosocial lying is always the best policy." There's no singular, cohesive way to understand or talk about deception. In my view, this is actually good news, and here's why: On one hand, we're likely *worse* than we thought when it comes to lies of self-interest, because we have a fudge factor—even though we don't like to admit it (publicly), we *know* that we do. But on the other hand, we're likely *better* than we thought when it comes to prosocial lies. They come from a good place. Sometimes it's misguided and not as great as we think (paternalistic lies), but on the whole, we're trying. The reason I say this is all good news is because both sides of it are learnable. We can learn to notice our fudge factor. We can also learn how to be more conscientious prosocial liars.

If I'm going to take the time and energy to learn a new skill, I want a good reason why I should. So . . . why should we take the time to learn how to both stomp out and increase deception? Or put another way: Why does it matter?

"If Donald Trump Can Say It, I Can Say It"

Several months after the 2016 presidential election (but before I started my journal), I found myself doing a phone interview with a cardiologist. I do a lot of writing for hospitals, helping them turn clinical and scary health language into consumer friendly messages people can more easily understand. This doctor and I were talking about his hospital's electrophysiology program, so I could write a web page about it. Electrophysiology deals with treating people for arrhythmias, or irregular heartbeats, and one of the treatments is ablation. The more ablations a hospital does, the better they tend to be at performing them. This is why volume is an important claim—consumers like to know that doctors have done the procedure a bunch of times and have the right experience. When I asked this cardiologist about their ablation volume, he said, "It's the highest in the region." While that was an impressive claim, part of my job is to check the facts on all the claims I write. So I asked him if he had actual numbers to back it up. He hemmed and hawed a bit, and finally said, "Listen, if Donald Trump can get up there and say whatever he wants, we can say that we have the highest ablation volume in the region."

I was stunned. I laughed nervously, because I was caught off guard.

I think I said something like, "Okay, I'll follow up with marketing then," before I changed the topic. I was a freelancer for an agency the hospital had hired to write the content, so it wasn't really my place to give him a speech about integrity and truth. Not to mention, it would have been poor form for me to be so righteous. But still, did he really think that? This was an educated person. A person of science, who had been through years of schooling and had relied on facts and evidence his entire career. Had his belief in facts been that rocked by Trump? Did he really think truth didn't matter anymore?

All during Trump's presidential campaign, I thought, No one believes anything this guy is saying. The American people are smarter than this. And then, well . . . we don't need to belabor what happened. That he won was one thing. But that he (and his press secretary) could continually tell lies, exaggerate, and flat out make things up once he became president, seemingly with no consequence, really did have me wondering if anything mattered anymore. What was the incentive to tell the truth, when someone lying and spewing paranoia was rewarded with the highest office in the land?

I forced myself out of that place, because it was too tragic a location. But it frightened me that others might take up more permanent residence there. And I wondered: What effect would our president's unchecked lying have on an entire generation of leaders? On our children? What if this was the beginning of not caring about honesty anymore? As I said, a big motivation for starting my honesty project was to turn the lens inward, to focus on the one thing I could control—myself—versus catastrophizing and name-calling. If I was going to start calling out lying, I really should start with my own. Shining this light inside ourselves, doing this work of untangling deception, separating hard truths from kind lies, calling bullshit on self-delusion, checking our privilege, attaching alarm bells to our fudge factor—this all matters, because the minute we start to believe it doesn't matter, we'll be in that tragic place of not caring. Nothing good comes from that place. This work we do is so much bigger than any one elected official. It's part of human consciousness, and as we'll explore in the next chapter, we've evolved as human beings to care about honesty for very specific reasons. No matter what Trump—or anyone, for that matter—gets away with, all is not lost. As long as we do the work of honesty and support others doing the work, all will never be lost. I call that the "poetic" reason of why this honesty work matters, and why it matters *now*.

There are practical reasons, too. Let's start by addressing why we should care about the clear self-interest lies, even the small ones. Why should we start paying better attention to our fudge factor? It's pretty simple: The cumulative effect of all of us lying *just a little* adds up. Those small instances of dishonesty regarding money add up to a chunk of change over time. There is also the matter of small lies having the tendency to lead to even bigger lies. Yael Melamede made a documentary called *(Dis)Honesty: The Truth About Lies*, featuring a handful of people who were very publicly caught lying, whose lives unraveled as a result—they were shamed, fired from their job, fined, even sent to jail. "Each of these stories started with a small infraction which led to more and more, until these people were in very deep trouble. We can look at them and wonder how did they fall so far, but it's important to realize that for them the thirtieth infraction is relative to the twenty-ninth, not the first. All along the way, it is just an incremental buildup," Melamede explained to me. Lies can stack neatly, until they all come tumbling down.

And then, there are the little one-and-done half-truths we tell, such as when we don't speak up to correct a falsehood (e.g., your boss credits you with a successful campaign that was really your co-worker's idea and you don't correct her), or when we purposely mislead or parse words to the point that we are technically speaking true words but with a dishonest intention. Sometimes, this is on purpose and for a specific reason tied to self-interest (like you *really* want that promotion). Other times, our dishonesty slips through our consciousness almost undetected. *Almost.* Because these decisions have a tendency to leave a radioactive trail behind, filled with toxic by-products like guilt, shame, and judgment (of ourselves or others). You might have adrenaline in the moment—when you post that picture on Facebook, successfully shift the blame, bullshit your way out of something, or exaggerate in a way that makes you look better. What happens in the next moment, though? You know the icky feeling I'm talking about, like a sugar crash of bad emotions and second-guessing.

We know from polygraph (lie detector) technology that lying can be accompanied by physiological markers—like an increase in heart rate and blood pressure, and sweating. Of course, simply being nervous causes these responses as well, which is why polygraph tests are controversial and some psychologists, scientists, and law enforcement personnel don't consider them reliable (not to mention they can't be used as evidence in court). Still, they may have some use in certain situations (like in the study mentioned below). Either way, the idea that our physical body may respond to our emotional choices about honesty is worth thinking about—especially when there is some evidence that consciously telling the truth can make you healthier.

A University of Notre Dame study by psychology professor Anita Kelly found that people who consciously worked to avoid lies for several weeks were healthier—with less sore throats and colds—and also reported feeling less stressed. Her study included 110 adults, ranging from eighteen to seventy-one years old. Half of the participants were told to stop telling lies for the next ten weeks, while the other half didn't get any special instructions. Both groups came to the lab weekly to fill out questionnaires about health and relationships and to take lie detector tests to help assess how many lies they had told that week. Over the ten weeks, the no-lie group reported better health. When they told three less lies than they did in other weeks, they had four fewer mental health complaints (like feeling stressed or sad) and about three fewer physical complaints (like headaches and sore throats). The control group—the group without specific instructions to avoid lies—also had fewer mental and physical symptoms when they lied less. It wasn't as significant as the no-lie group, because, on average, they were still telling more lies (since they weren't instructed not to). This is only one study, and it's hardly conclusive evidence that honesty improves our health, but it's compelling enough to pay attention.

Emma Levine, the prosocial lying scholar, has also done some research that looks at honesty from the communicator's perspective, and what it feels like to tell a difficult truth. She and her research team conducted a study where they asked one group of people to aim for complete honesty in all encounters, with everyone, for the next three days. They instructed the other group to be kind or conscious of their words. The complete honesty group dreaded the task, predicting it would cause unhappiness and would have an adverse effect on relationships if they couldn't use lies to cover up awkward situations. But, surprisingly, it didn't have the negative effect people expected. It actually made them feel . . . good. "People think honesty is going to be worse than it is. It turns out that honesty is more pleasurable and socially connecting than you expect it to be," Levine says. To summarize, when you focus on being honest versus indulging in your own self-interest, it's better for the economy, less likely to lead to bigger lies, and better for both your mental and physical health.

That leaves the question: What about the "good" kind of lying? If we're all telling prosocial lies, and they benefit others, why bother focusing on them? Who cares if we don't really understand it? Can't we just leave well enough alone and go about our merry way? We can. But there is a cost.

"You're Either Honest or You're Not"

University of Massachusetts psychology professor Robert Feldman, author of *The Liar in Your Life*, studied lying for several decades. He was one of the first people to break the news that we lie way more than we think. Feldman found his way to deception research by accident. He was conducting a series of studies about non-verbal communication, and one of the areas he was looking at was whether or not our non-verbal information (body language, expression, etc.) could clue others into whether we were being honest or not. He did several studies trying to determine whether we could tell when someone was being deceptive, anticipating that study participants would be able to tell when they were being lied to. He was wrong. Over and over, he found that people couldn't tell when they were being deceived. That's when Feldman started looking more directly at lying and began researching deception. "I started off by assuming that people didn't lie very often, and that's why we weren't very good at discerning it. In fact, I found the opposite—that we lie frequently. We lie so much and we're not even aware. I had to do a 180-degree switch in my thinking," he explains to me.

In one study, he found that 60 percent of people lied at least one time during a ten-minute conversation with another person. He had pairs of students talk to each other for ten minutes. Some were told to appear more likable, others were told to appear competent, and a third group didn't get any instruction. After the conversations were over, the students watched recordings of their conversations, and researchers told them to identify any lies they told, no matter how small. In watching their conversations, the students had no idea they had lied as much as they had. One person told twelve lies in the ten minutes. Some of the lies were of the conversation-building kind—like agreeing they each liked someone or something. Others were bigger, but also pretty funny (especially when you keep in mind these were college students), like claiming to be the star of a rock band. Students in the likability group told more lies than those in the control group (the group given no instruction)—mostly lies about feelings. Students in the competent group tended to tell lies about future plans.

Feldman's takeaway from the study wasn't that students are big liars (though I do imagine him chuckling at some of the things these students said). Rather, his point is that there are mixed messages around lying. "We teach our children that honesty is the best policy, but we also tell them it's polite to pretend they like a birthday gift they've been given. It's part of being a socially successful person in our society," he says. We not only tell these lies; we want to hear these lies. He gives me the example of when he has a speaking engagement. "There has never been a time when people come up to me afterwards and tell me it went too long, or it was boring. Rather, they say, 'Oh, it was so interesting!' If I analyze the interaction, that's what I want to hear. At some level maybe I want feedback, but the reality is the adrenaline is running, I'm feeling good and I want to maintain that feeling," he says. As a person who does a fair amount of public speaking, too, I understand exactly what he's saying. I try to imagine how it would feel if someone came up to me after a talk and said, "I noticed the three places you stumbled, and it made me think that you weren't as smart as I thought." How awful would that feel?! Of course, not saying anything is always an option—rather than brutal honesty or made-up things. But the minute we begin speaking to another person in a manner that suggests feedback, the stage is set for us to either say a truth or say a falsehood. We need the truths. But maybe we also need the falsehoods.

The way we tend to talk about lying is inherently confusing and contradictory, says Thomas Carson, the philosophy professor. He finds that when he asks students their views on lying, many of them will say that lying is wrong, and recount how they've been told lying is wrong. Then, he walks students through scenarios, such as a Polish woman hiding Jewish people in Nazi Germany. If the woman hadn't lied to the Nazis, she, her family, and the people she was hiding would have been killed. The students agree that she—and scores of other people who hid Jewish people in Europe, people who escaped enslavement in nineteenth-century America, or women fleeing from violent husbands whenever and wherever— did the moral thing by lying. "When you say that lying is always wrong, then you are elevating that as the most important moral obligation. But obligations can conflict. There might be obligations to others, to not hurt their feelings or even to protect them from being killed. You can't make lying as a principle more important than those considerations," Carson explains. Someone may try to argue that it's wrong to lie, but you "had" to do it. That's incoherent, he says, because a moral judgment is supposed to tell you what to do. If you are saying something is really morally wrong, you are saying *not* to do it, period. A better way to think about it is that lying is wrong *in the absence of other reasons to the contrary*.

Instinctually, most of us develop a framework to figure this out, because—in the hysterical words of George Costanza—"You know, we're living in a society!" It's a scaffolding that remains mostly hidden, though, and the way we talk about lying is still fairly nonsensical, filled with truisms that aren't, in fact, true. The cost of not understanding prosocial lies is our emotional health and how we regard both ourselves and other people. And guess what? All that nonsense we endure as children has a real effect on how we behave as adults. For example, a person may behave by saying accusingly to another person, "You're either honest or you're not, and you're either raising your children to be honest or you're not." I know, because this is exactly the accusation that was leveled at me, in one of the most contentious and infuriating public spaces that exist: the reader comments section of *The New York Times*.

THOUGH KEEPING THE JOURNAL at first made me feel worse, after a few weeks, it started to make me feel better. Even though I had some failings around honesty, I was being honest with myself about those things for the first time in a while. The idea of *who I was* and the reality of *how I was being* felt more closely aligned. I pitched an essay about my honesty journal to the editor I sometimes wrote for at *The New York Times*, and he liked the idea. I worked on the piece over the summer, and it ran that fall. In the essay, I talked about my experiences keeping the journal, pulling out examples like explaining to my then eight-year-old son what the word *pimp* meant. I highlighted the research Dan Ariely, Seth Stephens-Davidowitz, and others had done around dishonesty, and also explained what behavioral scientists were currently studying in the world of prosocial lying. My takeaway in the piece was that the act of focusing on honesty could make you feel better. I concluded, "The bottom line is that focusing on honesty is a way to actively engage with the world, versus passively complaining about it."

By the time the piece ran, I already had an inkling that I wanted to write a book about the topic. There was just too much there, and though at times it all felt rather obvious, honesty also felt like this hidden world of weirdness we weren't supposed to notice. I was noticing in a big way, and I didn't want to back down. I knew the *Times* piece was just the first step. Though I usually try to avoid the brutality of *Times* reader comments, I wanted to get a sense of how people were reacting to this idea of honesty as a way to engage with the world. I took a deep breath, and opened the comment panel below the article after a few days. There were the requisite nasty and/or snarky comments, which I ignored. There were also several constructive comments—mostly positive, but some semi-critical—that engaged with my argument in a thoughtful way. I appreciated those comments, and they helped me push my research to the next level.

Yet, the comments I found myself really studying were the ones from people who were convinced that (a) honesty was so basic, there was no need to write about it, and (b) they *themselves* were above reproach when it came to being honest. One woman wrote, "It's interesting that truth-telling is presented as a novel lifestyle experiment, akin to a juice cleanse or a day without using your cell phone. When did telling the truth become so exotic?" Another commenter said, "I have totally gone through life as an honest person and could not imagine otherwise." Obviously, I assumed he or she was full of complete and utter shit. Perhaps the most illuminating comment was from someone who called me out for taking a moment before I gave back a McDonald's cashier the extra dollar in change she'd given me. Remember how I thought for a moment before I handed it back, and that I realized a motivation for giving it back and being honest was the fact that I was keeping an honesty journal? But how I didn't struggle at all with the bigger instance of sending the $1,000 check back to the children's hospital? This commenter did not like that. *At all.* They questioned why I would struggle with the small instances of honesty so much, when it was clearly black and white. "You're either honest or you're not, and you're either raising your children to be honest or you're not," the commenter wrote.

For a moment, I felt slapped. Was this commenter right? Was I actually a lying piece of shit, raising my children with some kind of disastrous moral relativism? I panicked. And then I took a deep breath and remembered second grade. And fifth grade. And sixth grade. And high school. And college. And last year. And last night.

And the illusion that it is simple, when in fact, the only people who think it is simple are the ones who haven't taken the time to examine it, because it's deeply painful, deeply shameful stuff. After all, if you were admonished as a child to always be honest, but then excoriated for not being kind to Aunt Edna when she asked you if you liked your birthday gift, the weight of that weird dissonance echoing in your brain for decades could perhaps lead you to say, "You know what, screw all of this! You're either honest or you're not!" when you see some writer poking around in areas you really don't want to deal with. And why would you? Those places are likely confusing and related to uncomfortable memories. It's hard to go there; however, you can't pop the bubble of shame or clear away the confusion unless you confront what's behind your actions. Maybe you're actually trying to be a jerk. We're all jerks sometimes. I get it. Maybe, though, you're trying to be kind and helpful and principled. That might mean you need to tell a prosocial lie, or it might mean you need to take a deep breath and spill the truth.

I wrote in my honesty journal, "An honest life isn't some life lived in a vacuum of purity. It is a life lived in gray areas. It's about stepping into that gray area and looking around and being truthful about what you see and feel." That was a new insight for me, and it was the beginning of truly noticing those mixed messages I internalized growing up. You can be a good person, living an ethical and kind life, and tell a prosocial lie every single day. In fact, it's hard to be happy and enjoy meaningful relationships if you don't. It's also hard to be happy and enjoy meaningful relationships if you continue to lie to yourself and fail to notice your own behavior. How could I possibly sort through that "life lived in gray areas"?

Two Honesty Principles to Start

I originally thought of my honesty journal as a practice, like yoga or meditation. But as I continued to journal and explore honesty more fully, I realized I was documenting a journey. I began thinking about some organizing concepts I could use—principles I could distill down, like fence posts for the journey. I liked how Gretchen Rubin had outlined her "Twelve Commandments" in *The Happiness Project*. I was seeking similar guiding wisdom. I didn't know most of my principles yet, but I was solid on what my first honesty principle should be: *First, be aware.* There is a reason mindful meditation has become so popular—it helps people cultivate awareness. The biggest hurdle for most of us is just training ourselves to pay attention. To stop and notice. To pause and listen. To take a beat. The first big hurdle of focusing on honesty is the *focus* part. This is why awareness is your best tool. Being aware can help you:

- Spot your own fudge factor
- Avoid saying an untruth you'll regret
- Deliver a hard, but necessary, truth
- Determine that a kind lie is the best course of action
- Catch your conflicts of interest
- Check your privilege
- Escape your default setting of not noticing

Being aware is a simple concept. That doesn't mean it's easy. Running ten miles is *simple*—put one foot in front of the other about fifteen thousand times. But it's hardly *easy*. Simple and easy are not true synonyms. The point is, even simple things require training. The only way that I could train myself to be more aware about my honesty choices was to write them down. The benefit of writing a thought down is that it usually makes you pay attention to that thought at least five times. First, you have the thought, perhaps during a conversation or digital exchange with someone. Two, you make a note in your brain that you're going to write about it in your journal. Three, you write it down in your journal. Four, you re-read what you've written in your journal after you write it. Five, you think about it again when you reflect on what you wrote that day. Then, if you're like me, you re-read the entry several times and continue to think about it in the days and weeks that follow. Before you know it, you may have reflected on a situation more than a dozen times—a situation that before would have slipped by with barely an acknowledgment. This is how awareness builds, through repetition of paying attention to situations that make you examine your thoughts. Perhaps it sounds tedious, but you get more efficient at it the longer you do it. If you ever nursed a baby, or watched your significant other nurse a baby, you know that in the beginning, the baby nurses twenty or thirty minutes to get enough milk. Like, *forever* (speaking as someone who nursed both my babies). But by the time they are a few months old, they are highly efficient and get their fill in less than five minutes. (True, they often spit it back up all over you. Let's just set that aside and focus on the *efficiency* part.) You will become more efficient with your awareness practice if you stick with it.

While I got pretty good at being aware in situations that involved honesty—from conversations with my kids to arguments with my husband to email exchanges with clients—I felt overwhelmed by trying to decode all of it *at once*. There was family life, work life, social life, married life, social media life, spiritual life, political life, interior life, and iterations that combined these. Some areas were more difficult than others, and yet, I wanted to improve my honesty game in all these different aspects of my life. There was so much swirling in my head on any given day, so many ideas that seemed to conflict, and so many theories that I wanted to figure out how to apply. But did every interaction in my life carry equal weight? I knew, practically speaking, that it didn't. My relationship with my husband was more important than my relationship with an acquaintance I only saw once a year. And yet, every interaction was important, because the work of honesty meant being aware all of the time. I wanted to continue to cultivate awareness. I also didn't want to lose my mind by expending energy in the wrong places. While I always needed to be aware, some situations required more energy and thought than others. I needed a principle that would help me move forward and not get stuck in my head.

I decided the second honesty principle was this: *Not every situation is the same.* This didn't mean that I could stop paying attention in certain situations; it just meant that I didn't need to regard every situation as equal and allocate equal energy to it. It also gave me a framework to compartmentalize, for lack of a better word. Ultimately, I believe we should be who we are all the time. One of my coach's favorite sayings was, "How you do anything is how you do everything." I liked the saying, too. I also knew that trying to tackle kids, husband, family, work, friends, and social life all at once would be like deciding to become a vegetarian, stop eating sugar, get nine hours of sleep every night, get rid of my television, and start boxing five times a week all at once. I had written enough articles about goal setting and change management to know that when you focus on too many things at one time, you set yourself up to fail. If I was going to get somewhere with honesty, I would have to start with the lower hanging fruit and work my way to the harder-to-reach areas. The best course of action would be to start by focusing on honesty in the relationships that were of less consequence and work my way to the most important, most intimate relationships, keeping in mind that while honesty always mattered, *not every situation was the same.*

The *Times* commenter had taken me to task for how I behaved in the drive-thru at McDonald's, so why not start there? Not literally at McDonald's, but with my social behavior and the world of small talk, social niceties, and those common interactions that we tend to just sweep under the rug. I wondered, what did it actually look like under that rug? It was time to find out.

Reviewing the Honesty Principles

First, be aware.
- Stop, look, and listen. Pay attention to situations versus living on autopilot. (*Writing something down makes you think about it at least five times.*)
- Simply being aware is an excellent first step to prevent dishonesty.

Not every situation is the same.
- Different areas of your life have different stakes; not every decision deserves the same amount of energy. (*If you have too many goals at once, you won't do any of them.*)

CHAPTER 4

Honesty in Social Situations

ONE TUESDAY AFTERNOON IN APRIL, about a year into keeping my journal, I found myself at the YMCA pool, swimming laps. When I only had about ten more laps to go, I felt someone whoosh by me in my lane. I came close to hitting the person, and it startled me. The etiquette for sharing a lane is that you always get verbal confirmation from another swimmer before you enter the lane. You never assume they will see you, because swimmers' heads are down in the water and goggles fog up quickly, making it hard to see someone in the distance.

I made the adjustment of scooting over in my lane for the rest of my laps. I passed by the swimmer a few times. I could tell from the presence in the water that it was a man, and that he wasn't a very strong swimmer. He was probably a beginner, I thought. After I completed my laps, I hung out at the wall for a minute, waiting for him to swim back down. I saw that it was an older gentleman who didn't look all that proficient at swimming. I knew right away that he wasn't trying to be rude; he simply didn't understand the etiquette. As he bobbed toward me, I took a deep breath. I didn't like "correcting" people when they screwed up, because I know how shameful it feels to be called out when you've made an innocent mistake. On the other hand, he needed to know; otherwise he risked getting hurt, or hurting someone else.

"Excuse me, sir?" I said tentatively.

"Yes?" he said.

"I'm always willing to share a lane with another swimmer, but it's really important to make sure you get my attention—or any swimmer's attention—before getting in the lane," I explained.

"Oh, I thought you saw me. I waited until you were halfway down," he said, surprised.

"I know, but I can never see anything when I'm swimming. My head is down and my goggles are all fogged up. You just have to make eye contact or get my attention verbally."

"I'm sorry," he said. "I just started swimming." He looked embarrassed. I felt his shame as my own, which created a panicked feeling. At that point, I made a decision. Actually, it was more instinct than decision. "I totally did the same thing the first time I swam here! I thought the person saw me, and they had to tell me this was the etiquette. It's not necessarily obvious to a new swimmer that the person in the lane can't see you. Don't worry!"

That was a lie. No one had to tell me, because it *did* seem obvious to me the first time I had to join someone's lane that I better make sure they saw me. This carefulness undoubtedly came from years of running on the road, and never crossing in front of a stopped car unless I made eye contact with the driver. I could see that another person not as used to navigating the life-and-death of exercise might not get it.

Immediately, he brightened. "Thank you for telling me," he said genuinely.

"No problem!" I said. We chatted for another minute, and then I hoisted myself out of the pool.

I had just successfully executed a prosocial lie. It's the kind of thing I would have done before keeping my journal without even noticing. Now, however, I noticed. (*First, be aware.*) I also reflected on how it made me feel. It made me feel happy. Lighter. Like that feeling of holding in a smile. Prosocial lying worked!

But then a week later, I had prosocial lying fail.

I was at a writers' conference, and an editor I had worked with many times was there. The first few times I had worked with him, it went well. But increasingly, I found him difficult to work with because of his editing style. His edits back to me often felt brash, bordering on rude in the comments. I talked with other writers, and they reported similar experiences. Though it had never come to it, I had told myself I would turn down a project if he were the only editor working on it. I had never met him in person before, though, and when I met him at this conference, he was such a nice guy—unassuming and slightly awkward in a charming way (which describes a great many writers and editors). His personality didn't seem to match his editing style. Had I been wrong? Had I been too sensitive? I wasn't sure.

He cornered me during one of the breaks, and abruptly asked me, "Do you get more edits back from me than from any other editor?" He didn't ask it in a menacing, demanding way. It was more like a hurt little boy way. I was caught off guard. I stammered and said something like, "Um, I don't think so?" I did manage to say something about him having a very exacting style, to which he agreed. He said another writer had leveled this charge at him, and he was trying to see if others had the same experience. I was immensely uncomfortable. I wanted to be honest and tell him, "Yeah, dude, you need to chill. Nobody wants to work with you because you can be a dick." He even opened the door for me to be honest, but in that moment, the truth wouldn't come to me. I brushed it off and tried to change the topic. I didn't want to hurt his feelings.

I felt terrible after the exchange. I knew immediately that I had failed. I had told a prosocial lie, just like the swimming lie, but this was different. This was a case where I should have been honest.

How we approach honesty in our day-to-day interactions with people—including the way we feel after telling either a prosocial lie or a lie of self-interest—is indicative of what we value. You can learn a lot about yourself by noticing your go-to responses in these social interactions. My lie to the swimming lane interloper showcased my desire to be empathetic. Empathy is the antidote to shame. I know how shame feels, and I want less of it. Empathy-building is a strength of mine. It's something I like about myself. On the other hand, my lie to the editor points out a weakness of mine: my inability to manage confrontation in a fruitful way. I want to, but I'm often scared. What am I scared of?

Hurting someone. Looking stupid. Being judged or told to shut up already because I clearly don't know what I'm talking about. It's not lost on me that both of my examples above are with men, but I'm an equal opportunity chicken, and have struggled just as mightily to have the uncomfortable conversations with women. I'm far better at having these conversations now than I was at twenty, when my solution to not wanting to date a boy anymore was to simply never call him back. Still, giving people honest feedback, especially when I have an emotional investment in it, is something I struggle with. And yet, not doing it makes me feel as terrible as knowingly cheating would make me feel.

To recap: I sometimes feel bad when I lie, but do it anyway because I think being honest would make me feel even worse. On the other hand, I sometimes feel as good when I lie as I feel when I'm honest.

I'm guessing that you know exactly what I'm talking about. So . . . how in the world did this complicated relationship with honesty come to be an everyday part of the human experience?

The Evolution of Honesty

That human beings are honest at all is a puzzle for evolutionary psychology. How did it benefit our ancestors to be honest? After all, to be honest is to pay an opportunity cost—to say "no" to a dishonest option that is likely to provide more immediate material benefits. How could individuals survive and thrive if they were continually paying opportunity costs? And yet, honesty, as a trait, hasn't disappeared. So how did something that seems to be a weakness (from an evolutionary point of view) become so essential to human beings? This puzzle fascinated Christophe Heintz, associate professor of cognitive science at Central European University. He isn't the only evolutionary psychologist trying to account for how a seemingly detrimental behavior—honesty, or forgoing opportunity—was actually beneficial for our ancestors. Figuring it out may seem like a mere academic project. But it can actually tell us a lot about our behavior today.

On a cool June morning, I call up Professor Heintz to walk me through this business of honesty inside of human evolution. Though he lives in Budapest, he's in Paris on the morning we talk, in what I can only imagine is a bustling part of the city, because several times during our Skype call, I hear the wail of European-style sirens. I'm in Ohio, looking out on my suburban landscape—with trees softly blowing and dogs barking. Neither one of us is in an environment remotely like our ancestors on the African savannah. And yet there is something so fundamental in how we approach honesty that connects us through time to those ancestors, which is the presumption of cooperation. I assume that he will be honest with me in our conversation about his work, and he assumes that I will be honest with him in discussing the project I'm working on. So why did it turn out this way?

Heintz and other researchers theorize that honesty became a desirable trait because of *partner choice*. To be honest is to exhibit prosocial behavior, because it means that you're foregoing benefits so as not to deprive others from the benefits they rightly deserve. Humans are ultimately a collaborative species, and we benefit from cooperating with each other and acting together. Being prosocial and honest makes you a better cooperator. Good cooperators are desirable because they don't take more than their share or start fights about how much they get. When good cooperators are involved, there are more benefits for everyone, and less fighting in general. So, imagine you are in a village and you want to hunt. There are benefits to hunting in a group—it's safer, and people working together are more likely to catch prey than someone working alone. You want to find good partners and also convince others that you are a good partner to go hunting with. "You have to become the person people want to go hunting with," Heintz says. We learned to make choices that would eventually provide benefits, which is what helped us survive and reproduce. The function of honesty, then, was one of managing reputation, because a good reputation was the best protection against being ostracized, or prevented from participating in fruitful cooperative actions. But how does honesty actually *work*? What is the mechanism for it? How does it play out among human beings? In other words, how can partner choice theory account for the fact that we feel good when we're honest and bad when we're dishonest? Heintz says that he has wondered the same thing. There are multiple psychological mechanisms that work together. I like to think of these mechanisms as Door No. 1, Door No. 2, and Door No. 3.

Behind Door No. 1, we have the Machiavellian mechanism: You are honest because you understand it's good for you. Heintz gives an example of a group of Jewish diamond merchants that many scholars have studied. In the diamond business, there is a huge incentive to cheat because the industry works on a system of credit. But as this group of merchants has figured out, there is a stronger incentive to be honest, because if you cheat and you're found out, you will lose your reputation. If you lose your reputation, you won't be able to trade anymore. The diamond merchants understand this, and are able to enforce honesty standards that go beyond what the law itself can do. It is why that particular group of merchants has been so successful. So, honesty can lead to things that are good for us, and that material benefit makes us feel good. But Machiavellian thinking alone doesn't explain the range of honest behavior observed, because following this logic, a person who was only motivated to be honest because it was beneficial to them might still cheat when they didn't feel their reputation was on the line (i.e., there was a very slim chance of anyone finding out). For example, Heintz offers, tipping decently in a restaurant where you often go might be a way to make sure that you will be well served next time you come. But then why do people still give tips when they are traveling and know they will never come back to the restaurant? "What determines honest or generous behavior is more than Machiavellian calculation," he says. Ultimately, Machiavellian thinking is too risky, because there are too many potential social interactions to account for. We can't possibly compute them all, and we are bound to make mistakes.

Door No. 1's Machiavellian approach gives us a partial answer, but we really need to hit up No. 2, behind which we have another psychological mechanism, and it has to do with *esteem*. In short, we have a preference for being esteemed by others. Rather than always being calculating about whether a potential situation will pay dividends if we're honest, we have a shortcut, and the shortcut is always being esteemed by others. Put a more simpler way: We love to be loved. So even in those situations where we're not expecting our honesty to pay material benefits, we break toward honesty because it makes others like us. "From an evolutionary standpoint, in view of uncertainty, a mechanism with a preference for being esteemed by others is the best trade-off. It's a good thing that we like to be esteemed by others, because it's a preference that leads to more benefits," Heintz says.

There is one more key piece, though, and it's behind Door No. 3: We also like to be esteemed by *ourselves*. Basically, we are judging our own behavior as if we were judging someone else's behavior. "We look at ourselves as a potential cooperator, and if we evaluate ourselves as a potential cooperator, we feel good," Heintz says. We fundamentally want to like ourselves, because if we like us, then why wouldn't someone else like us? If other people like us, maybe they'll ask us to go hunting and we don't die from a life of lonely, pitiful starvation. We needed a way to know if we truly liked ourselves—which means we needed to be familiar with the feeling of not liking ourselves. You know the feeling I mean. I knew it when I was seven. It's universal. It's the five-letter-word that feels as familiar as the fetal position, yet we try to do whatever we can to avoid it. *Shame.* Shame, or the bad feeling we have when we think badly of ourselves, is the output of an evolved mechanism, Heintz explains. "We feel shame to avoid choices that will lead to decreasing opportunities for cooperation," he says. If all else fails, shame comes in and keeps us in check. It's hardwired into us. It's cruel, of course, and if allowed to flourish in our psyche unchecked, it leads to all kinds of problems for people. But shame does serve some evolutionary purpose, which is fascinating to me.

Now, there is just one more caveat—a giant asterisk that complicates it all. Because remember, we do lie for self-interested reasons and cheat. *A lot.* We're actually kind of terrible. Sure, we feel bad about it. But we still keep doing it. Why? Because we are able to *justify* some behavior. Whether it's baked into human nature or we learn it as we go, we're pros at justifying. Remember the actor/observer bias? How we judge others more harshly for doing the same things we do? We fail to judge ourselves as we would others because we can justify our own actions. And if you can justify your actions, others still esteem you, you can still esteem yourself, and the mechanism is still in place. This works for both prosocial lies and lies of self-interest.

When I was laid off the second time within six months way back in 2002, I actually stole an entire roll of stamps. I packed them right up with my stuff while the human resources person stood a few feet away. I had just bought them (with the company credit card), and I was so caught off guard and utterly crushed that this company was laying me off *the day before I was supposed to sign a contract for a house* that I poached the stamps. I must say, I never really felt that bad about it. Did I mention they laid me off the day before I was going to buy a house?! No one ever knew I took the stamps, and at the end of the day, I could still like myself. In reflection, I see that it was dishonest. At the time, I justified it, though. I esteemed myself just fine, and the world continued to esteem me. As for the truly prosocial lies? I absolutely justified telling the lie to the man at the pool who got in my lane. I hate for people to feel stupid. My lie made him feel less stupid. He definitely esteemed me, and I esteemed myself. Voilà, justification!

The decisions we absolutely cannot justify, or that we justify *for a while* but eventually can't, we feel guilt around. But also perhaps shame. People have various ways they define the difference between shame and guilt. I define the difference in this way: Guilt is a tangible thing related to specific actions, whereas shame is shadowy and about your personhood. For example, this past Christmas, I didn't give money to the GiftCrowd holiday collection for the school bus driver because I was feeling nickel-and-dimed with holiday requests and didn't want to enter my credit card information in yet one more platform. I feel kind of guilty about it now. But that feeling of guilt is specific to an action. If I extended the feeling into a sweeping self-judgment about the kind of person I am, that would be shame. Guilt says, "I didn't give money, and I FEEL bad about it." Shame says, "I didn't give money, and I AM bad." We often feel shame and guilt together, but the shame is deeper and has a tendency to stick to our soul. Guilt you can often counter by apologizing, making a correction, or some other constructive behavior. Shame, on the other hand, tends to linger, often without specifics. I find it helpful to understand that evolution has shaped us to feel shame, and that it's part of a mechanism that tries to keep us honest for our own survival. Shame isn't an overly constructive emotion, though. In fact, shame can be a highly destructive emotion, and as we'll explore in the chapter on self-honesty, identifying your shame triggers is a key part of the journey toward a more honest life.

The Role of Emotions

Talking to Professor Heintz gives me the ten-thousand-foot view of honesty. And in some ways, we are still those primitive creatures, knowing we need to find good cooperators to make a go of it. For example, who do you want to invite to your progressive dinner party? Mark, who makes the most amazing peach cobbler but is uptight and stingy, never making quite enough, so some guests are left cobbler-less . . . or Marianna, who always makes people laugh and whose tiramisu is good, but not as good as the cobbler, yet there is always enough of it? Most of us—at least those of us who know what it feels like to be the ones holding an empty plate—would opt for Marianna. We are still primed to look for good cooperators in social situations.

Of course, we're far more emotionally intelligent creatures than our ancestors. We are able to balance several competing values at once, and assess when there is another value on the table that's more important than honesty (because as the second principle tells us: *Not every situation is the same*). This ability to balance competing values is a good thing, but it also complicates our honesty story, because it means that emotion can get in the way. Remember my example of not being able to be truthful with the editor who asked me what I thought about his edits? My emotion was in the way. At first blush, I might have labeled the emotion "fear"—as in, fear of hurting his feelings. However, because I had read a study Matthew Lupoli conducted when he was a doctoral candidate at UC-San Diego (he's now a lecturer at Deakin University), I knew there might be more at work.

Lupoli has been studying the effect of compassion on prosocial lying. One might expect compassion would lead people to be more honest, Lupoli explains. "We all have experience with dishonesty and the harmful consequences of lying, so given these negative effects, you might think compassion would make people more honest," he says. On the other hand, compassion could also motivate someone not to cause any more harm, and thus tell a prosocial lie. Previous research has shown that compassion induces people to give more money to charity, and even to receive painful electrical shocks in place of someone else. (Whenever I read about studies involving electric shocks, I'm always glad that I'm a writer and not a researcher.) So, how would compassion—defined as being "emotionally motivated to alleviate others' distress or suffering"—affect honesty? Lupoli and his colleagues tested this by having study participants evaluate a poorly written paper. Participants were split into two groups, and each participant was told that they would be evaluating an essay from a student who had written about why they should be part of a graduate school program. Although participants thought they were each getting a different essay, the participants all got the same essay, and it was a rather mediocre piece of writing. When participants had to evaluate the essay in private (they didn't think the essay writer was going to see their evaluation), they gave it poor marks. Then, the researchers told the participants that they were going to get the chance to read a message from the essay writer, so they could get to know the essay writer better. The compassion group read a message about how a family member of the essay writer had recently passed away; the control group read a message about how the essay writer had recently been grocery shopping.

Both groups of participants were told that they could now offer feedback to the essay writer to potentially help them strengthen the essay so they could resubmit it to an essay contest, where money was on the line. Participants were reminded that this round of feedback would be shared with the essay writer. This time around, the people in the compassion group (the group that read the story about the relative dying) wound up inflating their assessment of the essay to a greater extent than those in the control group. In other words, they told a pro-social lie to the essay writer, telling the writer the essay was better than it truly was. Why? Because they felt compassion. "Compassion attunes people to the suffering of others. So if a person sees lying as a means of preventing suffering or harm, it might increase dishonesty," Lupoli says. Indeed, that's what it did for these study participants. They felt sorry for the essay writer who had just lost a family member, so didn't want to add more suffering by offering a harsh critique of the essay. Even though the study participants were told that their feedback could help the essay writer revise and re-submit and potentially win money, they still struggled to see beyond the feeling of compassion.

In another study, Lupoli and his team also tested the spillover effects of compassion. They wanted to see if emotions elicited in one context would show up in another context involving a potential pro-social lie. They randomly assigned two groups of people to either see neutral images of household items followed by a short movie clip of two people talking (a clip that past research showed produces a neutral state in people) or to see images of helplessness and vulnerability, followed by a short clip talking about child malnutrition and starvation. Then, researchers had all the participants do a perceptual task where they had to look at a screen and decide which side of the screen had more dots filling it. They were told that every time there were more dots on the right, they would earn ten times more money than when there were more dots on the left, but that they were earning the money for a charity that fought malaria. (Participants were told that it was easier to identify the number of dots on the left than the right, so that's why they could earn more money for the charity if they were able to discern when there were more on the right.) The compassion group—the one that saw the compassion-inducing stimuli—cheated more for the benefit of the charity than the other group, both when it was obvious there were more dots on the left than the right, and when it was ambiguous. (All the money earned was actually donated to the charity.) This suggests that if you are feeling compassionate in general, you are more likely to bring that emotion into your next interaction with someone.

Emotions: The Good, the Bad, and the Ones That Make Us Lie

On the surface, lying to benefit others seems good, right? Imagine you are one of these study participants. You've just watched a video about hungry children and then you have to do this strange dots test. You're already feeling compassion, and then you are given an opportunity to lie to benefit others. I can certainly imagine clicking the box that said there were more dots on the right if it meant one less child might get malaria. But now imagine that you work in the accounting department of the charity that is helping to end malaria. You know the good work the charity is doing on behalf of people who need it, and your heart goes out to these people. How might that compassion affect the way you fill out the charity's tax returns? If you cheated the government out of tax money owed, you could frame it as a Robinhood-esque prosocial lie for the benefit of people who needed it. But would that ultimately be the *right* thing to do? Compassion can lead people astray because it creates bias. "Compassion doesn't give us an accurate gauge of what the greatest good is," Lupoli explains.

The same may be true of an emotion like anger. Imagine that you are in the stands watching your kid play football. Or soccer. Or basketball. Or whatever sport you can relate to. Because your best friend is the coach, you have insider information about which kids easily made the team and which ones barely made it. You happen to know that the kid of the parents sitting next to you barely made the team. The dad is being obnoxious, and it's making you angry. Maybe he's trashing your political party. Maybe he's trashing the kind of car you drive. Maybe he's yelling that No. 32 (your kid) needs to learn to hit the ball. The point is, you are getting angry with him. He makes one more rude comment, and bam! You go off and spill the honest truth that his precious kiddo barely made the team! Of course, you know immediately that you have behaved like a jackass. But still, anger clouded your ability to know what information to hold on to and what information to share.

This is all to say: When it comes to honesty, emotions are a bitch.

I realized when I started keeping my journal that emotions were at play in my honesty decisions, especially in social situations, where it's easy to get drawn into drama. This is why the third honesty principle is *Be mindful of emotions*. Emotions can be good. Compassion, for example, is a key human emotion. So is anger. You don't need to avoid emotions (as if you could); rather, you just need to pay attention to them when you are faced with a dilemma of whether to lie or not.

Going back to the prosocial lie to my editor, it was being mindful of my emotions that led me to realize I had messed up and needed to correct the situation. A few hours after I told him the prosocial lie, I texted him and told him that I may not have been completely honest with him because I had been caught off guard. I had a chance to think more, I said, and I would like to find a time for us to talk further about my perception of his editing. We wound up sitting by the pool the next afternoon and had a very nice chat. It was difficult for me to get the words out at first. I knew that compassion had been at work in my decision to lie to him the day before. It isn't that I felt sorry for him exactly. It's that I had seen him as the underdog, the unpopular kid being accused of doing something wrong. By being aware of my emotions, I was also aware of the bias they had created, and I was able to see the right thing to do more easily. He may have been hurt by what the other writer said, but he was asking for feedback. He wanted to know, so that he could perhaps make adjustments. I saw that lying to him was a cruelty, not a kindness. Lying had kept me from having to have the difficult conversation, but it had only hurt him. We talked for over an hour. I got to know him better and told him the way his edits made me feel. He apologized and explained some things to me about his situation that helped me see where he was coming from. Will everything always be wonderful and conflict-free if we work together again? Probably not. But now, I feel like at least we have an honest relationship, and the groundwork to have honest conversations.

I know that I use prosocial lying as a form of empathy, and while I think that is a good thing, I also see the shadow that lurks behind it. Sometimes a person needs to feel the sting of failure or disappointment or even embarrassment to find their motivation to act differently or respond differently. While piling onto their feeling of failure or heaping shame upon them is unkind and unnecessary, trying to eradicate their negative feelings may be doing them a disservice, because screwing up—and having to face your screw up—is what makes a person grow. There is something almost narcissistic about the notion that I can single-handedly wipe away someone's pain, or help them avoid it altogether. Number one, I can't, and number two, it's self-serving to try to do so, because I'm trying to avoid the uncomfortable feeling of watching someone sit with their mistake. Analyzing my prosocial lying tendency has helped me see that. I still believe that a thoughtful prosocial lie has the ability to build goodwill and benefit everyone. I do see that it's complicated, though, and it's worth thinking about and clarifying for yourself where your urge to tell a prosocial lie is coming from. This kind of deep self-work can tell you far more about yourself than rattling off a tired truism about honesty being the best policy.

Use Your Honesty Project as an Excuse to Be Honest

To break the ice in my conversation with my editor—the second conversation, where I had committed to being honest—I told him that I was working on an idea for a book about honesty. I laughed and said that it was working on the book that made me realize I had done a terrible job being honest the day before. Making this disclosure that I was focused on honesty lowered my inhibitions to speak honestly and released me to actually be honest. It's not unlike when you start a sentence with, "To be honest," or "Frankly." It was a stronger effect than that, though. I have since noticed this many times, whether I am talking with my kids or giving advice to a friend. Simply saying out loud to the person that I am consciously focusing on being more honest frees me to share my honesty. I thought about including, *When you admit that you're focusing on honesty, it can help start an honest conversation*, as one of the honesty principles, but it's more of a useful tactic than a true principle. Still, I highly recommend you try it next time you are struggling!

What About Not Saying Anything at All?

Could simply not saying anything at all be one way around all of these struggles? Think back to the example of Robert Feldman, the University of Massachusetts psychology professor and author of *The Liar in Your Life*, when he talked about people coming up to him after a speech and telling him he did a great job. He reflected that these people may be telling him a prosocial lie, but that it's seemingly part of a contract with others. Others will fib a bit to make us feel good and we'll fib a bit when they're in a similar situation to make them feel good. "We are motivated to accept the lies of other people because it makes us feel better and the other person feel better. This is fine at one level, but it can also create misperceptions of who you are," he says. For example, you may think you are a far better public speaker than you are if people keep puffing up your ego. But nobody wants to tell you your missteps. Would it be better if they simply said nothing at all? Neither gave you praise nor honest feedback?

It depends on who you ask. If you are the communicator, it may be easier for you to say nothing rather than to be honest. Remember, though, how emotions get in the way of seeing a situation clearly? (*Be mindful of emotions.*) Your word on which is better is not the most reliable word. The other person, that is, the target of the communication (or non-communication, as it were), may have a different view of it altogether. Not having any feedback at all may be worse than having negative feedback. Think about it, if you give a presentation and nobody says anything, isn't that stress inducing? Don't you assume that it was terrible (at least if you're neurotic like me)? Which is the worst among these three things: (1) being slightly deluded that you're a better speaker than you think, (2) feeling slightly down that the guy with the purple tie said he wished that you had focused more on the first story and not so much time on the second one, or (3) being a mass of anxiety because of your feeling of uncertainty since nobody said anything at all? I would venture to say that "3" is the worst option (at least for me).

This is also what Emma Levine has found in her work on prosocial lies of omission in health care settings. In certain settings, such as with terminal cancer, doctors often believe that saying nothing is better for the patient than providing false hope. But patients find that false hope from a doctor is better than a doctor not saying anything. Hope can help a patient and improve their mental state. That matters for their quality of life when they are fighting a disease. Being told by a doctor they have a chance to beat the cancer (even if, from a medical perspective, it's highly unlikely) can provide comfort, whereas it's upsetting for a patient to hear nothing at all from the doctor about a prognosis. Levine's research has found that false hope at least gives hope, whereas omission has no real emotional benefit. So, while not saying anything at all may seem kinder, in some situations, it's actually crueler.

Do we all just need to be mind readers? Well, that would help immensely. A more practical approach is to think like a negotiator.

Are You Ready to Haggle?

My sister Laura and I adore flea markets. We've been to flea markets all over Ohio, Kentucky, and Indiana, and I've collected everything from vintage sewing patterns to old restaurant drinking glasses to jewelry (one of my favorite flea market finds is a necklace I got for a dollar with a little "J" charm, for "Judi"). Flea markets are vibrant and unexpected and full of wonderful kitsch. I love that all of the objects had a previous life. I also love the joy of a bargain. As all flea market pros know, the real bargains are to be had by haggling. A good haggle starts with the phrase: "Will you take . . ." followed by your price point. Sometimes the answer is no, but if you are reasonable (and you're making an offer to take multiple items off a seller's hands), it's often successful. The reason the haggle is successful is because both parties are equally motivated. At the end of the day, the flea market vendor doesn't want to pack up all the same wares they came with, and the flea market shopper doesn't want to leave empty-handed. They both want something, and they are both willing to part with something else to get it. It's a classic negotiation.

I like to think of prosocial lying as a kind of negotiation, too. If it's truly prosocial (not a lie of self-interest), the communicator (the person with the decision to make about honesty) and the target (the person receiving the lie or the truth) are in it together—aligned in a way, similar to the flea market vendor and the flea market shopper. The communicator wants to be a good person (while avoiding emotional distress), and the target wants to feel respected (while also avoiding emotional distress). Sometimes, it's necessary to haggle a bit, meaning each party will need to experience a bit of emotional distress to get to the best deal possible. If we go back to the public speaking example, I certainly don't want to be picked at by an audience member for things I cannot control, like my thighs appearing too big on stage, or to be on the receiving end of other mean-spirited comments about my intelligence or general delivery. But I would like to know if my presentation was effective or not, even if it means you telling me that you wish I had done XYZ or that I should speak more slowly or make better eye contact. I want to be a better speaker, and one of the ways I can improve is to receive feedback. I may have to get my ego knocked down a bit, and you may have to have that awkward moment where you fear hurting my feelings. But ultimately, that's the best deal.

What makes it tricky, however, is that we all have different preferences. "If you are the target, one thing you can do is make it clear to others: If you have feedback on X or Y, it's not helpful. I only want to hear about Z," Levine says. What about if you are the communicator and you don't know someone's preference? If it's an ongoing relationship, especially a working relationship, you should ask them. We'll talk about strategies for this in the next chapter on workplace honesty, because alignment is particularly important in professional situations. In any given circumstance, it's easy to think of honesty as an absolute—an either/or where the only two options are crushing someone or leaving someone in the dark. In fact, it's negotiable. You can haggle. Because sometimes, the price is simply too high.

"My Husband Is Not Actually from Portugal"

My friend Sarah is a corporate lawyer, and one of the things she both likes and dislikes about her job is getting wined and dined by other attorneys who are making a pitch to help with her company's spillover legal work. She likes it because sometimes these dinners are interesting, but she dislikes it because just as often they're draining. She was at one of the more exhausting variety dinners several months ago, sitting at a big table with several attorneys from both her company and the vendor company. Conversation was loud, and she was trying to find her way into it. She heard one of the vendor attorneys mention something about Portuguese sweet bread. Her ears perked up. He was talking about how he and his wife visited Portugal and loved the bread. This caught Sarah's attention and seemed like a way into the conversation, because she and her husband also loved Portuguese sweet bread and had recently bought some at a market. She explained this—that they got some at the market and loved it—but the attorney didn't understand her quite right, and thought that she was telling him her husband was Portuguese. This excited the attorney very much! At first, Sarah didn't understand this was what the attorney was saying as he continued to rave about Portugal and how fantastic it was that her husband was from there. The attorney was loud and talkative and by the time Sarah realized she had been misunderstood, she couldn't get a word in. He was soon on to something else. She didn't know whether to try to take the conversation back and correct him, or just let it go. As an attorney, a big part of her job was untangling the facts in any given situation. On the other hand, she was also tired after a long day and a draining dinner full of people who were talking too much.

Sarah told me this story over dinner one night when my husband and I were out with her and her husband, and we cracked up about it. "At some point, it just wasn't worth trying to correct this guy. Plus, I knew I wouldn't see him again." Still, she didn't like the idea of a mistruth floating around out there. She mused that perhaps she should track down this attorney (who lived in another state) and say, "Hey, remember me from that one dinner? You really weren't listening closely to what I was saying, and you misunderstood. You thought I said my husband was Portuguese, when in reality, I only said that we loved Portuguese bread. My husband is not actually from Portugal." But what would the point of that be?

When does it matter that we correct misinformation? We run into this dilemma in social situations frequently. Someone has misinformation about you, perhaps it's humorous and of not much consequence—like a random person you'll likely never see again thinking your husband is from Portugal—or perhaps it's misinformation to your benefit. What if it starts out harmless, but then leads to larger scale deception? There was a story in *The New York Times* in 2018 about a Massachusetts antiques dealer and woodworker named Harold Gordon who took an ordinary secretary and turned it into a masterpiece that was impossible to tell apart from a true Civil War–era antique. He wound up selling the forged secretary to a collector, who then sold it to a museum in Hartford. Eventually, Gordon was questioned when someone in the antiques world finally got suspicious, and he confessed. Gordon said that when he created the piece, he never intended to sell it. He only wanted a fun project. But he told the *Times* that people kept commenting on the piece every time they came into his living room, praising it as an antique. The *Times* article didn't specifically say whether or not he corrected his houseguests, but I'm betting he didn't correct them. And eventually, when he needed money, he went ahead and sold it as the antique everyone had been praising it to be. Now, his reputation is disgraced and he's finished in the business.

How do you know when something is a slippery slope, versus a funny story to share over dinner with friends? How far do you need to take the notion of transparency? No answer to this question would cover all situations (*Not every situation is the same*), but the two key questions to ask yourself are: (1) Will this false information about me tempt me to get away with something I know I shouldn't? or (2) Could this misinformation about me lead to someone else feeling like a fool? I faced down these questions myself while keeping my journal.

In December 2017, I performed the wedding ceremony for my niece Rachel and her fiancé, Rafeé. They had asked me shortly after they got engaged if I would preside at the ceremony, and since Rachel is like a little sister to me, I was very honored. My husband and I had a friend get ordained online to marry us, and I was glad to pay the tradition forward. I logged on to Universal Life Church's site; five minutes later and for a price of $9.99 (the cost of the certificate), I was ordained. What marries two people is the marriage license from their county, as regulated by their state. As far as I've been able to figure out, the person who performs the ceremony is, well, ceremonial. Most people don't know this. They assume that if you are performing a wedding ceremony, you are a judge, a ship's captain, or a "real" minister. The thought of me being a woman of the cloth is hilarious to anyone who knows me, seeing as how I avoid organized religion. But many of the wedding guests didn't know this, certainly not Rafeé's family. Rachel and Rafeé's wedding wasn't just the merging of two lives; it was also the merging of two cultures, because Rachel is white and Rafeé is black. For some of Rafeé's family members, religion was an important cultural tradition, and despite my own disdain for organized religion, I respect other people's traditions. So, at the rehearsal dinner, when extended family members from the groom's side started asking me about what kind of minister I was, I felt uncomfortable. While it may have been easier to let them believe that I was a real minister, ultimately, that pretending would have made a fool of them. I had a series of awkward (and sometimes comical) conversations with people, explaining that I got ordained online. I wasn't a religious person, I said, but I loved Rachel and Rafeé very much and was excited to be playing a part in their big day. I'm not sure everyone was pleased. But I had been honest, and that mattered in this situation. I have to say, after the ceremony, almost everyone I had spoken to came back up to me and told me that I did a very nice job with the ceremony. Had I gone another way, and allowed people to think I was actually a minister, not only would I have felt bad for duping them and potentially making a fool out of them, the lie most likely would have come back to me.

Now, thinking about that situation—and the situation of misinformation in general and how to handle correcting it—it dawns on me that these social honesty dilemmas are not merely philosophical or ethical questions. They involve etiquette questions. And with that realization, I know exactly who to turn to next.

Polite Benevolent Honesty

I'm nervous when I dial Lizzie Post's phone number. I'm eager to hear her thoughts on where etiquette meets honesty, but I'm intimidated. After all, she is the great-great-grandchild of etiquette queen Emily Post and co-president (with her cousin, Daniel Post Senning) of the Emily Post Institute, the most well-known etiquette brand in the United States. The minute she answers the phone, my intimidation falls away and I'm immediately at ease. It strikes me then that there is etiquette on paper to guide people, and then there is the ability to be a naturally warm and generous conversationalist. Lizzie Post possesses both. We start to chat about my book, and I almost forget she's an etiquette expert.

Almost.

Because as the voice of etiquette, her perspective is slightly different from mine when it comes to prosocial lying. "Polite benevolent honesty" is what the Emily Post Institute recommends, she tells me. At first, her description of it sounds a lot like prosocial lying. "We don't believe in white lies," she explains. Knowing that white lies and prosocial lies aren't the same thing, I'm still following. "We believe in getting around having to tell a white lie by focusing on having a positive interaction," she says. Citing an example of a friend who has just bought a new winter coat and asks for feedback, Post says, "Maybe I think it's the ugliest coat I've ever seen. It would be true to say that, but it would be mean. Also, it's not necessary to share every thought I have in my head. Instead, I could say, 'That looks like it will keep you warm,' or 'I love when I purchase something new that I really love!'" Essentially, she says, it's a side step.

It sounds a bit like a prosocial lie of omission to me, or like paltering—saying something true to deflect from not answering honestly. But Post doesn't like the idea of thinking of it as deception. This echoes what Emma Levine has found—that people tend to regard deception as negative. In an effort to explain how deception can potentially be positive, I tell her about my swimming story, recounting how I told the man who got into my lane that I had made the same mistake before, even though I hadn't. Post laughs at my story and applauds my intent, which was to help the man not feel bad. But it was a lie, she says, and unnecessary to solve the problem. "Instead, we suggest people find something positive about the interaction. You can express honest sympathy without a lie," she says.

As it turns out, honesty is the third of three principles of etiquette the Emily Post Institute has identified. The first two are consideration and respect. Together, these three principles—consideration, respect, and honesty—create a formula for navigating tricky social situations. "Etiquette asks us to take not just our own perspective or experience into account, but also the perspective and experience of the people around us or in a situation with us. So, the goal of any social situation is to build the relationship positively in the best way you can," Post tells me. When faced with a dilemma about what information to share or what feedback to give, the first thing you do is identify who is involved and how they will be affected by your actions (consideration). In my swimming example, the players included me and the man, as well as other swimmers at the pool—because he could wind up hurting another swimmer. Next, you run through the various solutions. In my case, solutions ranged from not saying anything to confronting him angrily. Being kind and offering a prosocial lie was in that continuum of solutions, and I chose it because I was following the second principle: respect. "Respect means that in your own mind, you regard someone as having value and worth simply because they exist. You acknowledge that your actions may affect them positively or negatively. So, while not saying anything or lying may be good for you, it may not be good for the other person. An option that may seem good in the moment doesn't always have long-term positive effects," Post explains.

The real trick is in the *refinement*, and that comes after the third principle: honesty. I knew I had to speak up to this gentleman for his sake, my sake, and the sake of other swimmers at the Y. I wanted to respect him in whatever I said and take into account how my words and actions would impact him. The refinement came in my extension of empathy and decision to tell a prosocial lie. I could have refined my response slightly differently. For example, when I saw the man was embarrassed about his mistake, I could have simply said, "I know how difficult it can be when you start something new, but it's really great that you're here." Whatever you say in a situation like this, it should be based in the truth, Post says.

I was feeling pretty good about my benevolent lie before, but now that I'm talking to Post, I'm questioning it. Why *did* I go right to telling a lie? Why didn't I see other alternatives? Other means of being empathetic? Post knows exactly why. We always think we need a story that justifies how we feel, she says. When there is no significant story, we create a white lie, or maybe stretch the truth. The problem with the white lies and the story-stretching is that you have to keep track of them. In other words, they can come back to bite you on the ass (I assure you those are my words, not Post's!). Also, we panic in the moment, especially if we haven't trained ourselves to be ready for those moments and learn how to refine. This is true in situations where we have to practice the side step, as well as in situations where we need to have the uncomfortable moment of honesty, Post says.

"Like correcting misinformation?" I venture.

"Yes! We get so many questions about that!" she says. The classic question they get is this: You introduce yourself to someone and the other person gets your name wrong. Instead of correcting them, you let it go. The only problem is, you see the person again—maybe multiple times—and that person still continues to call you by the wrong name. At some point, it's embarrassing for you, and you know it could be potentially embarrassing for the other person. Rafeé, my nephew-in-law (and whose name rhymes with "coffee"), told me that a man at his old job—someone high up in the company, but not his direct boss—spent an entire summer calling him "Jafeé." The first time it happened, Rafeé wasn't sure if the guy had said Jafee or Rafeé, but the second time, he was sure. It already felt too late to correct him, Rafeé told me. Plus, the guy was fairly senior in the company, and Rafeé worried he would come across as rude. After a few months of this, the man finally realized he had Rafeé's name wrong and he said to Rafeé, "Why didn't you just tell me?" The man wasn't angry with Rafeé, just more befuddled. Rafeé replied that he wasn't sure when would have been a good time, to which the man said, "Anytime would have been good!" They laughed about it (and Rafeé and I laughed about it), but there is a lot of truth in what the man said—anytime would have been appropriate, but yet it always felt inappropriate to Rafeé. Post's advice for this situation is to be apologetic, but honest. "I would say something like, 'I'm so sorry. When we first met, I should have said something, but didn't, and now I'm embarrassed. You didn't have my name right and I should have let you know right then. My name is actually Lizzie, not Livvy,'" she says. This works just as well when the situation is reversed—like if someone introduces themselves to you, and the next time you see them (which may just be five minutes later), you can't remember their name. You can take the same approach—apologize, admit you're embarrassed, and tell the truth that you don't remember their name.

So why are these exchanges so painful? "Because we have a fear of not knowing what happens if we admit the truth. But ultimately, it's much easier to take the personal hit and tell the truth in a way you feel good about that seeks understanding from the other person," Post says. It sounds like my theory of honesty as a negotiation, or a flea market haggle. Absolutely, she says. "I am always concerned about being rude to others, but sometimes I forget that others also have a social obligation to be polite to me as well." It's easy to pre-emptively fear someone's rudeness and let that govern your behavior, instead of remembering we all have a social contract with each other to be polite—you could even say to be "good cooperators" if you think of it in evolutionary terms. No matter if you practice the "side step" or you tell a straight-up prosocial lie of commission, where you say an untruth for the benefit of someone else, it's about the same thing: intention.

After talking with Lizzie Post, I know my next honesty principle needs to be around this idea of intention. Intuitively, I've always known that intention matters, and Emma Levine's prosocial lying research found this, too. Recall that she had told me if people see your good intentions, they will usually see your prosocial lie was the right thing to do. But if they determine your intentions were self-interested, they will see your lie as bad. The viewpoint from the world of etiquette complicates this slightly. Some of it is a question of semantics: side step versus prosocial lie of omission, or focusing on the positive interaction versus a kind of paltering. The vocabulary may well be important, but more important is the refinement. There are ways to refine that employ less deception, and that matters, too. As we know from our discussion of emotions, intention alone can lead you astray. After all, an accountant who works for a non-profit can have the best intentions of helping more people, but if they use dishonest accounting practices, it still isn't right. The refinement has to follow the intention. My fourth principle, then, is this: *Intention matters. So does refinement.* You start with what's in your heart, but then you educate yourself and use your brain to figure out how to shape your response or your actions, whether it means telling a prosocial lie of omission or commission. My intention with the man at the pool was to help him be aware of his mistake (because it could have been dangerous if he did it again), but then to help him feel less ashamed of that mistake. The best way I know how to do that is to offer empathy. After I was honest with him about his mistake, I chose to refine by telling him a prosocial lie. It was a lie of commission, and there were other choices, including not saying anything or offering a statement of encouragement. While I don't regret my choice and very well may make the same choice in the future, understanding the range of possibilities that come with refinement is quite helpful. My other lie—the one to my editor—also started with a good intention: I didn't want to hurt his feelings. But I didn't refine in that situation. I stopped with intention and made the wrong call because my emotion was in the way. My refinement came when I revisited the situation, thought carefully about it, and corrected my honesty fail. *Intention matters. So does refinement.*

One of the things my discussion with Post helped me realize is that we're in this etiquette business together. Though the actor-observer bias pulls at us strongly (recall this is the bias that makes us judge others' actions more harshly than we judge our own), that's only part of the story. We are far more complex than any one bias. In fact, I think perhaps we gravitate toward "refining" an honesty situation in the same way we prefer that someone else refines a situation for our benefit. For example, while working on this book, I found myself traveling with my daughter, Georgia, who was then eight. We went to Charlotte, North Carolina, to attend a wedding of a friend of mine, leaving very early in the morning to make our seven a.m. flight. After landing, I rented a car, plugged the hotel address in my phone, and navigated my way across the city while Siri gave me directions. I wound up having to circle the block of our Hampton Inn a few times before I found the parking garage, and once I finally made it inside, I accidentally parked on the Hilton Garden Inn side without realizing it (they were sister hotels and were attached via the garage). I went into the Hilton Garden Inn (not realizing I was in the wrong place) and started the check-in process while Georgia pirouetted around me in the lobby. My nerves were fraying fast, and the very nice young man behind the desk said something like, "This is actually the Hilton Garden, but the Hampton is just across the way."

Of course, I was embarrassed and said something like, "I'm a moron." He assured me that it happened all the time, and pointed to where I needed to go. Back outside at my car, I still found myself confused about where exactly I needed to move my car (did I mention I had been up since four o'clock that morning and Georgia had not once stopped talking?) and had what I can only guess was a confounded look on my face. "Can I help you?" the valet parking attendant said. I told him that I was trying to understand where to move my car. "I swear, I'm not usually this dumb," I said.

"Trust me, I spent most of my day helping people who are confused about this. Everyone goes to the wrong hotel at first. It's a weird setup and it's so confusing!" he said as he walked around the bend and pointed to the exact spot across the walkway where I could park. Did I really think he spent *most of his day* helping people trying to check in at the wrong hotel? No. Was the setup actually *that* weird once I took a breath and really looked at it? No. In truth, the signage was pretty clear. I had been bleary-eyed and distracted, and hadn't looked that closely. But I sure appreciated what he said, whether it was a prosocial lie or not. This young man certainly dealt with all kinds of people, and he intuitively grasped how to soothe a situation, especially when an overwhelmed parent was feeling like an utter idiot. In fact, his prosocial lie lifted my mood, and when I checked in at the correct hotel a few minutes later, I noticed with fresh eyes every nice amenity the hotel had—free internet, a nice indoor pool, friendly staff, comfy beds, and free breakfast—including a waffle bar with chocolate chips, whipped cream, and multiple sauces. Tell them lies and feed them waffles? That's okay by me.

Why We Feel the Need to Save Face

My husband recently confessed something to me, which he thought was rather comical. When he has to make a small purchase at the hardware store or the mini-market, he prefers to use cash versus a debit card. Apparently, using a debit card to make a small purchase embarrasses him. When he has no cash and must use the card, his solution is to open his wallet as if looking for cash, and then say to the clerk, "Oops, looks like my wife got in my wallet and got my cash again! I guess I'll have to use a debit card."

While it is pretty funny, I actually have a few issues with this. Number one is his strange embarrassment at using a debit card. Why does he need a story? There's also this: No part of it is true. While we do often share cash back and forth, it's always with full knowledge. His little lie feels like it propagates a stereotype about women. I don't like him spinning stories that pit me as a shopping-obsessed wife who sneaks off with "her husband's" money. Not only does this completely misrepresent me, there is also the fact that I make my own money. We both like the economic system we've created and are excellent partners in money management. So why in the world is he walking around telling this silly lie when he's out of cash?

Because he is trying to *save face*.

I realize as we are laughing over this ridiculous wallet story one night at dinner that saving face is yet one more dimension of social honesty. We often associate the concept of "face" with Asian cultures, and in fact, the notion of saving face has origins in China, but it is also pervasive in Japan. A quick search turns up many articles written for Americans who are doing business in Asia (especially Japan) to try to explain this idea. One piece of advice I see several times is to avoid disagreeing with people who are senior to you in a group setting. American businesspeople are also advised that Japanese companies may shy away from talking about mistakes. Not only is saving face part of the culture, it's also part of the culture to avoid actually *talking* about saving face. Coincidentally, the very day I'm searching for information about saving face in Asian cultures, there is a piece in that morning's edition of *The New York Times* about a young woman who made a video letter to come out to her parents in China. She explained to the reporter that while she felt certain her parents would still love her, she was very nervous because of the tradition of saving face in China, where the stigma of being gay is very strong. Saving face may be a silly anecdote in my world, but it's a very strong force in cultures around the world, with often serious consequences, so I don't want to make light of it.

Though Americans are rarely afraid of challenging authority or criticizing superiors, we do practice elaborate face-saving rituals in our social interactions, mostly in the form of telling untrue stories, exaggerating, and justifying. These face-saving stories may fall along the prosocial lie continuum, but they have a tendency to be born of self-interest more than for prosocial reasons. For example . . . have you been late to a meeting and you told a story to explain why? How about forgetting someone's birthday, only to wish them a belated happy birthday the next day, along with a quick apology for forgetting because you were so jet-lagged (you don't include the fact that the jet lag was from three days ago)? I was telling these stories, too, until my journal made me more aware of them.

I go to my mom's just about every Sunday with my daughter. My two sisters visit, too, and we basically have a mini-salon in my mom's living room. We talk about politics, culture, family, history, books we're reading—you name it, we talk about it. I love these afternoons. I'm often the last one there, though. In fact, in the last few years, I've gotten later and later. I would often make an excuse of why I was later than usual, explaining that Allen had to go to the grocery store and I had to wait for him to get home, or that I had to finish up a story I was writing. These stories were a mix of untrue and paltering (e.g., Allen did go to the grocery store, but it was hours before I had to leave for my mom's). Though my mom and my sisters probably didn't care what time I got there, I was feeling guilty that I was the last one there, and the excuses were all about saving face. Through doing a lot of thinking about this tendency (which I only noticed because I was keeping an honesty journal), I realized that for me, lying to save face usually had to do with some element of my personality that I was either trying to justify or to protect. For example, I'm not great at being on time. I know this about myself, and it frustrates me and sometimes embarrasses me. Hence, I try to save face around it by spinning silly stories. I think my husband tells a face-saving story when he's out of cash because, in his mind, always having cash is the mark of a prepared person, and being prepared is a huge part of his identity. I suspect that looking at saving face in this way—through the lens of individuality—is a particularly American take on it, and is different from the role that saving face plays in other cultures.

I have stopped with the Sunday afternoon excuses, but I still catch myself on the precipice of telling face-saving stories. Each time, I stop, breathe, and consider the other options. Option one is sitting with an uncomfortable truth—like the fact that punctuality is not one of my strongest traits—instead of trying to justify or manage it. Option two is offering a sincere apology, if an apology is in order. And option three, which is the case more often than not, is *don't say anything at all*, because commentary just isn't necessary. Most of the time, we are so caught up in our narcissism that we fail to realize that nobody actually cares. Nobody at the hardware store cares if my husband uses a debit card. Now, when I hear other people telling me these face-saving stories, I want to just say, "Stop. Just stop. You don't need a story." This echoes Lizzie Post's advice about avoiding untruths or stretching a story to explain things. If you don't want to attend someone's event, don't lie and say you're sick if you're not. In reality, that's a self-interested lie, because while you may believe you are lying to spare someone's feelings, it's more likely that you're lying to benefit yourself, and potentially spinning a story that is likely to create more lies. Instead, regretfully decline and tell them you have plans. You *do* have plans, even if your plans are to sit and scroll through Instagram on your couch.

I've spent a lot of time in this chapter introducing the background and concepts we will use as we continue on this honesty journey, including how we evolved to value honesty, how emotions cloud our judgment about honesty, how prosocial lies can build trust, how honesty is a bit like negotiating, the dilemma of whether or not to correct misinformation, the overlap between honesty and etiquette, and why we feel the need to save face. But much of that is just what happens before nine a.m., after five p.m., and on the weekends. So . . . what in the world is going on where we seem to spend the bulk of our time: at work?

Reviewing the Honesty Principles

Be mindful of emotions.

- Emotions, like compassion, can cloud your judgment about whether a lie is truly prosocial and benefiting the other person. (*Worrying about my editor's feelings originally kept me from telling him a truth that would help him.*) Don't let your fear of hurting someone guide you into a potentially paternalistic lie, if they can benefit from knowing the truth.

Intention matters. So does refinement.

- Even good intentions can lead you astray (*e.g., an accountant at a non-profit who commits fraud to help the non-profit keep more money to help more people*). Refinement helps you see all of the options and make the best choice possible.

CHAPTER 5

Workplace Honesty

Wʜᴇɴ ᴡᴇ ᴛʜɪɴᴋ ᴀʙᴏᴜᴛ ʜᴏɴᴇꜱᴛʏ in the workplace, we tend to focus on the stories of corporations who deceived the public and were brought down by whistleblowers and investigative reporters. From Enron to Theranos, these are the stories that dominate the business news. They are right to get our attention, because they deeply affect individual people's lives, as well as the fabric of society in general. I heard John Carreyrou, the *Wall Street Journal* reporter who exposed the Theranos scandal and wrote the book *Bad Blood*, speak at the 2018 Association of Health Care Journalists conference. I was captivated by his talk. I'm grateful for solid investigative reporting like his that uncovers corporate wrongdoing and fraud, as well as for the employees who make the brave decisions to come forward.

All that said, this chapter isn't really about that—at least not directly.

Instead, it's about the exchanges you have with people on a daily basis in the space inside of and around work. It's a little bit about ethics, but ethics tends to be highly scenario based. In fact, ethics researchers *love* scenarios, the more gripping and heart-wrenching, the better. Pore over the ethics literature (or just Google "ethics scenarios") and you'll find them. These hypotheticals involve lifeboats with a limited number of seats, vials of disease cures to be saved from crumbling labs, and side-by-side houses engulfed in flames. In every scenario, there is a nearly impossible decision to make: Save five members of your family, or five people who can wipe out cancer; put out the fire in your own house where your dog is sleeping or the house next door where your neighbors who are consistently rude to you are sleeping. I've also come across more than one ethical scenario that involves finding Bill Gates's wallet on the street. Most of us will never see a lifeboat or a house fire (let alone two on the same street!), and are not likely to stumble upon Bill Gates's wallet. These thorny hypothetical situations are supposed to make us think carefully and rationally about a tough ethical dilemma, teasing out various motives and weighing the greater good against self-interest. In theory, how we work out these ethical dilemmas informs how we behave in everyday life.

In theory.

And that's the problem. It's all theoretical. While they are interesting intellectual exercises that help us sort through theories from various philosophers, you don't have much skin in the game when you're reading from the comfort of your couch about lifeboats with limited numbers of seats. I love an intellectual exercise as much as anyone, but does how we work out these extreme and highly unlikely dilemmas have anything to do with how we will behave when it's time to do team evaluations or when we are trying to sell a product to a customer?

Taya Cohen, associate professor of organizational behavior and theory at Carnegie Mellon University's Tepper School of Business, wondered the same thing. "Academics love difficult philosophical dilemmas that ask people to make hard choices. But how people reason through these tough ethical decisions is not what will determine people's everyday behaviors," Cohen says. She researches moral character, specifically focusing on the workplace, and has found that while the big ethical dilemmas, like whistleblowing, get most of the attention in the literature, there is a wealth of interesting information to glean from the smaller decisions we make every day. Many times throughout each day, we make both split-second and intentional decisions about whether we will behave selfishly or in a way that helps others. These decisions are rarely about life or death (though of course, if your job involves being a first responder or a doctor, they may be), and often, are not even about money or cheating. What's at stake in these everyday interactions and decisions within the space of work—whether our work involves a physical or virtual place—are things like our ability to take pride in our work, to form solid workplace relationships, to succeed in our career and feel fulfilled, and to be productive members of society.

So far, we've talked about why honesty matters for the furthering of the species, how emotions both help us and hinder us when it comes to honesty, and the intersection between honesty and etiquette. In this chapter, I want to examine how the work you do, as well as who you are at work, affects your choices around honesty. We'll look at the role of moral character and identity, talk more about how prosocial lying is both a key element of certain jobs and a survival technique for the workplace, and dig into conflicts of interest.

What a Stolen Fifteen Minutes Taught Me

Here is a dose of honesty: Originally, I wasn't going to include a chapter about honesty in the workplace because I've been a freelance writer most of my adult life. Compared to most people, I've had very few jobs that involve an actual workplace or being an employee. However, as I began to think more about it, I realized that I had to include a reflection of honesty inside of work, because our work experiences are so much a part of who we are and how we spend our time. Furthermore, I realized that I didn't have to focus on only one sliver of what a workplace is, because when you break work down, it's really just you, plus other people, trying to do a job that's needed in some way by some people somewhere. That alone makes it a social experience. Even if you're a long haul truck driver, or you work from home (as I do), or in a quiet lab, or with animals all day, you most likely still face people-related issues that involve honesty questions. Ultimately, that outer circle of social honesty isn't complete without thinking about how we interact with others on the job. The other important reason I knew I had to include a chapter on work is that most of us have formative experiences and lessons related to work and honesty that shape how we come to know what work is and who we are inside of it.

My first experience of work was at age thirteen, when I started helping out with teaching gymnastics lessons at the YMCA. The Y was essentially my second home, because I also competed for the gymnastics team there. I wanted as many reasons to be there as I could. Plus, I was very anxious to make money. I desperately wanted a pair of Guess® jeans (when I wrote about my deep desire for the jeans in my diary, I always drew the little R in a circle). My mom said they were too expensive, and I'd have to earn the money myself. It was 1987 and minimum wage was $3.35/hour. My first paycheck was about twenty dollars, and while it was twenty dollars more than I had before, I could see that my three hours a week was not going to add up super fast. At that time, we had paper time sheets that we signed in and out. I noticed that the head instructor (who was also my coach and the one in charge of the whole gymnastics program) was always there and signed in before me because she was planning the lesson. She got paid for an extra fifteen minutes. It occurred to me that maybe I could get there a little early and sign in, too, even though I had no reason to be there early, other than to sit in the lobby. I decided to try it the following Tuesday, signing in fifteen minutes early. No one said anything, so I did it on Thursday, too. I remember that when I left Thursday night, I was really second-guessing it, getting that shameful feeling in my stomach that you get when you know you're doing something wrong but don't want to admit it. Sure enough, the following Monday before my own gymnastics practice, the program director called me into his office. He was a very nice man who seemed impossibly old, though I now realize he was probably only about thirty. He reminded me that I was only allowed to sign in for the time I was actually teaching or preparing the class, but preparing was generally only the job of the head instructor. He asked me if I was preparing the class for those fifteen minutes I had signed in. I started to cry, and said, "No." I don't remember his exact words because I was so embarrassed and wanted to get out of there as fast as I could, but I do remember that he was kind.

I felt like I had been punched in the gut. The shame rose up through me. More than thirty years later, I still remember the texture of that shame, the heat of it on my cheeks. Did everybody know I was a cheat? Did my coach know I had lied? I was mortified for weeks, thinking about it each night before I fell asleep. Why had I done it? To earn money for the jeans a little bit faster? It wasn't worth the feeling of shame. Getting called out was mortifying, but the fact that I had done it at all was even worse. Looking back, I'm so grateful that I had that lesson. It stuck with me through all of my time at the Y (I worked there in some capacity until I was twenty-two) and at my other job at the fabric store I had throughout college. I would put on my employee smock and punch in just before I walked out onto the floor, and punch out the minute I got back to the employee room. Ditto for the campus writing center where I worked in college. I may have had other shortcomings as an employee, but I was never going to try to cheat time again. (This is one reason I try to avoid hourly rates as a freelancer, because I think such rates are mostly a strange little lie about time and value, and I'd rather just tell you what I think a project is worth, regardless if it takes me twenty minutes or three hours. But I digress . . .)

I came out of graduate school with the best of intentions regarding work. I was fresh off reading pages and pages of heady theory, full of ideas about better understanding humanity, the subjugation of women, institutional racism, and the complicated nature of human history. My ideals about the world and people were so strong that I assumed everyone shared them. So it was quite a shock when I got my first job with a highly dysfunctional publishing company, working in—of all things—sales. Never mind the fact that I was supposed to sell search engine directory listings (something that even in 1998 was ridiculous to be selling), the culture there was a complete disaster. The forty-something married president of the company was working his way through sleeping with several of the young women, the head of human resources was selling weed out of her office, and my friend was stalked by one of her co-workers—who had everyone fooled into thinking he was just a darn nice guy—and then fired when she spoke out in an email to someone. I felt a strange sense of something like guilt, mixed with indignation. These were bad things, and not at all what I thought the work world would be like. At the same time, wasn't I colluding in it somehow, because I was taking money from this company?

As it turned out, I was lousy at sales. Mostly because I had no training, but also because I didn't believe in what I was selling and had only taken the job because I thought maybe I could eventually get an editing job. After about six months, I realized I needed to get the hell out of there, and I found a job proofreading at a design firm, with the potential to do some copywriting. The production manager who hired me was a capable, no-nonsense middle-aged woman. I liked her immediately. Surely, there would be none of those same shenanigans here.

Um, yeah.

I will say, it was at least a different kind of dysfunction. I enjoyed many parts of the job and the people. It's where I learned how agencies worked, and that writing was actually worth far more money than I ever thought. I made a terrific group of friends and I came into my own as an independent adult. But on the negative side, the HR guy routinely commented on my breasts (all of the women's breasts actually), the leadership was fragmented and inconsistent, and lower level people were routinely thrown under the bus when something went wrong. When one of my co-workers was blamed for not catching a mistake on a package proof before it went to print, she wrote the dollar amount that it cost the company on a Post-it note (something like $17,000) and kept it on her cubicle bulletin board for months, like some kind of hair shirt. Her manager never told her to take it down.

The real turning point for me was when one of the company principals called me into her office and questioned whether or not I was a team player, because I, too, had made a mistake in proofing something—a catalog, as I recall. At first I felt the familiar shame, but it quickly turned to resentment. It was a mistake, and I hated that I made it, but it certainly wasn't on purpose. I was trying to do my job the best I could. But it didn't seem to be a place where people had each other's backs when mistakes were made. There was no encouragement to grow and learn from your mistakes; instead, you were blamed and chastised. After that day, I simply started trying a little bit less, and figured this was just how it was. Work was not a thing to be cared about too much, because it would always disappoint you, and you would always be disappointing someone.

I often wonder what would have happened if I hadn't been laid off from that job during the 2001 recession and found my way to freelancing after a short stint at another job. If I had stayed there, would I have found my strength and purpose and re-oriented, or would I have sunk into mediocrity—not just in what I produced, but also in how I treated others? I feel certain I never would have embezzled, flagrantly lied, or committed outrageous ethical breaches, but what about my sense of goodness, fairness, and the betterment of humanity? Would that have been drained out of me, with every yearly review, every mindless meeting, every scolding, every leering glance from the HR guy? Would I have been less likely to help others, and more likely to spread gossip? More likely to be sarcastic, apathetic, or complacent? I want to think I would have found my way. After all, I was a conscientious person—someone who was responsible and self-directed, but also eager to please and make people happy. I think I would have had ups and downs, but would have stayed steadfast, upstanding, and decent in all of my dealings with people.

I think.

I don't know for sure. But I do know who I am—and according to Taya Cohen, who we fundamentally *are* may be what matters the most.

Personality or Situation?

Do we have a moral character that determines how we will act, no matter what our surroundings? Or do our surroundings determine the greater share of how we will behave? As it turns out, that question has gone back and forth among psychology and workplace researchers over the years. For a while, there was a push toward the situation determining everything. You may have heard of the Stanford Prison experiment, a study that tried to determine if good people would essentially go "bad" if you put them in a bad situation. The answer seemed to be yes. You can read about the study at PrisonExp.org (it was also a movie), but frankly, there are many ethical problems with the study, and that such a study even happened seems horrifying. But it's where the thinking was in the 1960s and 1970s. Within a decade or so, the zeitgeist moved back to favoring personality as the determinant of how you will behave in any given situation. Researchers came up with five essential personality traits: openness (how well do you handle change?), conscientiousness (how thoughtful are you?), extraversion (how outgoing are you?), agreeableness (how cooperative are you?), and neuroticism (how emotionally stable are you?). They said those traits were your roadmap for behavior.

Both views of what determines behavior—all situation or all personality—are too narrow, Cohen explains to me when I ask her to walk me through the person-situation debate and where it is now. Who you are matters, but so does who you're with (as Dan Ariely has shown in his work). That neither is the right answer by itself seems rather obvious to most of us. But what isn't as obvious is what's missing from the equation. And that, Cohen says, is the moral piece. Specifically, people's moral character. "Our big questions when starting this line of research were, What is moral character? What about a person will help us predict harmful versus helpful behaviors? And why does it matter to know?" Cohen says. As she began to dig into defining moral character, she realized that you could boil moral character into three basic components. First, there is the motivational component, which is essentially your *desire* to do good things and avoid doing bad things. Second, there is your *ability* to do this—can you really follow through on your desire to do good and avoid doing bad? Finally, there is your *identity*, which means you've made being a good person central to who you are. In terms of traits, people with high levels of moral character are highly conscientious, and they tend to have high levels of honesty and humility. The reverse is true as well, so that people with low levels of moral character tend to have low levels of honesty and humility, and aren't as conscientious. Cohen found that people with high moral character are also more guilt-prone, meaning they are more likely to feel bad about being selfish or doing harmful things.

People with high moral character can certainly have some blind spots. People make errors in reasoning and get aligned with groups that exert undue influence on their decision-making. Throw religion into the mix, and you can pretty quickly have a hot mess where people are killing each other in the name of moral values. Cohen and her team acknowledge that having high levels of moral character is not a guarantee against being unethical. But low moral character people still cause the bigger share of problems—at least within the space of work.

Cohen's research looks at two types of behaviors in the workplace. One type of behaviors she calls organizational citizenship behaviors, or OCB. Examples of OCB include advising and mentoring co-workers, being a good listener and being compassionate to others, helping co-workers out by changing shifts or schedules, and generally being helpful to others. The other group of behaviors she labels counterproductive work behaviors, or CWB. This includes nastiness and rudeness, being self-centered in interactions, taking tools or supplies home without asking, leaving work early, and generally being a jerk.

For the study, Cohen and her team used work diaries, self-reports, and surveys of colleagues to figure out if someone was of low or high moral character (most people were average). They found that low moral character employees committed an average of sixteen acts of CWB each week, according to their own reports. By contrast, high moral character employees averaged just one CWB act a week. (She also had co-workers observe and keep diaries, which corroborated the patterns.) The low moral character employees also had more lenient attitudes toward unethical negotiation tactics as compared to the high moral character ones. The upshot of Cohen's research is that low moral character people, especially clusters of low moral character people, can do a lot of damage in an organization, essentially sinking the ship for everyone. Considering the fact that so many people are of average moral character, potentially swayed either way on any given day, just one or two low bad apples—like an HR guy staring at breasts, or a manager with a penchant for blaming people—can subtly and slowly contaminate a culture.

None of this is shocking for the lay person to read. But the influence of moral character on everyday work behaviors hadn't been specifically studied before in the way Cohen did. One of the discoveries she also made is that moral character was far more likely to determine how people would behave in the workplace than ethics codes. "The presence and enforcement of an ethics code in the organization did not have a reliable effect on CWB or OCB, and neither did income or organizational sector," Cohen wrote in the study. She isn't suggesting that companies shouldn't have codes of ethics. But rather, she's saying that "ethics" as we know it doesn't have much to do with whether or not Trey will monopolize conversation in the marketing meeting and belittle anyone who doesn't agree with him, or whether Trinity will share her fantastic Excel hack with Ethan, who is tied up in knots trying to get the budget ready for the big client presentation and really needs help.

I was at the pharmacy picking up my son's prescription recently when I saw a small example of an employee who was motivated beyond a code of conduct or set of rules. One of the pharmacists had his keys in hand and sunglasses on his head and was waving good-bye to his fellow pharmacists behind the counter who were both helping other customers. He noticed me waiting, and as he walked by the counter on his way out, he asked me my name, grabbed my prescription from the bin, and quickly checked me out. I thanked him for taking the time to check me out after he was already done for the day and off the clock. He smiled and handed me the bag, saying, "Nah, don't worry about. This is just what we do." I had just read Cohen's moral character study, and wanted to say back, "Actually, I bet there is nothing written down that says you have to wait on me after you're off the clock, but you probably have high moral character, which makes you more likely to participate in OCBs like this!" Instead, I smiled back and thanked him again, because it would hardly be an OCB to force someone who has just worked a long day to listen to you talk about psychological studies (even fascinating ones).

Can Moral Character Be Strengthened?

Perhaps you have the desire to be upstanding at work and stop engaging in a CWB—like consistently getting to work late and asking a co-worker to cover for you or being passive-aggressive in situations that involve conflict—but you need a little bit of help strengthening that muscle. Or maybe you have a co-worker you feel has a good heart, but you see engaging in CWBs like gossiping, and you're wondering how you might exert some subtle influence. Research from social psychology and organization behavior has some suggestions for people who want to become more considerate and make moral character more central to identity.

For example, one study found that people didn't lie as much for money when the person leading the experiment said, "Please don't be a cheater" instead of "Please don't cheat." A related experiment with kids found that kids between the ages of three and six were more likely to help the experimenter leading the study with toy cleanup when the experimenter said, "You could be a helper" rather than "You could help." Cohen (who was not an author on these studies) explains that statements like these help people better connect to their desire to see themselves as good, decent, and helpful, instead of bad, uncharitable, and unhelpful.

Researchers have also found that having employees write a letter to themselves in twenty years can help foster more honesty and integrity-filled work environments. When researchers at Netherlands Institute for the Study of Crime and Law Enforcement in Amsterdam compared a group of employees who wrote letters to their future selves in twenty years with a group who wrote a letter to their future selves in three months, they found that the twenty-year group was less likely to make bad choices in a decision-making task. Cohen, who was not an author on that study, either, summarizes, "We assume that writing a letter to one's self in twenty years helps people recognize the long-term consequences of their behavior, and as such, helps with self-regulation."

OCB versus Don't Bother Me

What does all this morality business mean for you and me in how we approach our work life each day? One way to look at it is that in any given situation involving a decision about honesty, integrity, or decency, act as the high moral character person you are (I'm going to assume that if you're reading this book, you either are a high moral character person or you are working hard to become one). Ask yourself: What would a person who is motivated to be decent, is capable of being decent, and regards themselves as decent do in this situation? Then do that thing. The reminder of who we *want* to be is one of the best motivators for being that person.

So, let's say you've just finished printing a document at work, and you notice the copy machine is now out of paper. To load the tray, you have to open a brand-new ream. Not only did you get a paper cut last time you opened a ream, it will take at least thirty more seconds, and you really just want to go back to your desk. Do you take the time to load the paper for the next person printing? Maybe 10 percent of the time you don't, because some days are just not our best days. But most of the time, you probably do this simple OCB, right? It matters, not just for creating a nice workplace, but also for how you think about yourself. You're a person who loads the copy paper so the next person doesn't have to do it, because you know it's the right thing to do.

At this point, you may be thinking: Judi, did you seriously decide to include a chapter on workplace honesty just to remind me to load the *freaking copy paper*? There is more to it, I promise. For example, let's consider this situation: You've been putting off responding to someone who has emailed asking for advice about being a writer, and wants to "take you out" for coffee. They seem genuine and eager, and their email was polite, not demanding or entitled. You don't want to say no, because you want to be helpful (and you remember how many people helped you when you were getting started). On the other hand, you're on a book deadline, your days are jam-packed as it is since all hell breaks loose as soon as kids are home from school, and frankly, if you have a free hour, you want to spend it at yoga. So, you put the email into your "things to deal with later" pile. All day long, there is a nagging voice telling you to respond, because it's the decent thing to do. But what to say? As it turns out, this very situation happens to me with some frequency. A similar situation has probably happened to you before, too, when someone presents you with a reasonable request in the professional realm, and you just don't want to do it.

Now, we're getting deeper into person-to-person dynamics, which is where moral character gets muddier. For example, I feel that I have high moral character and participate in many OCBs, like paying it forward by recommending colleagues for gigs, sending thank-you emails to people, and being on time for conference calls. Yet I am protective of my time and don't want to do every favor I'm asked. If I lie to get out of doing something, that feels wrong. If I tell the truth that I don't want to do it, it feels mean. Etiquette expert Lizzie Post would advocate for a side step that keeps the interaction positive, but doesn't offer complicated stories or white lies to explain. Something like, "Thank you for thinking of me. My calendar is consumed by a book deadline, and I am unable to meet with you." That's a solid, honest, non-asshole response, and I have used that tactic before. You probably have, too. Why do we sometimes still feel so bad about it, though?

Here's what I've realized about these exchanges that involve someone asking you for something you don't particularly want to give: How you feel about the exchange has far less to do with the other person than it does with how you feel about yourself. Let me explain what I mean. As I write this, it's election season, and we are getting any number of people ringing our doorbell. I've been a lifelong Democrat, so if a Democratic candidate or campaign worker comes to my door, I will most likely talk to them for a few minutes—if only to tell them that they've got my vote, or express concern that they don't seem committed enough to an issue I care about. But when it comes to Republican candidates I don't support, I have no problem with total honesty. I open the door and politely say, "Thanks for your efforts, but I'm a Democrat and I'm not voting for your person," and then gently shut the door before they can engage. Why don't I feel bad at all doing this, but I do feel bad turning down a freelance writer newbie for a cup of coffee?

The answer has to do with identity. I identify as a Democrat. It doesn't mean I won't be civil to all people, but it does mean that my identity as belonging to this particular group provides me with a license to be honest in that specific exchange. "I'm a Democrat," I say, and the Republican campaigner understands. They don't like it, and they think I'm highly misguided, but they get that I don't want to do what they're asking (vote for their candidate). Yet when the newbie freelance writer emails me asking for help, my honesty—no matter how polite and benevolent—still feels bad, because I identify not just as a freelance writer, but also as a person who actively wants to help other freelance writers. I simply have conflicting interests: My identity as a helpful person to other writers versus my desire to stick to my schedule and not get sidetracked. When I turn down a writer's request for help, a part of me feels like I'm not being true to who I say I am. That causes an internal struggle.

Now, there are a zillion possibilities between yes and no, and I've refined over the years how I answer these emails. What I usually say now is something like, "That's great that you are starting to freelance! The freelance community is very helpful, and here are some resources to check out [here I link them to blogs, message boards, and writing coaches I know]. I can't commit to coffee right now, but I am happy to answer one or two specific questions you have." I preserve my identity as helpful, but by asking something of them—to come up with a specific question for me—I still keep a safeguard on my time. And if they respond back with a specific question, I take a minute to answer it.

If moral character is one determinant of honesty decisions we make inside of interactions with others, then the identity we claim for ourselves is the other. Your identity can act as a license to be honest in situations where honesty might otherwise be difficult. If your co-workers ask you out for drinks after work and you really don't want to go because you don't much like hanging out with them (but your identity as a nice person is important to you), you may face a dilemma of how honest to be. But if those same co-workers ask you to come to the Pepsi festival with them, which is the biggest event of the year for people who love Pepsi, you can point to the Coke posters in your cubicle and the can of Diet Coke in your hand and say, "Oh sorry, no. As you can see, I'm a Coke fan!" Professing your identity or belonging to a group sometimes helps you avoid the side step or the other social maneuvers we employ to get out of things we don't want to do.

Related to this idea that belonging can inspire honesty is the notion that most identities come with "prototypes" for how we should behave, and even how we should think, says ethics researcher Keith Leavitt, associate professor at Oregon State University. Research has shown that this phenomenon—called the situated identity effect—can be powerful. One of the best places to observe and study it is in individuals who have multiple occupational identities nested inside of them. For example, Leavitt and his colleagues studied Army medics—people who had both a solider identity (which could include using lethal force to defend their nation) and a medical identity (which emphasizes the preservation of human life). By triggering one identity or the other, researchers found that the Army medics responded differently to a question about the value of a human life. "We found that simply manipulating the cognitive activation of one role or the other in very subtle ways is enough to change people's moral judgments. They start behaving according to the prototype you activate," Leavitt says. In his study, the Army medics primed with a medical identity were significantly more likely to avoid putting a dollar value on human life, compared to those primed with a military identity. Army medics in combat clearly have a difficult job, and deal with competing interests on a level I can't even imagine. However, the takeaway for all of us is that it's possible that the group we feel most connected to in a given moment underscores how we believe we should behave, to the point of clarifying some aspect of our identity we might struggle with otherwise.

Now, obviously, we can take this argument to a dark place, and see how identifying strongly with a group is connected to cults, gangs, terrorism, Nazi and white nationalist groups, and other violent and dangerous segments. The last thing I want to do is link honesty with oppressive extremism, since extremism so often stems from fear and lies. It's also worth noting that citing "honesty" doesn't excuse despicable, violent actions.

So, to get back to our original argument—on the mundane level of Pepsi versus Coke, Democrat versus Republican, vegetarian versus meat eater, cat versus dog, bicyclist versus runner—some kinds of identities provide shorthand for communicating with others who want things from us, enabling us to be honest with them. Identity is a kind of truth serum, empowering us to give truthful answers without the fear of being judged, because we have the weight of a collective identity behind us (Diet Coke fans unite!). However, this is only one way to look at identity. The other is that it's an extremely powerful motivator to lie. Especially at work.

Who Are You, and Would You Lie for It?

Because Leavitt studies both ethics and workplaces, he is interested in why people fib, hedge, exaggerate, and cheat at work. There have been two prevailing ways that people have understood workplace dishonesty, he says. The first is that we are dishonest when we think we can get away with it—when the benefit outweighs the cost. The second is everything we just talked about regarding personality and moral character. But there is also a third way of looking at why we tell lies in the workplace, and that's the one Leavitt is currently most interested in. It has to do with social motives, specifically the identity you claim related to your job. "To understand why people lie in the workplace, we need to understand their identity motives," he says.

If someone asks you, "Who are you?" you may have several identities you use to describe yourself. I would answer the "Who are you?" question by saying that I'm a writer, a mother, a wife, a runner, a swimmer, a gardener, and (when appropriate) a Democrat. "But ultimately, we have a pattern of how we construe our identity, one dominant way we define who we are," Leavitt tells me. We mostly fall into three buckets around identity: the personal, the relational, and the collective.

With the *personal level* of identity, you define yourself by what makes you distinct. It could be your accomplishments and the things you're proud of, or simply the ways in which you are different from others. It's an identity based on standing out. For example, you are the top salesperson, the youngest person to make partner, or the author of a book you're proud of. With the *relational level* of identity, you define yourself through your obligations and the roles in which you serve others. You take pride in their accomplishments; their wins are your wins. For example, you are the right-hand person for the CEO, a coach of a team, or a campaign manager for a political candidate. Finally, with the *collective level* of identity, you define yourself through belonging to a group. Instead of standing out, you prefer to disappear into the group, because it's how you understand your place in the world. For example, you're part of an NGO trying to accomplish something, or an employee of an iconic company.

You use your interactions with others to maintain who you are and reinforce your identity, Leavitt says. The workplace is full of these kinds of social interactions. It's also full of hierarchical structures and public displays of performance. Hence, we are continually managing threats to our identity. These threats can ultimately drive people to engage in all kinds of dishonest behavior, including lies that protect others. I don't know about you, but my job is a huge part of my identity and how I define myself in the world. There are clear things at stake—like my sense of self-worth—that are worth protecting if they come under threat. It makes sense that an identity threat could compromise my thinking around how to respond in any given situation. For example, part of my identity is being a successful writer. If I'm talking to another writer about my negative experience with a publication, I may be more apt to put all the blame for why the relationship didn't work out on the publication, possibly even exaggerating or saying unexamined statements, versus admitting that I failed in some way. We can think of many examples of how people in all categories of identity may respond when that identity is under threat. A star performer who falters and doesn't capture the top spot may feel the need to tell a lie to explain why they didn't win. A teacher who prides herself on her students' success may be tempted to lie about test scores. Another teacher who prides himself on his high student evaluations may be tempted to round up the numbers if someone asks. An employee of a nonprofit whose funding is threatened may be motivated to fudge a number. "We tend to tell three kinds of lies at work: lies that protect my own accomplishment, lies that protect someone I'm close to, and lies that protect my company," Leavitt says.

Of course, we may be motivated by different identities at different times. I certainly have been. And in fact, Leavitt finds that being able to prioritize different identities at different times is one of the best ways to avoid dishonest behavior. For example, if a professor who builds some of her identity around being a great teacher gets bad evaluations, but she has another identity to fall back on—like perhaps she is an excellent collaborator on a research team—then she's less likely to engage in dishonest exchanges. "A threat can become intractable and build if a person doesn't have other identities to escape into. That's when lying can take place," Leavitt says. Pigeon-holed people often double down on their identity and go to great lengths to manage the threat. Elizabeth Holmes of Theranos is a classic example. She was so desperate to maintain her sense of herself as visionary high-tech entrepreneur that she protected it at all costs, to the point of extreme dishonesty and illegal behavior.

You don't need to embrace black turtlenecks and minimalist design to let yourself be seduced by an identity. It happens at all levels, and to a range of consequences. This is why our fifth honesty principle is, *Think about who you are being.* When you are in a situation and there is a temptation to engage in deception for your benefit or another's benefit, ask yourself if the temptation is related to an identity you need to protect. If you understand who you are being, you have a better chance of seeing the situation more clearly, and not letting yourself feel backed into a corner, where a lie feels like the only answer. This holds true for the big lies and the small interactions that happen every day. As we've seen, small decisions around honesty add up—not just in that you may create a story for yourself that you have to keep track of and potentially have to add more lies to, but also, you just wind up feeling increasingly worse about yourself. I've noticed that if I am feeling stressed out because I don't know how to respond in any given situation, if I simply say to myself, *I am a person who tries to tell the truth, even when it's difficult*, it helps me—as basic and almost silly as that sounds. For example, I was on a deadline for a magazine story not long ago, and it had the potential to be somewhat high-profile. A source pulled out at the last minute for extenuating circumstances, and I suddenly had to replace them. I panicked, because it wasn't easy securing a source to begin with (it was a very specific type of experience I was looking for) and I worried whether I could find another who matched. I put dozens of feelers out to my network, and got several leads—most of which were dead ends. But then I got lucky and acquired two solid leads within about fifteen minutes of each other. Both people were thrilled at the prospect of being in the story, but I could only include one (and truthfully, the second one wasn't as strong). The thought of having to tell the second person that I couldn't include them made me feel awful, especially since they made it clear they would drop everything to do an interview. I knew they would be disappointed, and I would look like a person who didn't follow through. I avoided responding to their email for an entire day, and when they followed up that night to ask if I would be sending questions or scheduling a time to talk, I felt terrible. I seriously considered spinning a story, but then I had this moment where I remembered that I was a person who tried to tell the truth, even if it was hard sometimes. Right then, I emailed the person and thanked them, telling them that while I couldn't use them for this particular story, I would keep them in mind if I wrote about the topic again (which is true). Thinking about how I was going to respond caused dread in me all day, and yet, once I simply remembered who I was, it was remarkably obvious, and all the drama I had created for myself seemed so unnecessary.

But what about the ability to "pivot" to another identity when one identity feels threatened? Leavitt tells me his own story about that. Presenting research and publishing papers is a big part of his identity as an academic. A few years ago, he had three papers rejected within one week. Naturally, this was disappointing. Timing wasn't on his side, either, since he was attending a big conference full of academics in his field that very weekend. While at the conference, he happened to bump into Adam Grant. Anyone who follows organizational psychology knows that Adam Grant is famous for being a brilliant and bestselling author, and an all-around influential thinker who continually publishes important studies. In other words, pretty much the last person in the world you want to talk to if you're not feeling great about yourself. Leavitt knew Grant because they finished their PhDs around the same time, and Grant had served as an editor on a few of Leavitt's publications. So naturally, Grant asked Leavitt how his research was going. Leavitt could almost physically feel the identity threat rising through him: One of the most successful researchers in his field was asking him about his research, days after a chunk of it had been rejected! It could have been a must-lie situation. Except that Leavitt had a few things on his side. For one, he's an ethics researcher who actively studies this stuff, so he had awareness (*First, be aware*). He also had other professional and personal identities to slide into, from being a teacher to being a mountain biker. He knew this setback in one area of his professional life didn't determine everything, and didn't need to be rationalized, justified, or just plain lied about. So what did he wind up saying to Grant? "I just said, to be honest, ask me again in about a month," Leavitt tells me.

Leavitt's advice for companies and managers is to encourage employees to be able to move about their different identities, versus pigeon-holing them. For example, if a manager only values or rewards a team member for one identity—such as being one of the top salespeople—that team member can start to feel unduly threatened if their sales numbers drop, versus if that same manager values the team member for being a top salesperson *and* a strong mentor to junior salespeople. Employees also need to ask themselves if they are over-identifying in one area. Leavitt gives the example of college professors who would be mortified to have anyone discover their radio not tuned to NPR at all times. Talking to Leavitt helps me see ways that I have sometimes over-identified and could do better to think about who I am being. For example, one tweak I'm making is being careful not to over-identify as this successful, veteran writer who knows the business inside and out, because this can make me miss things or interpret feedback incorrectly. Instead of doubling down on that identity when I feel a threat (*Oh no, Judi, you're going to be exposed as a fraud writer!*), I'm trying to embrace pivoting to another identity. For example, instead of sending a terse email recapping the ways in which I am right, I may need to assume the identity of a lifelong learner, to find some humbleness and embrace the notion of always learning and trying to improve. Or, if my business is slow, and I hear my colleagues talking about their successes, I need to give myself a moment to feel the jealousy and notice the identity threat snaking around my legs. And then I need to remember that in addition to being a successful writer with bylines in lots of big publications, I am also a person who learns from others, is supportive of others in my field, and believes in the collective power of good writing and good ideas.

And if that doesn't work, I go for a nice, long run.

Are You a Time Traveler?

People have a tendency to temporarily time-travel to the future, to what we *think* will be true in the future. If your identity is that of a standout achiever who accomplishes things, you might optimistically think, *I'm sure I could be proficient in this. I'll just say I am, and then I'll get proficient before anyone notices that I'm not.* No one notices at first, so you forget, and then a few weeks (or years) go by, and eventually, you've been lying on your résumé so long, it's like white noise you don't even notice.

"Borrowing from the future is a lie that's disruptive in organizations," Leavitt says, noting that it's often what's behind accounting fraud. You fudge a number because it's soooo close, and you'll make it up next quarter, and then next quarter comes and you rationalize why you didn't make it up, but now you're in a little deeper, so you need to cover it up and continue borrowing from the future. Focusing on what is true in the here and now is not always easy to do inside of an organization, but you'll be thankful in the future if you can.

When Should You Lie at Work?

We've covered what tempts us to be dishonest at work and how dishonesty is related to both the big and small decisions we make every day. We've also learned some strategies we can use when we face various dilemmas. This is helpful information, since it's clear that more honesty in the workplace is a better thing.

Except when it's not.

Work is clearly not a place for total honesty. In fact, there may be no better place to exercise your prosocial lying skills than at work. We learned from prosocial lying researcher Emma Levine that telling a prosocial lie is seen as a viable way to build emotional trust. However, honesty and prosocial lying are equally essential ingredients for building trust and goodwill. It's one thing to debate about whether or not to tell a goodwill-inspired prosocial lie at the YMCA pool to the old guy who gets in your lane and then feels like a dope because he didn't understand. It's another thing altogether if your daily job relies on building trust and goodwill. How can you possibly know when to reach for honesty and when to craft a trust-building prosocial lie?

While working on this book, I got an answer to that, in the most unlikely of places: a "ride-along" with a member of my extended family who happens to be a police officer. This relative, who asked me not to use his name, is a police officer in a midsize Midwestern city, where he works the seven p.m. to five a.m. shift in a tough inner city neighborhood with a high crime rate. I took a road trip to where he lived, and spent half of a Friday evening shift with him. (If you're interested, most police departments allow citizen ride-alongs. I highly recommend it.) We went on various calls, and at one point in the evening, a woman reported that someone had stolen the radio out of her truck.

I had no idea people still stole car radios, but off we went to check it out. The woman's story made absolutely no sense to me—it included so many confusing extraneous details (she had diabetes; her friend was on heroine; her mother stayed with the kids sometimes), and I couldn't follow along. Meanwhile, my relative took copious notes. I wondered, what on earth could he be writing? None of this makes any sense, and it's a *radio*! When the woman was done telling her convoluted story—which somehow he seemed to follow (he knew some of the players involved in all those extraneous details, like a thief named Fat Joe)—he handed her a card that assigned her a case number and told her she could follow up with a zone misdemeanor investigator, who would investigate. He answered her questions and told her a little more about the process. As we walked back to his cruiser, he asked me: "What do you think the chances of that case getting solved are?"

"Probably not very good?" I ventured.

"Pretty much zero," he said.

"So, why bother with it then? I mean, I guess you have to, but if it's just pointless, why not just be honest?"

"If she pursues it, we will, too. We'll try. But in situations like this, people want to be heard. They want their story heard," he said. "Most of what we do is just listen to people."

He could have been honest with the woman and said something like, "Yeah . . . we'll fill out the paperwork and put it in the system, and you could get lucky, because, hey, anything's possible. But these kinds of petty crimes are virtually unsolvable. So sure, call the zone misdemeanor investigator. Just don't hold your breath." After all, we value people who "tell it like it is." That's not what she needed in this moment, though. What she needed was a little hope, and to be heard. She needed a prosocial lie.

Recall that there are different types of prosocial lies—the paternalistic lies (you only think you know what's best for the other person) versus the trust-building prosocial lies (you have insight into what the person needs). My relative had that insight, not because he had ever talked to this particular woman before, but rather, because he had talked to hundreds of people just like her. To be able to do his job effectively, he needs citizens to trust him. He needs them to call the police when something is wrong. He needs them to tell him what they saw. He needs them to believe that he cares (he does). He needs them to work with him, and then with investigators, to solve crimes. With the public perception of the police currently so divided, he has to work extra hard to foster trust. In some situations, that might mean he needs to take a "no bullshit tell it like it is" approach, dishing out some hard truths to someone and calling it as he sees it. Other times, he needs to offer hope and instill confidence. In his job, the downstream effects of that decision can literally be life or death. For example, that night, the woman was only reporting a stolen car radio. But the next time she needs the police, it may be a much more serious situation. She could be a key witness. She could be the one who can provide the missing information the police need. If she knows and believes that the police are there to help and can be trusted, she is that much more likely to come forward or cooperate. That cooperation could mean the police get one more gun off the streets and save one more life.

Are You a Humble-Braggart?

Do you often say things like, "Apparently, I got chosen for the fellowship. I'm just as surprised as you!" or "It's pretty annoying to be the only competent person in my department," or "I don't blog that much because it's so time-consuming to moderate all the comments I get when I post."

This is called humblebragging, and behavioral scientist Francesca Gino, professor of business administration at Harvard Business School and author of *Sidetracked: Why Our Decisions Get Derailed, and How We Can Stick to the Plan*, has studied the effect it has on other people. In a 2018 paper she co-wrote on humblebragging, she defines the practice as, "bragging masked by a complaint or humility." Humblebragging is common—most of us have uttered a humblebrag at some point—but ultimately, it's not the effective tool we think it might be, especially if it becomes our go-to tool for trying to present ourselves in a better light. We try to humble ourselves by complaining about how difficult our success is (*Poor me, with all those blog comments to wade through!*) or by channeling self-deprecation (*No one is more surprised than me that I won this awesome and prestigious thing!*). We think it makes us seem the right combination of modest, deserving of sympathy, and successful, but ultimately, Gino finds, we just come off as insincere.

The next time you feel a humblebrag forming on your lips or working its way to your preferred social media feed, try this instead: Say nothing.

Now, you may not deal with those life-or-death consequences in your line of work. In my job as a writer, I don't, either. But I do have to deal with navigating stressful situations that require deft and careful thought about how honest to be. For the past several years, I've worked as part of a production crew that puts on live corporate events (I write the scripts for the events and the speeches for many of the executives presenting at the events). I've told people presenting on stage they did great, while flagging certain areas in my mind to help them work on for next time. I've worked with executives on speeches, and when—mere minutes before they are set to go on—they are second-guessing if they can pull it off (and I'm wondering the same thing), I've instilled confidence in them, saying things like, "You know this material and you are ready!" At the same time, I've also thrown up red flags when I'm working with someone and the day before, they want to make changes that I think aren't good. It's my job in that moment to be brutally honest and say, "I don't think this will help your message. In fact, it might hurt it." The latter is definitely more difficult, because I do run the risk of offending them. When I know they are nervous and not feeling particularly confident, I start to feel compassion (*Be mindful of emotions*).

However, I know that they rely on me to give them feedback because they trust me. They trust me both because I know when to sidestep with a prosocial lie and when to let the truth spill forward. Since I work for myself, I've got my little "culture of one" mostly figured out. I know how I'm going to be with a client, or with a source for a story I'm writing, or with a colleague I'm collaborating with.

When we move this scenario to the organizational level, we run into problems, though. Emma Levine points this out in her work on how to bring the conversation about prosocial lying into organizations, many of which have codes of conduct that have blanket statements about honesty, holding it up as a fundamental value. Meanwhile, employees may be actively encouraged to lie in certain situations—or on the flip side, admonished not to lie only to see a manager lie, whether for prosocial or self-interested reasons. Employees may then feel confused or stung by hypocrisy. "Having an open conversation about the appropriateness of deception can help managers promote honesty when it fosters development and learning, and discourage honesty when it causes unnecessary harm," Levine writes in her paper, "Why We Should Lie."

The place where miscommunication around honesty can do the most damage is when a manager—or even a lateral co-worker—is faced with giving feedback. Let's imagine that you're in a meeting (because if you work in an office, you probably spend a good part of your day in meetings), and someone newer and more junior is giving a report about a project they are working on. Her presentation style is lacking and the information is poorly organized. You know that she will need to deliver this report in front of the client next week, so it will need work. When she is done with the presentation, she asks, in front of the entire team (which contains some intimidating people): "So, what do you think?"

Maybe you happen to know this junior team member pretty well, and you know that she needs tough love, and in fact feeds on brutal honesty and has an extremely thick skin. Then by all means, you can say, "Ay ay ay, this needs a lot of work! What are you thinking? We've got to go back to the beginning and clean this entire thing up, or you'll tank with the client!" I'm guessing that most people aren't like that, though, at least not when they are new to a company. In fact, let's say that this is an employee who lacks confidence and experience, and is easily embarrassed. A prosocial lie solution, or a side step that focuses on staying positive and building trust, might be to say, "Good job on a solid start. How about we connect after the meeting and build on what you have?" That way, you've focused on the positive, she's not embarrassed in front of the whole team, and you will still have a chance to help her strengthen her report. Imagine that this tactfulness and desire to truly help people thrive was the established culture of the company, that managers were trained to prioritize fostering development over some hypocritical standard of honesty. If that was the case, then you wouldn't have to worry about your team looking at you like you're nuts, and you having to initiate side conversations that are gossipy in nature ("I had to tell her she did a good job because I didn't want to embarrass her, but I know it was shit and we'll lose the account if that's what she presents next week!").

A better corporate motto than "We are honest" might be, "We use honesty to help people be better, not to harm." I'm guessing that it's easier to walk a cat on a leash than it is to change an entrenched organizational culture. But even if you are inside a bigger structure, you can still practice your own "culture of one" and use every opportunity to explain your methods and your thinking to others. Your decisions matter—for you, and for those around you.

I think back to the manager at the design firm who called me into her office to scold me for my mistake. The frustration I felt that day was the beginning of my resolve to figure out a way to work for myself. I feel about her the way I feel about going to a conservative all-girls' Catholic high school: It showed me exactly what I didn't want, so that I could find the path I did want. Her inability to balance honesty, encouragement, and kindness turned out in my favor.

I'd still like to make sure I do better than that, though.

Can You Spot Your Conflicts of Interest?

Whenever I write a piece for *The New York Times*, I get a slew of PR firms who want to send me free things or give me subscriptions to services. Some days, it's like a virtual swag bag in my inbox. The *Times* has ethics rules against taking things from companies related to a story you're writing for them. Even if they didn't have such a rule, I'd still turn down the offers from PR people, because it could be a conflict of interest. It's not that I would knowingly fabricate something to appease a company that sent me a free coffeemaker. It's that I have a fear of owing people things, and I would second-guess myself far too much. I'd wonder things like, *I didn't include such-and-such—what if the brand gets mad?* Or if I decided to shift the way I wrote about something, I would wonder if it was my independent idea to do it, or if I was subconsciously trying to keep someone happy. I also stay vigilant about keeping my streams of money very separate. For example, I produce videos for a children's hospital here in town (the very same one who sent me the duplicate check!), so I would never then try to write about them in an article for an outside publication.

A journalist taking gifts from a public relations person or using a client as a source are obvious conflicts of interest. But conflicts of interest are not always so obvious. Just ask Ivan Oransky. Trained as a medical doctor, Oransky has spent most of his career as a journalist and professor (he's currently vice president, editorial at Medscape, and a distinguished writer in residence at New York University's Arthur Carter Journalism Institute). He is also the co-founder (with writer Adam Marcus) of the site retractionwatch.com, a blog dedicated to covering retractions in the world of scientific papers. This may sound like a dull pursuit, but it's one of the most fascinating science blogs around. Oransky and Marcus are tracking everything from the "oops" type of screw-ups to full-on misconduct, lying, and cheating, as well as general shenanigans in the world of science. "We're trying to look at how good the scientific correction process is," Oransky tells me. The short answer is that the process is having to work pretty hard lately.

Oransky moderated a panel discussion I attended at the 2018 Association of Health Care Journalists conference (he is the current president of the association) about what happens when science turns out to be wrong. I was intrigued with the topic for a few reasons. First,

I often include scientific studies as part of pieces I write (or, ahem, books I write) and I worry that I'll rely on a study with bad information. And second, there is a whole transparency movement within science that ties in with this book and is relevant for people who are not scientists. Because, at its heart, "when science gets it wrong" is mostly a story about conflicts of interest—specifically, the conflicts of interest that people don't want to talk about, because they are inextricably linked to their livelihoods.

The scientific world has been doing some reckoning with itself for the past decade or so, after a small group of scientists started seriously questioning some of the studies they were seeing published. A lot has been written about this (if you're interested, search "replication crisis"), and it's a bit confusing with a large cast of characters. So let me attempt to simplify it by using a hypothetical situation. Let's say I'm a runner (which I actually am) and I have a blogging gig with a running shoe brand (full disclosure: I have blogged for running shoe brands. But this is a purely made-up scenario). As a blogger, there is continual pressure on me to come up with new ideas. If I don't, I fear the brand will move on to another running blogger. Furthermore, I really want to become a senior blogger, but to get to be a senior blogger, I have to generate a certain amount of social media traffic on my pieces. So I've got to come up with clickable headlines and juicy, surprising content. I get the idea to look through my running log for ideas. I notice that after the birth of each of my children, after I recovered from the initial postpartum period, I got faster in my running times for about six months until it evened out again after getting sick and having to take a few weeks off. I feel a tinge of excitement. This could be a breakthrough finding—giving birth makes you temporarily run faster! I imagine the headlines I could write and how much social media traffic that could bring!

I open up a spreadsheet and start plugging in running times for the two years before I had kids, the year after having each one of my two kids, and then the two years after that. I control for the fact that sometimes I ran different routes, only matching route to route. I control for the time of day, which isn't hard, since I always ran at the same time. I plot my dataset in a chart, and there I see a subtle curve. It appears that I got faster after each kid for about six months, until each time I got sick and lost some fitness when I had to take a few weeks off. The data tells the story: My pace in the two years before kids averaged 9:10 per mile. From three months postpartum to nine months postpartum, my pace averaged 8:50/mile. Then, it slowed back down to its 9:10/mile average.

I publish my findings in a blog post, it gets more clicks than any of my other stories, and the brand loves me! Averaging twenty seconds faster per mile is a big deal for runners, even us recreational ones. I'm onto something. I can just feel it! If I can spin this finding into a bunch more stories, my blogging gig will be secure and that promotion to senior blogger will happen.

And then . . . people in the running community begin to get suspicious. They look at my data, and say, "Is this all of your data?" to which I say, "It's all of my relevant data." Now we have a problem, because my idea of what's relevant and their idea of what's relevant may not be the same thing. They ask which categories I track in my log, and I tell them that I have data for the route, the time, and the time of day. They ask me if I kept any notes on my runs. I tell them that, yes, I made notes about things like how I was feeling, and . . . the weather.

I had excluded weather from my dataset because it didn't seem relevant. But now, when I go back and look again, I notice that those two postpartum stretches were during the winter. When I look further at my data, I notice that I've been faster in the winter every year I've kept data—or least, about half of my winter runs have been faster. The other half of my winter runs were greatly slowed down by snow. So, on average, my fast times in the winter are canceled out by my slow times because of all the snow. But guess what? During those two winters after each of my children were born, it turns out that we got absolutely no snow. So for those two winters, and those two winters alone, there was nothing to slow down my natural inclination of running faster in the winter.

No snow.

Uh-oh.

I must retract it. I'm frustrated. I'm ashamed. I'm wondering how I missed this. Now, pretend that I'm an academic and the running brand is the institution I work for and the senior blogging gig is getting academic tenure. Because if you plug real science, real studies, and real data in place of my silliness, my little scenario is close to what's happening in the scientific community. Peers are calling into question studies that don't seem quite right because of findings that seem too surprising, too good to be true, or too much of a departure from previously published studies. Furthermore, when these peers try to replicate the study, they can't produce the same results. While some study authors of these discredited or retracted studies seem downright seedy, I'm guessing that the majority of these researchers did not set out to lie. They did not set out to mislead. In fact, I venture to say they are curious and well-intentioned people, who are believers in the scientific method and eager to contribute to the literature.

So what in the world happens? It's not just one answer, Oransky says. But a big part of it is that researchers and academics are under enormous pressure to publish studies—and not just *any* study, but studies that wow and are accepted at prestigious journals. It's not merely ego that motivates, it's their livelihood. To keep their job, to get tenure, and to get grants, they need to publish. And you don't publish negative results (though there is a movement to do that). "The same way a reporter needs that big scoop, a scientist needs it, too," Oransky says.

What Does Honest Work Really Mean?

Leo Tolstoy famously said, "Honest work is much better than a mansion." He basically grew up in a mansion before he became an anarchist and started wearing peasant clothing, so I get his point.

But what is honest work? As a cliché, it refers to physical work or hard labor. After all, whoever coined the phrase, "An honest day's pay for an honest day's work," probably wasn't referring to the work of a social media strategist or an investment banker. Getting beyond the clichés, what do we know about this idea of honest work? Is it determined by the person or the profession? We're not quite sure, says Taya Cohen. According to her research, 20 to 30 percent of working adults in the United States have low moral character. "However, we do not know whether these individuals are distributed randomly across different occupations or whether they are more concentrated in certain sectors, positions, or industries than others," she writes.

Most of us probably have some theories about where low moral character people tend to hang out—at least if you equate trust with moral character. So, which professions do we trust the most and which do we trust the least? According to a 2017 Gallup poll on honesty and ethics in the various professions, the most trusted profession in America—for the sixteenth year in a row—is a nurse. Military officers and grade school teachers have the next two spots. As for the least trusted profession in America? Lobbyist. Car salespeople and members of Congress fill in the bottom rungs. Auto mechanics and bankers are squarely in the middle of the list—sometimes trusted, sometimes not. While all Americans polled agreed on the most and least trusted professions, there are some partisan differences. Republicans rate police officers, members of the military, and clergy higher than Democrats do (although clergy has dropped overall in the past several years). Democrats rate TV and newspaper reporters more trustworthy than Republicans do.

Car salespeople have been at the bottom of the Gallup poll since it started in 1977. This makes me wonder: What is it about car salespeople that we find especially untrustworthy? I've dealt with car salespeople a handful of times in my life and while I never feel like they are actively lying to me (i.e., telling me lies of commission), I always feel like there are things they aren't telling me, especially if I think about *used* car salespeople. In fact, if I were to make a list of who I think *palters* the most—remember, palter is to use a true statement for the specific purpose of deceiving someone—I would put used car salespeople at the top of that list, right along with the other two least-trusted professions, politicians and lobbyists. This isn't surprising since Todd Rogers, professor of public policy at the Harvard Kennedy School, found that people who discover they've been paltered to respond as negatively as when they discover they have been actively lied to. People find paltering especially unethical when they have asked someone a direct question and are met with a true statement that deceives them. Example: A member of Congress is seeking an endorsement, and the endorser asks, "Will you vote for this bill that protects the national parks?" The Congressperson responds, "I have a long history of protecting the things that are important to the American people," to secure the endorsement—and then votes against the bill. What do we say about that Congressperson? "Lying politician!" It really gets our goat when the lie feels so intentionally manipulative.

The thing is, Rogers finds, people who palter think it's this awesome negotiating technique. They think it adds value to the negotiation. And it might. But if they are discovered, the breach of trust is of the worst kind. Bad enough to keep you stuck at the bottom of the list of least-trusted professions for four decades.

A researcher likely doesn't start with a willful intention to deceive. The research is suggestive of something, so they begin to shape a narrative with the data. It's the classic confirmation bias: You want something to be true, so you look for evidence that it is, to the exclusion of evidence that it may not be true. Greater transparency in scientific data is one way the scientific community is trying to improve the process. But there is a more fundamental problem, Oransky says. "The incentives for researchers are misaligned." If job security and grants wind up being the reward for breakthrough research, it creates a baked-in conflict of interest. Does this mean that all scientific research is compromised? Of course not. But attaching stakes to outcomes will probably not get us closer to the truth—which is the goal of scientific research. The scientific community is trying different things to combat the problem, and as Oransky points out, it doesn't help that everyone keeps calling it a "crisis." "I describe it as science having a healthy awakening," he says. The fact remains that a good many institutions aren't setting scientists up to be able to get to the truth in an uncompromised way.

You could look at news outlets who have to push out content twenty-four hours a day, and need to impress advertisers with metrics—clicks and shares and engagement—as suffering from the same problem. So often, media outlets are just reacting to whatever the latest craze or viral video is, propelled not by the idea of getting to the truth of the matter, but by the thought of how much engagement they can derive from jumping on the bandwagon of whatever is trending. You and I—the people who consume the media—feed it. Even in writing this book and having heightened awareness, I still have to remind myself to stop before I react to whatever image or story springs onto my social media feed. It's really out of control, and the topic for a whole other book that I am certain someone is writing (and I will be happy to read).

Tangents aside, the real problem with conflicts of interest is when we don't acknowledge them, and let them play in the background of our lives. When you have multiple agendas, and one is tied to the other in a way that makes a narrative *have* to be true, it's a sign you may be dealing with a conflict of interest. For me, avoiding classic conflicts of interest in my work—like taking kickbacks—is fairly easy, because they are so obviously wrong. It's more challenging to ferret out the subtle ones and to spot my own confirmation bias, not just in any story I might write or read, but also in my relationships and in my parenting. This is on my mind, since we're about to jump headlong into talking about honesty inside of these more intimate relationships. We may be wrapping up talking about the workplace, but we're far from done talking about conflicts of interest and confirmation bias. However, within intimate relationships, the conflicts and biases are born of our hearts rather than our wallets. They are deeply tied to identity, to how we understand our feelings, and to our notions about blame. These heart conflicts can cause grave pain and intense confusion in their attempts to keep themselves safely stowed away, huddled in the darkest corners of our soul.

I know, because I spent several years trying to keep my own squirreled away.

It's time to unearth them.

Reviewing the Honesty Principles

Think about who you are being.

- Are you tempted to be dishonest because your identity—the key way you see yourself in the workplace—is threatened? (*Theranos's Elizabeth Holmes doubled down on her identity as a high-tech entrepreneur when it was threatened.*)
- How can you cultivate and embrace other identities and ways of being, to better be able to handle identity threats? (*I embrace the idea of myself as a lifelong learner instead of feeling threatened if I make a mistake in my writing.*)

CHAPTER 6

Honesty in Friendship

MAKING FRIENDS IN YOUR FORTIES IS HARD.

Keeping friends in your forties is hard.

Basically, friendship in your forties is just hard.

Now, not everyone reading this book is in their forties. I am, though, and as you've probably figured out, I like to start with me. As we get further into our discussion of honesty and friendship, I'll circle back around and try to find you, in whatever decade you're in. But I'm going to start right where I am.

The reason I find friendship difficult at this stage of my life is because I'm to the point where I guard my time more closely, don't want to deal with bullshit, and don't want to pretend anymore. So when I'm forming new relationships, it's not worth making the effort to connect with a person if I'm not willing to be honest, and they're not willing to be honest—which is not always an easy match. That same standard of honesty now holds for my current friendships. If honesty isn't already baked into a friendship (even a friendship I've had for a while), reverse engineering it now is challenging, and may or may not be worth it.

I don't mean this to sound like grousing. I think it's actually a good thing. As an introvert, I don't need that many friends. I prefer to have just a few close friends, and then a wider circle of interesting people I see sometimes, but don't feel the need to know very well. That said, I've felt compelled lately to convert more of those acquaintances into true friends. It might be because many of my friends are writers

I've met at conferences. I love them dearly, but they tend to be scattered all over the country and I don't get to see them very often. I find that lately, I've been craving the immediacy of having a friend right there to talk to and hang out with.

This is how I came to be giving myself a pep talk about making new friends as I walked down to our town's annual summer festival several months ago with my kids. Allen, who normally goes to these things with me, was at a concert with a guy friend. *This is your opportunity*, I told myself. My daughter, Georgia, spotted her friend and they immediately huddled together on a bench, squealing with joy. When had I been so happy to see a friend that I *squealed*? Ivy, the mother of Georgia's friend, started laughing, and so did I. We knew each other a little professionally (she oversaw publishing at a magazine I contributed to) and from chatting before and after play dates, so we struck up a conversation. We started off talking about kids, because in a pinch, they are a common denominator for smoothing the way. Eventually, we started talking about our careers. About life. About big ideas (like honesty). I told her about the book I was writing. I was enjoying talking with her like I hadn't enjoyed a conversation in a while. She was smart and funny and easy to talk to. Definite friend material. The conversation veered to exercise. It turned out we were both runners. We talked about some of the routes we ran. And then she said, "Oh, we should run together!"

I cringed.

Now, I used to make running dates. It was an important part of my social life when I was in my twenties. But these days, I run alone, on my own terms, and don't want to share that time with anyone else. I'm diligent about protecting it. Still, a few years ago, I would have said, "Totally!" with no intention of ever following through. And then I would have had that feeling of dread you have when you say you want to do something you don't want to do, and you're just waiting for it to come up again. Every day it doesn't come up, it's more and more awkward, until finally, you just don't even talk to the person anymore. Luckily, in this moment, I was actively aware that I was facing an honesty choice (*First, be aware*) and I knew emotions, like fear of rejection, were at play (*Be mindful of emotions*). I didn't want that cloud to forever hang around us, so I sorted through the emotional fog and made the decision to be forthcoming. "Actually, I have to be honest. I really like to run alone," I said, as earnestly and kindly as I could. I further explained, "It's my time to just unplug from the world. I need that, you know?"

I knew what I was saying was reasonable. Still, in that beat before she answered, I let all the worrisome thoughts surround me: Had I ruined things? Why couldn't I just be agreeable? What if I hurt her feelings?

Ivy looked at me with surprise in her eyes, but then she broke into a warm smile. "Thank you for being honest!" she said. "And I don't even know why I suggested we run together, because I like to run alone, too!" We laughed and both agreed that if we would have said, *yeah sure, let's run together*, we never actually would have and it would have always been this thing we felt awkward about. It was such a nice moment, and helped me feel more connected to her. We wound up chatting most of the evening, and she and her husband invited me and the kids back to their house, where the kids continued to play and the grown-ups sat in the kitchen and talked more. "I may not want to run together, but I'm always down to get a glass of wine," I said. We've since gotten together numerous times and always had a great time talking, with or without wine.

I let honesty be my guide, in large part because it's my project to do so. But still, why was my gut reaction that it was going to be worse than I thought? After reflecting, I remembered the answer: We are really bad at predicting what honesty feels like.

Why We Often Miss the Opportunity to Be Honest

Could my honesty have pushed my new friend away? Possibly. But it's also possible that the fear of honesty pushing someone away is greater than the reality. That's what Emma Levine's study found. Actually, it was a study that she and Taya Cohen, the moral character researcher, conducted together. Remember the experiment I referenced in chapter 4, where people were asked to be completely honest in their dealings with others for three days? Cohen and Levine found that while people dreaded the thought of being honest with others—predicting that it would harm relationships more than help them, and cause hurt and pain—quite the opposite was true. "People made big forecasting errors. Then in retrospect, they found so much meaning in being honest," Cohen tells me when describing the study. They feared rejection, but in many cases, found liberation. In fact, many of the quotes Cohen and Levine capture in the study reflect that sense of liberation, such as this one:

> Tension was building up with my roommate because I couldn't bring myself to tell her the things she was doing that were annoying, and while doing the study I told her all those things I had been avoiding to tell her for a while and it felt kind of liberating. Some of the things were kind of awkward, but others felt good and it helped ease some of the tension. I learned that it feels better to say those kinds of things instead of keeping them inside until it explodes.

In a related experiment, Levine and Cohen had pairs of people— either friends or romantic partners—come to a lab, where they were instructed to ask each other certain questions, with the direction to be completely honest. Again, while participants predicted it would be miserable and would potentially alienate their friend or partner, they ultimately found the experience meaningful. One participant said, "It felt good to tell her what I had been holding in, and I think it really helped to strengthen our bond, for me to open up to her about something in my past that I had always kept separate from my day-to-day life." Levine and Cohen conclude that so often, avoiding honesty means missing out on opportunity to connect and strengthen a relationship. For me, as someone who is touting the life-changing benefits of focusing on honesty, this finding is glorious. *See, I'm right! Honesty is the answer! It's how we can love each other more!*

You know by now that it's never that easy.

The reason I believe honesty becomes increasingly more challenging as we move further inward—from social honesty to intimate honesty—is that there is more at stake. Casual acquaintances, social connections, and co-workers are important, but you may or may not feel true fondness for these people. You don't want to treat them like shit, but they don't have the real estate in your heart the way people in your intimate relationships do. Your heart is both the most sacred place and the scariest place (there is a reason that sacred and scared read almost as the same word). Vulnerability is a variable in all relationships, but in the ones you value the most, it's an even bigger variable. What psychology researcher Brené Brown discovered after studying vulnerability for a dozen years, and what she writes about in *Daring Greatly: How the Courage to Be Vulnerable Transforms the Way We Live, Love, Parent, and Lead* is that we associate vulnerability with weakness, and with emotions like shame, fear, sadness, disappointment. We are so fucking scared of vulnerability, because it is the ultimate uncertainty. It is also, as she writes, "The birthplace of love, belonging, joy, courage, empathy, and creativity. It is the source of hope, empathy, accountability, and authenticity. If we want greater clarity in our purpose or deeper and more meaningful spiritual lives, vulnerability is the path."

To be honest—especially with someone you care about, someone whose love and acceptance you fear losing—is to be vulnerable. Compared with family or with romantic relationships, the vulnerability inside a friendship can feel even riskier. Unlike family relationships, which are based on circumstance and not choice, or long-term romantic relationships, which come with the expectation of ebb and flow and even a certain amount of turmoil, friendship is pure choice, without the same expectation of turmoil or having to "stick it out" through better or worse. When the "worse" comes inside a friendship, it's far easier to cut and run than in any other relationship.

In the story I told about Ivy, the vulnerability wasn't that great, because I didn't know her that well. I had the inkling that we could be friends, and I could envision it, but the stakes were fairly low. Even then, I still felt uncertainty about how my honesty would land. So when the stakes are higher? The uncertainty can be so intense that it stops us in our tracks. One of the biggest emotional shifts I've had to make in the past several years is embracing vulnerability, and embracing that moment where you just don't know what might happen to your heart and your ego, because I want to become what Brené Brown calls a more "wholehearted person," which is a person who walks through life fully engaged, with their heart open to others. I knew that I was continually afraid of letting others see me, but I didn't know what that fear was costing me. My journey through honesty is really one big journey through the landscape of vulnerability, crossing lakes of fear and scaling mountains made of emotional conflicts of interest. I say conflict of interest because your ego functions like a brand offering a kickback if you can just see situations in a way that most benefits it. *Don't tell her that truth of yours. She'll never understand. Here, take this judgment instead, and put it on her. It will make you feel better.* We incorrectly predict what honesty will feel like, especially with people we care about, because our ego is screaming so loudly "Red Alert, Vulnerability, Red Alert!" Part of what goes into any honesty choice is our principle, *Be mindful of emotions.* To be a wholehearted friend, we not only have to be mindful of those emotions, we need to find a way to quiet the ego long enough to even think straight and recognize the conflict of interest it's generating inside our psyche.

Is Honesty Always Worth It?

Recently, my sister Laura was telling me about a woman she used to be close friends with who now doesn't seem to want to have anything to do with her. "We were really close! We saw each other several times a week, and talked all the time," Laura tells me. They slowly started drifting away from each other after their kids graduated high school. And now, the woman is very cold to my sister when they see each other out. "She'll barely look at me, and if I do try to talk to her, she can't get away fast enough. I just don't understand: Did I do something?" Laura asks me rhetorically.

My theory is that the woman is jealous because some things in her life haven't turned out quite so well—nothing tragic, but little things, like some health issues, some weight gain, and losing touch with her grown kids, who have moved away. The other woman was always very "together," while my sister was struggling through her children's teenage years. But now, my sister has this amazing relationship with both of her grown children and is in fantastic shape. "I think you're a reminder that she isn't as happy as she could be," I tell my sister. I have no idea if I'm right. I barely know the other woman, and I only know my sister's side. I suggest to my sister that she just say to the woman in an honest, non-accusatory—and yes, vulnerable—way: "Hey, I miss you. We used to be such good friends. I've been trying to figure out what happened. Can we talk about it?"

Laura knows that she could do that. The vulnerability is a little scary, but she could do it. The question is, *Is it really worth it?*

We know that friendships—perhaps above all other relationships—are vital for happiness. In a large cross-cultural study of more than 270,000 adults, University of Michigan researcher William Chopik found that as people got older, the quality of their friendships became increasingly important, and was linked more closely with health and well-being than relationships with family. So friendship in general has great worth, and could absolutely merit some risk-taking in the honesty department. But as we already know from one of our core honesty principles, *Not every situation is the same.* The application to friendship is that not every friend merits that kind of emotional risk-taking. In fact, moving on is sometimes the best option. Chopik's research focuses on studying friendships across the life span, and in thinking about these findings, he theorizes that because we choose our friends, and choose whether or not to keep friends, over time, we wind up with the friends we like—the ones who make us the happiest—and weed out the ones who don't. As much as honesty can bring friends together, it can also be the thing that helps us recognize those friendships that aren't working for us anymore.

When I think about honesty in friendship, I often think about my good friend, Jodi. Jodi and I have been friends for more than fifteen years, and one of the things I love about our relationship is that we can be so honest with each other. She likes to tell me that I'm self-indulgent and obsessed with writing about myself, and I tell her she has major issues with vulnerability. We make each other laugh, and I can't think of any topics that are off limits for us to talk about. If I need tough love about something, she is my go-to person. In fact, I called her up because I needed a reality check for one of the concepts I was going to write about in this chapter. Actually, she called me because my text to her made so little sense. "I've read your text three times, and I have no idea what you're talking about," she told me when I answered the phone. When I tried to explain it, she said, "Okay, you're talking in circles. Let me tell you about why honesty doesn't always work in friendship."

Jodi then told me a story about a woman she used to be friends with who channeled a lot of negativity. This woman complained a lot, and had a lot of reactionary behavior, so that the smallest things could set her off. Jodi would listen patiently and empathetically, validating her friend first and then suggesting a different way to look at the situation. "I was very honest with her, in every way I could think to be honest. Like, I wasn't subtle," she says. The woman recognized that she had problems with negativity, but didn't know what to do about it. Jodi repeatedly tried to make suggestions, but the friend always had a reason why that suggestion wouldn't work. Finally, one evening they found themselves out to dinner with a group of other women. Jodi's friend and all the women at the table were essentially acting like mean girls, saying nasty things among themselves about all the other women and teenage girls at the restaurant, like "Who told you that dress was a good idea?" Jodi sat there seething and deeply embarrassed that these women were behaving this way. She considered saying something, putting forth the honesty one more time. "I just didn't think it would matter," Jodi says. So she left that night, and four years later, she still hasn't spoken to the woman. "I still feel extreme guilt that I couldn't just tell her the reason why I was leaving, or that we couldn't be friends anymore. I had just had enough, though," she says. I ask her why not tell the woman now—send an email or a text or something? It's been too long now, she says. "The bottom line is that honesty doesn't always get you where you want to be." She could have told the woman off, spoken her piece, left with that final dose of honesty. But why? In the end, to Jodi, it felt like honesty had let her down.

Cruel to Be Kind

Jodi's friend didn't respond to her tough love. I, on the other hand, rely on her tough love. I can't tell you how many times she has helped me get the fuck out of my own way. While I've certainly been defensive at times, I am grateful for every frustrating conversation. So . . . what is the deal with tough love? For the answer, I look to a 2017 *Psychological Science* study, ingeniously called, "Cruel to Be Kind" (yes, I am singing the song of the same name as I write this), which found that sometimes friends piss us off on purpose, for our own good. Specifically, you might try to make your friend feel negative emotions—to feel bad—if you think that those emotions will serve your friend well. The researchers manipulated conditions by using a computer game and a scenario where study participants were making specific choices for another person (not a real person, but participants didn't know that), after hearing about something difficult that person was going through (a breakup). Participants who were asked to empathize with the partner wound up trying to incite anger in the other person, because they thought the anger would be helpful for that person. For example, they chose anger-inducing clips of music for the partner to listen to (from among a range of music clips). We already know from research—and, you know, general life experience—that people can be assholes and try to make others feel bad on purpose. But this study was looking at whether we might try to make others feel bad to help them. Jodi doesn't get pleasure out of making me feel like a bumbling fool when I am telling her my (really dumb) plans about something. That feeling of *Wow, I'm a bumbling fool* and *I haven't thought this through* is precisely what I need, though. It should be noted, I do the same for her. In any given situation that involves a difficult truth, we seem to have mutually agreed to follow the principle, *Think about who you are being.* We are truth-tellers to each other. That's who we are. I can think of at least two other good friends this is the case with.

Why does this work in some friendships and not in others? For example, I think about another friend of mine—someone I've known for a long time—who I would never talk to in the same way as I do my truth-telling friends. She's a bit prim and I always suspect she's silently judging me (usually because my kids always seem to misbehave when she's around). While I enjoy things about her and her company, the kind of relationship I have with other friends wouldn't work with her. The answer may have to do with how well I know my friends' triggers, and how well they know mine. Researchers at Wilfrid Laurier University had pairs of friends each fill out questionnaires about how they would respond to certain triggers. These triggers were irksome behaviors and tendencies, like being insincere, displaying self-importance, acting selfishly, or—of course—being dishonest. After each friend filled out their own questionnaire, they filled out a second questionnaire, reflecting how they thought their friend would respond to the triggers (kind of like the TV show *The Match Game*). Some participants seemed to know their friends' triggers very well, whereas others . . . not so much. That mattered for the quality of the relationship, with researchers finding that the friends who knew their friends' triggers best had less conflict and a more meaningful friendship. In other words, friends who understood the triggers that set the other off—such as different types of lying, or even honesty that was too brutal—had better relationships with each other.

This finding makes total sense to me, so I ask Lara Kammrath, who is now an associate professor of psychology at Wake Forest University but supervised the study when she was at Wilfrid Laurier, if anything about the study was surprising. "Yes," she says, "what was surprising is that none of the existing research suggested it would work." Previous research had focused on whether understanding a friend's personality traits made for less conflict, and always found that it didn't. Kammrath theorizes why: "You can pick up someone's personality traits in a week. But their triggers? The things that drive them crazy? It takes way more time to learn," she explains to me. Researchers had been looking at the wrong part of personality. This finding about knowing triggers is related to the idea of prosocial lying only being effective when one person has insight into what the other person wants. Do you *know* what your friend would want in any given situation that requires a decision about sharing a difficult truth? Is there a tacit agreement? If we think about the principle, *Intention matters. So does refinement*, the refinement with friends comes in understanding their triggers. At the same time, just knowing their triggers doesn't mean you'll be able to connect with them in a vulnerable way. It only means you're more likely to avoid conflict with them. And in some friendships, that might be as good as it gets.

So in a way, we're kind of right back where we started with friendship: Honesty can foster connection, but it's still not always worth it. This is why it can be hard to make and keep friends the older you get, because you just have less and less tolerance for things that aren't worth it. My friend Jodi may have had a point when she said that I was talking in circles.

The Magic of Being More Direct

Everyone says they value honest communication, but man, we can be really bad about it. I've outlined a bunch of the reasons we're bad at it in this book. And here is one more: We want people to be mind readers, so we communicate too indirectly. Indirect communication is when your meaning is not explicit, but you hope it comes through, according to linguistic expert Deborah Tannen. We unsuccessfully use indirect communication with romantic partners for sure, but when we do it with friends, it can be even less effective. In her book, *You're the Only One I Can Tell: Inside the Language of Women's*

Friendships, Tannen spends a few hundred pages analyzing women's conversations with each other, picking out all of the nuances of how female friends talk to each other, for better or worse. The book is rich with ideas, but one that struck me the most is being more direct, particularly because it's something I've been working very hard on since I started my honesty journal.

In the book, Tannen shares an anecdote about hiking with a friend. She was struggling to keep up with her friend, and not much enjoying what would have been an otherwise lovely hike. "This pace is kind of fast for me," Tannen said to her friend. The friend merely replied, "This pace is fine." For whatever reason, Tannen didn't protest. She just kept on gasping for breath and following her friend on the trail. It wasn't a great experience, and as she eased her aching muscles the next day, she wondered why she hadn't just told her friend directly to slow down. "I had communicated the one way I knew how to; when it didn't work, I was flummoxed. Our own conversational styles seem so self-evidently the right way to speak, and our linguistic habits so automatic, that speaking differently, which seems like it should be easy, can actually be unthinkable," Tannen writes.

I know exactly what she's talking about. My conversational style is an empathetic, suggestive, and meandering one. I have always tended to talk how I write, which is to circle around an idea and look at it from various sides. I don't have a problem expressing a direct opinion (examples: Trump is a disaster; parents need to stop shaming other parents; aqua is the most glorious color), but I nearly always over-explain and often add a lot of qualifiers ("I'm just saying . . ."; "I appreciate your point of view, but . . ."; "I used to think this way, but then [insert story or anecdote here] happened and that's why I think this . . ."). Before I started noticing my honesty choices, I definitely tended toward the indirect in making requests.

One thing that changed that was taking a class about how to parent an ADHD child, after my kiddo Maxx was diagnosed when he was nine. I learned that all that extraneous stuff is overwhelming for ADHD kids and what they need are simple, direct commands.

"Hang up your backpack," "Wash your hands," "Get out of the tub now." Speaking this way was more effective, and also kinder, because ADHD kids need clarity and easy-to-grasp limits and directions. If you phrase it as a question ("Do you want to come for dinner now?"), a vague suggestion ("Let's think about following house rules a little bit better"), or a long-winded lecture ("I am so tired of having to tell you how to brush your teeth. You are nine years old. I shouldn't have to tell a nine-year-old how to squirt toothpaste on his toothbrush and put the brush to his teeth and move it back and forth without making a colossal mess!"), they get lost in what you're saying and lose the thread of what they are supposed to do. Keeping instructions brief and extremely direct sets them up for success, versus them feeling like a failure. The key is that when I would give these direct commands to my kid, I kept my tone even. I didn't say "Get out of the tub now!" through gritted teeth. I said matter-of-factly, "Get out of the tub."

Because this was successful with my kid (not successful every time, but more successful than my previous technique of begging and giving long-winded explanations), I started to wonder: Is it possible that we actually *all* need this? I started using it in business-type dealings. For example, I was helping Allen deal with getting his mother into a long-term care facility. It was an emergency situation because she had severe dementia and could no longer be left at home. My father-in-law was in the hospital, dealing with his own declining health. Family members, including my husband, had been staying with his mother, but we needed to get her to where people could better care for her. It reached a pitch one afternoon, and we knew we had to get her in a facility right away. We had already toured a property near our home and the administrator had a spot for her. The first step was to have her primary care doctor send her medical records to the facility. The woman who answered the phone at the primary care doctor's office was giving me the runaround, telling me that it could take several days to get the records and have them sent. I very calmly and directly said to her, "This is an emergency situation and my mother-in-law needs care. You will send those records within the hour."

And you know what? It worked. She sent me the release form, I got it filled out properly, the facility got the records, and my mother-in-law got where she needed to be. Never once was I rude. I was direct, and I didn't spend time over-explaining or beating around the bush. I realize that there is a difference between a customer asking directly for what they need and a friend asking another friend directly for what they need or being clear that they don't like something. It is more difficult with a friend than a stranger, but I am trying to incorporate directness as I can. When my sister Claire, who is eleven years older than me and lives fifteen hundred miles away, quite suddenly did a 180 and became an evangelical Christian when she was about fifty, it threw me for a big loop—especially considering she was once my role model for agnostic liberal humanism. Our conversations became circular and frustrating. She was desperate to get me to "accept Jesus as my savior," so that I wouldn't go to hell. I explained to her in my meandering, empathetic, suggestive way all of my issues with that concept, and how it was antithetical to everything I stood for and believed. But each long-winded challenge was only a reason to keep the discussion going, and the more she persisted, the more disrespectful it felt to me (though I understood that wasn't her intention).

I've had to learn to communicate with her differently; sometimes that means simply avoiding topics. It also means being more direct. When I told her I was writing a book about honesty, she told me she had a book to send me. When I received it in the mail, I flipped through it, saw that it was an evangelical treatise, and threw it in the recycling bin. When she texted me, asking me what I thought of the book, I panicked for a moment. I considered using one of the avoidance techniques I used to use, like telling her that I hadn't had a chance to look through it yet, or that I was still "checking it out." I also considered being passive-aggressive. Or aggressive-aggressive. Instead, I simply—and directly—said, "It's not for me."

I also added this: "But I love you." (And she texted back, "I love you, too.")

Hence, the sixth honesty principle is this: *Say what you mean, but don't be a jerk.*

Communicating more directly with people I love (as well as those I don't particularly love) is an ongoing project, but it's one very much related to my quest to be more open and less prone to let conflict fester. The example of directness with Claire is just one sister example. I have three sisters—Nancy and Laura are the other two—and now that we're all adults, they are my best friends. Granted, Claire lives far away, so our relationship has been long-distance for more than thirty years. But Laura and Nancy are my go-to people and I see them every week. We still have conflicts, though, usually around old wounds and childhood triggers—which are, of course, some of the most complex issues to have honest conversations around. Laura feels like she isn't smart enough. Nancy feels left out. They both think I was spoiled, and I feel like I don't get taken seriously enough. Every time we've had a tiff, it usually boils down to someone's trigger getting activated. When these tiffs happen now—which isn't that frequent, perhaps once a year—I make the effort to be direct and force the conversation. The last conflict a few months ago involved Nancy getting mad at Laura (and me getting stuck in the middle). It was the old hurt from childhood of Laura leaving Nancy out (though not on purpose), and though I felt like such a bitch telling Nancy that it was unacceptable to just stop talking to Laura, taking the deep breath and being direct made the conversation happen—which strengthened our friendship even more and helped to heal that childhood wound one more millimeter. I'll cop to the fact that being direct with friends and sisters is excruciatingly uncomfortable. The only thing that makes it bearable is that it's about love.

In fact, for me, the biggest challenge has been unlinking direct communication from being an asshole. That's the essence of what this principle is about. You can say what you mean without turning into an obnoxious, insensitive fool. This is a concept Sarah Knight deals with extensively in *The Life-Changing Magic of Not Giving a F*ck*. This little book is worth a read, because it is hilarious, and surprisingly poignant and insightful for a book that uses the work *fuck* approximately eight thousand times. She argues that when you stop giving a fuck about everything, you can focus on giving a fuck about only the things that bring you joy or are absolutely necessary. The number one thing to master is to stop giving a fuck about those draining interactions with other people, where you are worried what they think about you, for no real reason other than you want everyone to like you. This doesn't mean that you open up a torrent of insults on others because you no longer care what others think of you. You still care about being a good person and being well regarded, but you don't care about being all things to all people all of the time. It's still important to care about people's feelings, but you can care about someone's feelings, without agreeing with them or giving them a platform to go on (and on) about something you have absolutely no interest in. If you and a friend see something differently, and there is no longer joy in arguing about it—or there never has been joy in arguing about it—whether it's politics or how much screen time kids should be allowed, just be honest and say, "We see it differently," or, "There is room for various opinions." It's honest, it's direct, and most important, it's not rude or disrespectful. "You can sidestep the prospect of hurt feelings entirely when you view your conflict through the lens of simple, emotionless opinion," Knight writes.

Let me be very clear about something: Being direct with your honesty isn't a license to say whatever you want to say. This goes for intentionally hurting other people's feelings, or being uninformed, cruel, or bigoted. If a man says to a woman, "Hey, your tits look amazing," and then holds up his hands and says, "Sorry, just being honest," when she calls him out on being inappropriate, that's not a case of him merely being honest. It's case of him being a tone-deaf, disrespectful, and possibly narcissistic asshole. Speaking in a direct manner doesn't mean you get to subject people to your most deviant and deplorable thoughts or unexamined prejudices (even though my example was a man, this holds equally true for men and women). It doesn't mean you lift the filter and say whatever you want. Sadly, in the age of anonymous social media commenters, this very basic idea seems important to put in writing. What I'm really talking about is being direct as a function of improving a relationship or disarming a potential minefield so that the threads of friendship don't get lost in differences of opinion. When you're coming from that place of abundance and good intention, it's often kinder, more considerate, and more wholehearted to be direct than indirect. Will it always land well? No, it won't. It definitely takes courage to break linguistic patterns that keep us safe. But ultimately, being more direct can save a lot of heartache, second-guessing, and confusion.

Putting direct communication in the landscape of honesty gives you a kind of permission to try it. Remember my tip about how telling people that you're actively focused on honesty gives you a kind of permission to be honest? That absolutely applies here. The other interesting thing is that when your friends and other loved ones see that you're focused on directness and honesty, they start holding you accountable. For example, my sisters and I had a text thread where we were talking about how I should approach Allen about wanting to have a gathering at our house of all the siblings on a Saturday night (he feels that our house isn't clean enough or big enough for such gatherings and gets very stressed out by hosting), and Laura said something like, "Well, uh, shouldn't you just be direct with him?" It wasn't the first time that someone who knew about my efforts to pay attention to honesty gave me that suggestion. Quite frankly, it's contagious in the best way possible.

What I've learned is that you can say what you mean while still being empathetic, funny, supportive, and vulnerable. Calling up a friend who has just suffered a terrible loss, and saying, "I am very nervous to talk to you because I don't know what to say," is a lovely, vulnerable, and direct way to begin a conversation. It's probably better than beginning with the open-ended "How are you?" because that can feel too small and too generic. It's definitely better than avoiding talking to your friend at all, who undoubtedly needs a friend now more than ever. *Say what you mean, but don't be a jerk* takes effort, but I believe the effort pays off.

When It's Not Your Truth to Tell

We've all been in that dilemma with a friend, where you know something that might hurt them or anger them, and you don't know if you should keep the secret or tell them. As I was working on this very chapter, my friend Paige and I had some drinks and she told me about a huge dilemma she recently dealt with. I'm not going to share all the details, because it's long and complicated, and ultimately, private. But it's enough to say that it involved whether or not to tell a close friend something she had learned about the friend's daughter. The friend's daughter was an adult, and wasn't caught in an abusive situation, or something life threatening. But Paige was torn because this woman had been such a good friend to her, and while the daughter wasn't doing anything criminally wrong, the choice she was making would likely be hurtful to the mother, and it could possibly make her feel like a fool. Paige agonized, because she is a thoughtful friend, and because honesty is a key value for her. Ultimately, she decided not to tell the friend, because she realized that it wasn't her truth to tell.

The line between secrecy and deception is fuzzy indeed. Sometimes we hold a secret with the intent to deceive for self-interested reasons. Other times, we hold on to the secret either for prosocial reasons or because it isn't even really our secret, but it merely landed on us, like secondhand smoke we breathe in and then feel the effects of. In thinking about this dilemma of whether or not to disclose something to a friend, some key questions I consider are:

- Can the information benefit my friend *now*, or is the timing wrong?
- Do I know my friend's preference, and if they actually want to know the information I have?
- Do I know my friend's triggers? Is absolute honesty one of the things they demand above all else?
- Is the dilemma an actual truth to tell, or is it just me, wanting to have my say?
- Am I afraid of the vulnerability I'll have to muster to deliver the difficult truth, or afraid that my friend will be unnecessarily hurt?
- Is it really *my* truth to tell?

You can get through the entire list, and still get stuck on the last one about whether or not it's your truth to tell. It can be gut-wrenching to tease this out. That's why the seventh honesty principle is, *Is it your truth to tell?*

I phrased this principle as a question, because it *is* almost always a question, and often one without a clear answer. A big part of the journey toward living a more honest life is reckoning with that internal struggle and doing the work of discerning whether something is a truth to share or not. Some people may take the approach that the truth is the truth, and you must speak truth and let the chips fall where they may. I take a more utilitarian approach. Of course, this can backfire and come across as manipulative. It can also build connection, where an ethical mandate on absolute truth may have closed off the opportunity.

I'm thinking specifically of a recent experience where I grappled with this question of whether something was my truth to tell or not. A neighborhood family that my family has become friendly with had their parked car totaled by a drunk driver one night (it was parked on the street just in front of their house). I was out of town when it happened, so I was talking to them several days later about it. Ever the journalist, I was peppering them with questions, like, what happened to the person who hit the car? Eventually—not because they are gossips, but because I was asking and it became more awkward not to tell me than to tell me—they told me it had been my friend, Dan. I was shocked, and not completely shocked, because I knew Dan struggled with alcohol. Dan and I weren't terribly close friends, but Allen and I had socialized with him and his wife. The four of us often found ourselves at kids' events together and always wound up having good conversations. Dan was always ready to defend the underdog or support good causes—things I resonated with. Finding out what he had done, I wasn't sure what to say. I felt awful for my neighbor friends, awful for Dan's wife—who I knew was probably embarrassed and angry with her husband—and awful for Dan himself, because I believed him to be a person who would never set out to hurt anyone. I wondered, should I reach out to him? Should I reach out to his wife? My neighbor friends, who are lovely people in every way, said they had let it go (Dan had apologized to them profusely), and were simply trying to move on. I wasn't going to bring it up with them anymore. All that summer, I would see Dan's wife driving him around. I guessed that he had been charged with a DUI and lost his license for a while. Whenever I would see him, he would just smile and wave. I talked to him several times over the course of the year. When Allen's dad died, Dan and his wife dropped off the most thoughtful care package of wine, chocolate, and a gift card to a gourmet supermarket. I admit, I had a hard time reconciling this responsible, upstanding person I knew with a person who would drive drunk and endanger so many lives. That is, of course, the essence of addiction, and why it can be so hard for others to understand—even when you have your own experience of loved ones who struggle.

I felt conflicted and dishonest with every conversation, yet I decided to keep quiet and not bring it up. Partly, it was because I didn't want to seem like a gossip (and I hadn't told anyone other than Allen). Dan probably feared people had found out and were talking about him, and I didn't want to contribute to that. Also, the timing never seemed right. How did a person bring that kind of thing up? Had we been really close friends, maybe I would have found a way. But I stayed silent on it.

About eighteen months after it happened, Dan posted something on social media about being the survivor of a childhood gun accident, as part of promoting an awareness campaign. I had no idea of his history, and commented how sorry I was, and how brave it was for him to come forward and try to raise awareness. He wound up calling me later that week. It was initially to ask a writing question, but then we got to talking about his post. "I've got to tell you something," he said, and the whole story tumbled out, almost stream of consciousness. He told me about how he hadn't dealt with his childhood trauma for twenty-five years and when he finally started dealing with it, everything started to fall apart in his life. How it intensified his battle with his alcohol addiction and led to the terrible mistake he had made one night when he drove drunk and plowed into our friends' car. He knew that I had a brother who struggled with addiction his whole life, because I had written openly about my brother's struggle and death, and the effect on our family. "I've wanted to tell you all of this for a while," he said, sounding almost tortured. "I thought you would understand."

I realized then that he needed to tell me far more than I needed to acknowledge that I knew. Owning up to his story and his actions was part of his recovery process, and it wouldn't have been the same if I had just said, "So listen, I know you totaled my neighbor's car." There is a funny little space wedged almost imperceptibly between holding a secret for the benefit of others and holding a secret for the benefit of yourself—a space where you are holding it for the benefit that isn't yet clear. Sometimes it's just that the story isn't yours. It isn't your truth to tell. You don't need the catharsis as much as someone else does. And you have to let that person tell their truths according to their timing, not yours. We know this is true with children, and we often give them time to be honest about what they've done before we confront them, because we know it's important for them to develop that courage muscle. It's really no different for adults. We're just far more impatient with our friends.

Is it your truth to tell? Regard that question with sanctity and seriousness, and resist the idea that there is an easy and obvious answer.

And as for vulnerability, sending Dan what I wrote about him was terrifying (it wasn't the first time I was terrified, since I had been sending sections of the book to the many different people featured). I worried about invading his privacy, and tried to think of any other anecdote I could scrounge up to make my point. Like *anything* else. But the story so perfectly illustrated this concept that I had been struggling to verbalize. I also thought his story may be helpful for readers who have struggled with a similar situation. I made it clear in my email to him seeking permission that he could say no, and I wouldn't include it in the book, no questions asked. I took a deep breath and hit send, still wondering if I was making a mistake as I saw the email leave my outbox. Dan responded immediately and graciously said yes, because he was willing to be vulnerable, too.

Saying the things we need to say and being deliberate in how we approach honesty inside of friendship matters, because preserving our friendships improves our health and happiness. The scientific literature reiterates how important friendship is, but we intuitively know it anyway, as we belt James Taylor's "You've Got a Friend" alone in our car. The everyday language around honesty within friendship can be slightly less clear than the poetry of a great pop song, but it is worth trying to figure out the right words, no matter how young or old you are.

Reviewing the Honesty Principles

Say what you mean, but don't be a jerk.

- Try being direct, instead of indirect, when you need a friend (or anyone for that matter) to understand something clearly, or you need to express something honestly. (*"It's not for me, but I love you."*)
- Honesty is not an excuse to be an uninformed, sexist, racist, classist or generally offensive asshole, to be mean for the sake of being mean, or to stop caring about others' feelings. (*"We see it differently"* or *"There are room for many opinions on this topic."*)

Is it your truth to tell?

- Is the secret one that your friend needs to know for their safety, health, well-being, or happiness, or is it just a secret you feel compelled to reveal because you feel uncomfortable knowing it? (*Telling her friend that her daughter was doing something the friend wouldn't like wasn't Paige's truth to tell.*)
- Is there more benefit in waiting to see what your friend might do or say than there is in being candid and sharing what you know? (*Dan needed to tell me more than I needed to let him know that I knew.*)

CHAPTER 7

Honesty in Marriage

Arguably, my top two reasons for starting the journal and then deciding to explore the issues deeper in the form of a book were, in order, (1) my struggle to reckon with my infidelity and (2) the election of Donald Trump. Yet in my honesty piece for *The New York Times*, I mentioned neither of these things. It was easy to justify not overtly mentioning Trump, because that would have cast my piece as too political. Still, I think it was understood that the culture of his presidency underscored my argument. Leaving out my emotional affair was another matter altogether. I wasn't nearly ready to discuss it in the article, mostly because I was still in the middle of it. The closest I got to writing about my infidelity was talking about how I used my honesty project to bring up the idea of "open marriage" with my husband, after reading a big *New York Times Magazine* feature on it. That was a true statement, but it was a bit of a palter—an attempt to direct attention away from answering the most pressing honesty question in my life: How honest was my marriage?

Even once I began writing this book, I didn't know how I would tackle writing about my marriage. I knew how the story of confronting honesty in my marriage began, but I couldn't yet see the full picture because I was still trying to understand it and pull the narrative together. Honesty had tormented me, brought me to my knees, and made me second-guess everything. It followed no obvious course, there were no clear takeaways, and I still felt shame and sadness in the pit of my stomach whenever I would read back through entries in my honesty journal about my marriage. Unlike honesty in the other areas of life—which had a rough outline in my head, organized around some of my key learnings—honesty inside of my marriage was a giant web of contradictory ideas, less an outline than a wisteria vine tangled willy-nilly around some hapless branch of an old maple tree. There were many questions I needed to answer as it related to what I would write in this book. How much would I share in telling the story? What was private and should be left out? What had I even learned? Was telling the story just an exercise in self-indulgence?

And then there were the private questions that concerned my soul. The most pressing one was: Am I a good person?

I thought if I could get a handle on honesty in the less intimate relationships in my life, it would help me sort out the honesty questions within the most intimate relationship of my life. Even though that approach made sense—and I baked it into the very structure of the book—writing about honesty when I still had so much to figure out in this particular area of my life made me feel like a hypocrite. Yet I knew if I waited until I had it all figured out, I would never take on the project of sharing my honesty journey and challenging others to think about their own relationships with honesty—which is what I truly believed could make the world a little better. I had to begin my research and my interviews and my chapter outlines, even though I felt like a fake in so many ways.

It didn't help that the popular dialogue out there about honesty in marriage, and infidelity in particular, was lacking in complexity and thoughtfulness. The content in the blogosphere mostly presents an uncomplicated, somewhat judgmental view of what honesty in marriage is. The top results in Google searches on "deception in marriage" and "honesty in marriage" are dominated by Christian blogs that quote Bible verses and talk about God's plan. The next group of results are popular press pieces that try to estimate the number of married people who cheat and offer simplistic theories about why, usually presenting a shockingly one-dimensional view of honesty in marriage as non-negotiable and repeating the same tired talking points about what true intimacy is. None of this was particularly helpful to me as I started my book. I don't identify with religious interpretations and am uninterested in the notion of a divine plan. I don't particularly care about the so-called statistics on infidelity, mostly because I assume they are inaccurate and know they are inadequate. As for the advice columns and sound bites, every conversation my husband and I had was far more nuanced, textured, and complicated than any set of talking points.

In her book, *The State of Affairs: Rethinking Infidelity*, Esther Perel notes that our conversations around infidelity tend to be "visceral, loaded, and polarized." When we talk about affairs, we alternate between a moral tone and a fatalistic one, resorting to tidy summaries and clichés to understand why affairs happen and what they mean. Blame is key—we want to blame the one who strayed, and possibly punish. We make a lot of judgments, do a lot of shaming, and let the assumptions run wild. There is a problem with that, though, Perel says. "When we reduce conversation to simply passing judgment, we are left with no conversation at all," she writes. I knew there was more to it—at least in my marriage there was—and I wanted to be part of starting a richer, more nuanced conversation. Not because I was looking for a way to rationalize my actions, but rather, because I wanted to learn from my experience, and it seemed a waste to just reduce it to a Carrie Underwood song about slashing tires in anger. There was only one way to make the meaning I needed, to unravel the layers of fear and pain that were bound together with conundrums and terrible choices, to understand what honesty meant in the most important relationship of my life.

I would need to write my way through it.

A Marriage, in Two Parts

Let's go back to the beginning, to pick up the thread of the story I started in chapter 1. In setting up why I wanted to write this book, I told the story of how my emotional affair developed in 2013, how I kept it secret for months before being honest with my husband, how the other man and I ended it and cut off contact for a while, how we reconnected for work with strict boundaries in place, and how I started the work of compartmentalizing in 2014.

It was during this period, from early 2014 until around the *Times* honesty piece was published in September 2017 that I felt, on and off, like I was living a lie. To be more specific, I was working at cross-purposes—trying to strengthen my marriage to Allen on one hand while looking for all the things that were wrong with it on the other. Every time I went looking for what was wrong in our marriage, I found it. It was his temper, his impatience, his obsession with the kids getting too dirty outside, his sarcasm, his insistence on sticking to the same script about never wanting to have children and deciding against his better judgment to do it because he didn't want to lose me. Of course I had a role to play. I was impatient with his impatience, always ready to tell him what he was doing wrong and advise him on what a better response would have been. True, he was a difficult person to live with—something he freely admitted and gave me a speech about before we moved in together—but I never let him forget that he was difficult. When things were going well, our back-and-forth banter about him being difficult and me elucidating the ways in which he was difficult was a funny anecdote for a party. When I was on the mission to find something wrong, it was the reason to leave him for someone who wasn't so difficult and was more emotionally available, like the other man. Even though the other man and I kept our boundaries, thoughts of being with him remained in my head. The emotional affair, though over in one way, was still roiling underneath the surface, creating a fog around me. Some days it was so thick, I felt suffocated with confusion. Other times, weeks would go by where I would wonder if I was just making the whole thing up. The back and forth consumed my life. It was the last thing I thought about most nights before falling asleep, and the first thing I thought about each morning.

And yet, in the variable fog of those years, I did many things. I wrote articles and speeches. I ran half-marathons. I did yoga. I played with my kids. I had great sex with my husband (all that tension always needed somewhere to go). I hung out with my family. I had drinks with friends. I traveled for business and pleasure. I turned forty and enjoyed the surprise birthday party my husband threw me. I wrote two young adult novels (neither is yet published— stay tuned!). I lost and gained the same ten pounds three times. And I ate, slept, cried, laughed, and generally did all the things you do in the making of a life with someone. Allen and I would talk about the other man sometimes, usually in passing—like if the other man and I were working on a project together and I had a funny story to share. Allen had virtually no jealousy or worry. This is hard for most people to understand. It's hard for me to understand! If it had been reversed, I'm certain I would have had jealousy or asked more questions. It's simply not how Allen is wired, though. Allen is quirky, and has a way of seeing things that's rotated about ninety degrees from the way most people see things (my son is the same way, which is why they butt heads so often, but I digress . . .). He didn't have a problem with the fact that the other man and I were still friends and still worked together. Of course, he didn't fully understand that I was keeping my feelings on simmer, and letting them come to a full boil whenever we hit a bad patch in our marriage. Or it's possible that he did understand, but wasn't sure what to do about it. Allen knew the other man was an emotional outlet for me, and in a way, he was glad that I had him, because it took some of the emotional burden off of him. This is, after all, the role of a good friendship outside of a marriage. The problem with the friendship between me and the other man is that it always had the potential to tip back the other way, and keeping it in its platonic plane was exhausting. I had to, but I didn't always want to.

In the space of those years, I talked to two of my close girlfriends about what was going on and my attempts to let go of the emotional affair. It turned out that both of them had kindred experiences. In fact, one of my friends was in the middle of a very similar situation. She and I sent long, anguished text messages back and forth to each other, trying to help each other find some clarity. The second friend who had been in a similar situation had ultimately divorced her husband and was now remarried (but not to the man she had the emotional affair with). I also confided to another acquaintance-type friend one night when a bunch of us were hanging out at a writers' conference. She had her own story, too, but had never told her husband (she's now divorced). Yet another married girlfriend who I hadn't seen in a while invited me out to lunch one afternoon, and confessed she had a terrible crush on someone she worked with and feared acting on it. I also became friendly with the woman at the spa where I often got pedicures, and when the conversation turned to marriage and honesty, I confided in her about my emotional affair. No surprise, she had her own story, too. In fact, it seemed that whenever I brought up the emotional affair, my female conversation partner always had her own story about a frustration inside of her marriage and a resulting emotional affair. These were smart women. Genuine people who valued monogamy and trust. And they were all holding on to secrets. While I didn't feel good about the up-and-down nature of what was going on in holding on to my feelings for this other man, I came to realize that I was far from alone. Forming emotional attachments with an undercurrent of sexual attraction with someone other than your spouse—without "officially" cheating—seemed to be a very common occurrence, even in my small circle of friends. And in nearly every instance, the friend I was talking to with the experience similar to mine would always say something to the effect of, "There are so few people I can talk with honestly about this experience. I'm so afraid of being judged." I was afraid of being judged, too. But it got easier and easier to talk about in these one-on-one conversations, because I realized that sharing my experience mattered. Saying to these women, "I've been there, too. I'm still there now," helped me, and it helped them.

While I confided in friends, I still tried to stick to my internal narrative about what the relationship with the other man was about. We were friends. We had boundaries. We were each trying to make our marriages better. His wife and children needed him, and my husband and children needed me. This was a loop I played on repeat. Sometimes it would all get to be too much, and I'd send the other man an email reiterating that it was difficult, and that I still thought of him. I would ask, like some nervous schoolgirl, did he still think of me? And he would say yes, of course he did. But we both knew we were where we needed to be. And I *was* there, for every football game and spelling test study session. I loved Allen—I just didn't *like* him a good part of the time. I loved our family—but it was exhausting. I liked our division of labor, and still took pride in being the breadwinner—but it was a lot of pressure and forced me to take on projects I didn't particularly want to do. Still, I wasn't absent. I wasn't a terrible wife. I wasn't *really* having an affair. Allen knew the other man and I were still friends. He knew when we met for lunch or were working on a project together. I didn't hide my actions. I hid the confusion of my feelings, though, and that was the dishonesty that pulled at my edges. I hoped it would just fade with time. Either that, or I was headed for a breakdown.

When the other man told me he was getting divorced, I opted for a breakdown.

All along, I had worried that he and his wife might divorce. He had confided in me at the end of 2016 that things weren't going well, and while I gave my best pep talk, I was secretly terrified because of what felt like the deterioration of my own marriage. There was a lot going on as 2016 turned into 2017. Allen's parents were declining rapidly. Though they were substantially younger than mine (they married as teenagers), their health was growing worse quickly. His dad had a type of blood cancer, along with several complications that left him weak and in and out of the hospital. His mom had severe dementia—very similar to my own dad—and couldn't be left alone. As the oldest, a lot fell on Allen. Between the stress of caring for his parents and the stress of being a parent himself, he was a roller coaster of anxiety, and it wrenched me to watch him struggle. I alternated between empathetically excusing all of his outbursts and being angry with him when he took his frustrations and anxieties out on the children and me. So often, it was easier when he wasn't around. The house felt lighter and the day less tumultuous when he was gone. I would think about how it would be easier if he weren't here day-to-day—and then realize how ridiculous that was, because he did the lion's share of work around the house (all the grocery shopping and cooking, most of the laundry, cleaning, and other maintenance). I would feel spoiled and ungrateful, and I'd talk myself back from the edge. *This is who he is. He's a difficult person. He's doing the best he can. Stop nagging him. And for shit's sake, stop talking to the other man about him.*

If my cross-purposes were gently tugging in opposite directions before, now they were yanking with full force. As the stress of summer hit in 2017—summer is always the hardest time for us because the kids are home and it's one of my busiest work seasons—things became increasingly strained, and Allen and I were in a constant cycle of conflict. Talking to the other man once again started to feel like an escape, and I was looking for any way to justify it. When I read a piece about open marriage in *The New York Times Magazine* in the summer of 2017, I wondered if that was the answer. Allen read the piece, too, and we had a series of conversations about it. Neither one of us could quite imagine how it would work. Plus, I knew that on my end, I only wanted to open up the marriage so that I could spend more time with the other man. I didn't care anything about having random sexual trysts with people. And while my husband was naturally intrigued with the idea of random sexual trysts with other women, he was skeptical that he would have the time or energy. Our conversations about the whole thing were both funny and serious. In truth, talking about it turned us each on—him for his reasons, and me for my reasons (which, of course, were 100 percent related to the other man). While we admitted that it ultimately wouldn't work for us, it opened up some door in my mind that maybe it was okay to indulge my sexual feelings for the other man. To even act on them. *Just a little.* Remember how the confirmation bias works? That when you want something to be true, you will apply that filter to all of the evidence you see before you? I was doing that. Big time. I was working on a draft of the honesty article that summer, and I mentioned the open marriage discussion as an example of applying my honesty filter to my marriage. What else could I say? "By the way, as I write this, I'm both stoking the fires of and trying to extricate myself from a four-year emotional affair." That would have been honest! But that was private information, not for public consumption.

Toward the end of that summer—which, as I said, had been strained and conflict-filled—the other man and I traveled together for the yearly project we were still working on together. At the hotel, in another city fifteen hundred miles away, my life at home suddenly seemed like it belonged to someone else. For the entire week, the other man and I exchanged glances, each knowing what the other was thinking, but trying to stay focused on work. On the last night, after dinner and an evening out with other people working on the project, we wound up going to my hotel room. At first, we just lay down together on the bed and talked. After a while, I pulled his arms around me to spoon me, which was warm and wonderful. That was going to be all, I told myself. But then I turned and kissed him, and he reciprocated. After four years of keeping the boundaries, we couldn't keep them anymore, at least not for that one night. He held me tightly and said that he wanted to keep me safe. It was amazing to feel this thing I desperately wanted to feel and to be with someone who seemed so attuned to me—yet it was terrible to know the betrayal attached to it, and that there was no safety at all in what we were doing. We stopped ourselves from going any further (I honestly have no idea how), and he left and went back to his room. But I knew I had crossed a line. We both felt guilty the next day as we flew home, and I wasn't sure what was ahead for either of us.

It was only a few weeks later that the other man told me he had moved out, and he was getting a divorce. He said that it didn't have to do with me and he expected nothing from me. I didn't know all of the issues he and his wife had, but the one he would sometimes talk to me about—which I'm not going to share because it's not my story—truly did have nothing to do with me. Still, that we had shared such an intimate moment certainly didn't help his marriage. I knew it must have played some role. His wife didn't know the extent of our feelings for each other. He could never figure out how to broach the subject with her, on top of the other issues they were dealing with. She knew we were friends and I think suspected more. But it was a smaller piece of something so much bigger and historical in their relationship. Or at least, this is how I understood it. I felt awful for him because he said that he didn't want the divorce, but his wife had completely shut him out (and yes, I always realized I was only getting his side of the story). He seemed broken and lost. I both wanted to be his friend (because he needed one) and wanted to keep my distance.

In the days after he told me about his divorce, I continually repeated the mantra: *It is his life. It doesn't involve my marriage. It is his life. It doesn't involve my marriage.* And yet, I wondered if it was my opportunity to be with him and replayed the kiss hundreds of times. Since starting my journal that spring, I'd been writing about the ups and downs in my marriage. Now, I wrote, "I think my only escape from this conflict will be honesty. I've been studying it, noticing it, and trying to channel it. So often, I fail. Still, I think that honesty will be the thing that saves me." I believed that. I just didn't know what the truth was. Did I want to leave my husband for someone else? Could that awful thing be true? How could I do that to my children? Sometimes it felt like it was the only decision that would just put Allen out of his misery and alleviate his anxiety—to say to him, "You don't have to do it anymore. Just go and be." I was swimming in torment and indecision. What I had kept at bay for so long was now impossible to deny. "This isn't a sustainable way to live," I wrote on a terrible Tuesday. "I'm not built to live with secrecy, whether it's secret longing, secret motives, secret guilt, or secret confusion." What I needed more than anything was clarity: What did I truly want?

The next day, two days before our ten-year wedding anniversary, I came in from a run, stood with my fists balled up and sweat dripping down my face, and told Allen everything. Every wretched detail about my feelings for the other man, how all the indecision had resurfaced that summer, and how we had kissed in my hotel room. I told him that the other man was getting divorced, and I wondered if I should be with him. I knew the words coming from my mouth were hurtful, but at last, they were truthful. I didn't know if I wanted to separate, I told him. But I couldn't hide these feelings anymore, because in hiding them, I was giving them such power. That's what struck me the most: the power that the secrets and the emotional dishonesty had, and how the more it stayed in the dark, the more strength it gained and the more afraid of it I was. In finally saying it all—that I had never left the emotional affair behind, that I was tormented daily about it, and that now that the other man was divorcing, I felt an urgency to bring it into the light—I burst the bubble of its power, and it was such a sweet relief.

But of course, it came with a cost.

Allen was more upset than the first time I had told him about the emotional affair four years earlier. He thought I was deluded to think life would be better with the other man. He thought that what we were going through was simply the up-and-down of marriage and that I was expecting too much. I wanted him to be angry at me, to scream at me, to tell me I was ruining everything. I felt like I deserved that. But he didn't. He didn't feel betrayed as much as he felt like I wasn't seeing things clearly. Since we were both upset, we agreed to put it on hold for a few hours, so we could get the kids home from school, eat dinner, and get them to bed. We said that we would talk more that night. The minute I went in my office and shut my door, I was certain I had made a terrible mistake in being honest. I felt sick. What had I done? I made a pro/con list about separating, in an attempt to try to see things rationally. I talked to my sister Laura, who gave me the same advice she had given me four years earlier: "Your marriage has to be only about you and Allen. It can't be about anyone else," she said. She understood my struggles with Allen, and thought maybe a separation would give us each a chance to think through what we wanted and give us more appreciation for the other. I agreed and tried to sketch out in my mind what a trial separation would look like.

When Allen and I sat down that evening and started talking about the logistics of separation, at one point, he looked at me, fighting back tears (he rarely cries) and said, "Our kids need to be in their own beds every night." I don't know if it was what he said or the vulnerable way he said it, but a shock of recognition ran through me. It was such a simple statement, and something I had probably thought many times before. In that moment, though, it was a turning point. They *did* need to be in their own beds every night. That statement was like the first drop of dew. The first sign of a new day. The first time I felt clarity around what I wanted. I wanted the family and the marriage I had, right here in this living room. I wanted my kids to have one pillow and one dinner table. And I wanted their dad as my partner in it. I wanted it so badly and I felt panic that we might have destroyed it. I could see the panic in Allen's eyes, too. The pull of the other man—of that other life, that other opportunity that seemed to be sitting there waiting for me—loosened its grip enough for me to be able to see that making my marriage work was entirely possible, if Allen was committed, too. For the first time in so long, I felt like I had something to fight for—something I really, really wanted. I had to let go of thinking I made the wrong choice in marrying Allen, and he had to let go of thinking that he made the wrong choice in becoming a parent. We couldn't continue to hold each other hostage to our own resentment. We each knew these things already, but we saw them in a new way in that moment. That night started the process of Allen and I rediscovering each other.

It was around this time that I knew I needed to write a book about honesty.

The next time I saw the other man was several weeks later. He told me the whole story of how his divorce was unfolding and the agony of not getting to see his kids every day. I told him the whole story of finding my marriage again, of intuitively knowing that I had made the right decision, and feeling intensely grateful. I felt sorrow that I had won my marriage back just as he lost his, but he had no guile and no resentment. He may have been disappointed (I was disappointed, too, because there is a way to be both heartbroken and happy), but his relief for Allen and me was genuine. "Getting divorced is awful. Don't do it. Do whatever you can to keep working in your marriage," he said to me as he held my hand. I saw that he would go on to fall in love again, with someone else. He would find what he was looking for, but it wouldn't be me, and for the first time in four years, I was at peace with that. I would be jealous when he met someone, but I would be joyous, too.

I've struggled with how to say what I'm going to say next, mostly because I want readers to like me and not judge me harshly. At the same time, this book is not worth anything if I am not honest about the most difficult aspects of situations. So here goes. While I feel bad if my actions hurt Allen, and I certainly felt guilt at the time, over-all, I don't regret them. People often conflate emotions, but I think it's important to tease feelings out in these situations. You can take responsibility for your actions without disavowing them in a heap of guilt and shame. The intimate relationship with the other man, while tortured and confusing, meant something to me. I needed him and I am glad he was there. Some of the moments, I'd like to forget. But others, I cherish deeply and remember with fondness because they helped me understand so much more about who I was. Plus, Allen and I wouldn't have started down the path of more honesty without everything that happened. He knows that, and doesn't hold my actions against me, the same way I don't hold his actions against him. There is a peace and acceptance.

That said, where I do still feel guilt is in relation to the other man's divorce, despite how he reaffirmed that it didn't have to do with me. For me, his wife was always the silent fourth person in everything, and though I understood that they had their issues that made her opt for divorce, I couldn't help feeling that I had wronged her, because I had pulled her husband toward me when he felt unloved. Yes, I had sent him back and encouraged him to fix whatever he could. But he couldn't fix it, and there was nothing I could do about it. I know that, overall, I did not act in a stand-up way toward her. I willingly and willfully violated some code among women. Sometimes, we have to sit with knowing our actions caused emotional harm to someone, even when we have accepted why we did it. It's awful. But some things you can't smooth away with a prosocial lie or a side step of courtesy. Some things eternally are as they are. I often think about what I might say to the other man's ex-wife if I were to bump into her. Maybe she wouldn't even care. Maybe she knew and never cared because she had emotionally checked out herself. But maybe she would be angry, and she would confront me. In that case, I would let her speak her piece and take whatever she had to say. However, if she asked questions and wanted real answers, I would be honest with her, and do my best to both explain my behavior and apologize to her. I doubt my words would mean much to her, though. And perhaps they would be hollow, because the reality is that I wouldn't actually change any of my actions. It needed to unfold the way it unfolded. Of course, that's tremendously selfish of me to frame it that way. I believe that we are all selfish in these situations when it comes to our emotional needs. I'm just willing to admit it and to tease out the emotions instead of creating a simple narrative that's easier to live with. That's a big part of living an honest life—refusing to erase the complexity, and owning up to the fact that while you deeply regret how your actions may have hurt someone, you don't necessarily regret the action itself because it helped you to take the next step of your journey.

Honesty carved my marriage into two halves. For the first half, honesty was something to be afraid of. It felt unknowable, shadowy, and frightening. And now, in the second half, I've stepped into its light. It is such a surprise to see what those dark corners really look like. All of their messiness is illuminated and it's less than attractive. In fact, it doesn't look the way I thought it would, and I have to adjust my expectations. That is why I tell this story. If honesty in public or at work or with friends is really weird, inside of marriage it's downright *Twilight Zone* status. It has strange twists and turns, and surprise endings. There's a fiction that it shouldn't be complicated, that when you are committed to someone, honesty is the basis for everything. That's a noble concept, but the problem is that we are often not honest with ourselves first. Delving into honesty in marriage means touching on all the dimensions of honesty, from difficult conversations to prosocial lies, from dilemmas about revealing secrets to navigating conflicts of interest.

It also means being honest about our own beliefs about marriage. And that may have been the thing I missed from the very start.

Why Do We Expect So Much from Marriage?

By the time I started recording conscious memories, my parents had already been married for twenty years. As the youngest, I grew up in the shade of a mature partnership, one that had already been tested by having four children—including a child who was extremely difficult (my brother Paul)—in the first five years of marriage, and then three more children over the next decade. My parents had the system down by the time I came along. They had disagreements, but these arguments were about things like when to put in the storm windows for the winter (once the storm window was in, you couldn't open the window, so my mom always wanted to wait until after Thanksgiving because the kitchen got so hot when she cooked, whereas my dad wanted to install them in early November). I worried about one of them dying, but I never once entertained the idea they might get divorced. I understood that raising children was difficult, because my mom said it was (usually in the same breath that she expressed her gratitude for Dr. Spock). But marriage looked fairly straightforward to me. Also, our home life was steady and predictable. My parents built a house in 1958—the year they got married—and I lived there until I was twenty-one and moved out for graduate school in 1996 (as I write this, my mother still lives there). My parents genuinely enjoyed each other's company, and though they weren't overly sentimental or publicly affectionate, they had an easy shorthand with each other. They were a unit that seemed unquestionable and unimpeachable. Above all, they were happy people—happy in themselves and happy with each other.

By contrast, when my husband was a child, he would crouch outside his parents' bedroom door, sobbing with his younger brother as their parents screamed and sometimes threw things at each other from behind the door. While it wasn't an abusive environment, it was an explosive and scary one. His parents would have a screaming fight one day, and the next day, they might be dancing around the house in joy or spooning on the couch. Their relationship was unpredictable and fiery, and their children too often got caught up in it. His mother would manipulate Allen to take her side as she angrily listed all of her husband's faults, and then his father would complain to him about how difficult his mother was. (I witnessed this dynamic even after Allen and I were married, before they both started to get sick.) They were simply ill-suited for each other, yet they never knew anything but each other. They grew up poor in Mississippi, and married when his mom was a junior in high school and his dad was nineteen. His mother did finish high school before having children, but then had Allen and his brother by the time she was twenty. When Allen was six, the family started moving every year or two because Allen's father worked on building factories all around the southeastern United States. Virginia, South Carolina, Kentucky, Georgia, back to Mississippi, back to Virginia: It was always time to uproot. Allen makes friends easily, so he adjusted well to the moving, all in all. But it certainly didn't imprint on him a notion of stability. In their defense, his father did an excellent job providing for the family, and worked his way up from nothing to a top engineering position within his company. He had incredible ambition, and was the only one of his siblings to graduate from high school. As for his mother, she was very present for her children and took good care of them. Allen always said that his parents showed love to their children, but they didn't show love to each other. Their fighting took a toll on the family. By the time Allen came of age, he was praying daily for his parents to divorce, just to put an end to the volatility. His mom did leave his father once when Allen was about five, but other than that, they stayed together until Allen's father passed away in early 2018. His mom, who now has severe dementia, lives in an upscale memory care facility and doesn't seem to remember any of it. But Allen will never forget.

So it's fair to say we came into marriage with different expectations.

To be clear, I didn't expect marriage to be magical. But I did expect a degree of ease and sameness. I'm a creature of habit, and though I rely heavily on inspiration and intuition, and greatly enjoy the cosmic weirdness of the universe, I really like to know what to expect on any given day. This doesn't describe my marriage. Allen is a moody soul, capable of making me laugh incredibly hard in one moment, and become incredibly annoyed in the next. My own even temperament was like an antidote against this for the first six or seven years I knew him. I think the chaos of having children simply wore down my immunity at some point, at which point I started getting stuck in the fumes of his moods. There is no question that he is a good, solid, dependable person who always attends to the day-to-day of running a house. But emotionally, he's all over the board—usually without being in touch with how he's actually feeling, or how his words might impact me. In his mind, marriage is about two people balancing each other. I get to be the stable one and he gets to be the volatile one. To me, that makes the entire relationship feel volatile. But to him, nothing about our marriage even comes close to the volatility he witnessed growing up. Any marriage where people aren't throwing things at each other is a good one. So my expectation not only of the emotional stability I witnessed as a kid— but also the emotional fulfillment that modern culture has told me I'm entitled to—is like seven levels up from what he expects.

Esther Perel makes the point that we want it all from marriage. (I should be clear that I am using "marriage" in the same way Perel uses it: as shorthand for any long-term committed relationship, no matter its legal status, and including both heterosexual couples and same sex couples.) She writes about how we want our spouse to be our equal partner in everything, to offer unflagging support, to turn us on sexually and challenge us intellectually, to make us laugh and be there for us when we cry, to care about our inner life and help us be a better version of ourselves, to be interesting and surprising, and above all, to be loyal. We don't *need* to marry the way previous generations did (especially women). We *want* to. And because we're choosing it freely, our expectations for it are ridiculously high. "The human imagination has conjured up a new Olympus: that love will remain unconditional, intimacy enthralling, and sex oh-so-exciting, for the long haul, with one person," Perel writes.

Totally reasonable, right?

One of the first steps in teasing out what honesty meant in my marriage was admitting the fact that I did, in fact, expect all of this. Amazing sex. Endearing conversation. Emotional support. Unwavering adoration. I never needed Allen financially. I could have even had children on my own. But I wanted to re-create the family experience I had—turned up a few notches to reflect the way we understand marital intimacy now. One of my favorite things to say about myself was that I was low maintenance. What I meant by that was that I took responsibility for my own emotions and didn't need anyone to take care of me. Admitting that was somewhat false was extremely difficult. I like to be the contrarian. The girl who sees it all a little differently. So having to fess up to myself that I was, in fact, just like the rest of the wide-eyed masses who enter into marriage with these high expectations—and that my husband, whose emotional intelligence was seemingly so far inferior to mine (he doesn't even know how he *feels*!) was the one who saw things clearly—was an unpleasant reckoning.

Being honest with yourself is like trying to undo a tiny stubborn knot in a shoestring. It's *hard*. Inside marriage or an equivalent long-term romantic relationship, unwinding your own truths requires a pair of tweezers and a mighty magnifying glass, because not only is it agonizingly difficult, it's often nearly impossible to even see what in the hell you're doing. One way to start, I have discovered, is to pay more attention to how we talk to the person we love.

Do You Really Want to See Your Partner Honestly?

In *Daring Greatly,* her book about how vulnerability can be transformational, Brené Brown cracks open the myth that

vulnerability means weakness. One of the things she has discovered in her research is that while women say they want
their men to be vulnerable, the reality of a man being vulnerable before their eyes often frightens them. As women, we
criticize men for withholding and not being in touch with
their feelings, but we send all kinds of subtle and not-subtle
cues to *keep that shit in check.* "We ask them to be vulnerable,
we beg them to let us in, and we plead with them to tell us
when they're afraid, but the truth is that most women can't
stomach it," she writes. She quotes one of her male mentors,
who tells her, "Men know what women really want. They
want us to pretend to be vulnerable."

While I'm not a big fan of generalizations about men and
women, since my own husband and I have reversed the roles
in our marriage in so many ways, I do find this to be true
overall—though I see a shift when I observe my millennial
nieces and nephews in their marriages. I think as men and
women renegotiate their roles inside of romantic relationships,
we are also renegotiating the emotional work of relationships. I
think this negotiation is happening inside of same-sex couples,
too. When two men or two women are together, how do they
approach vulnerability? Does one partner ask for vulnerability
from the other, but then has a hard time seeing it? No matter
what your relationship looks like, the question is worth thinking about: Do you *truly* want to see your partner be vulnerable?
To what degree do you want them to pretend?

Where So Much of It Goes Wrong:
Our Conversations

One of the most helpful books I've read about honesty in marriage is
not a book about marriage at all, or even primarily about honesty. It's a
book titled *Difficult Conversations: How to Discuss What Matters Most,*

by Douglas Stone, Bruce Patton, and Sheila Heen, and it grew out of the Harvard Negotiation Project, which is a project that trains people to better negotiate and resolve conflicts. The authors explain that there are three different conversations inside every conversation that involves a disagreement or talking about a difficult matter: A conversation about *what actually happened*, a conversation about *feelings*, and a conversation about *identity*. "In each of these conversations we make predictable errors that distort our thoughts and feelings, and get us into trouble," they write. I'll explain how each of these conversations are connected with honesty in marriage, but first, I want to set up our next honesty principle, which is *Mine all parts of the conversation*. I'll explain what this principle means as we go, but the top level is this: A more honest marriage begins by searching inside your conversations. And you do have to search. Honesty generally won't come looking for you, especially not once factors like love, sex, expectation, children, and fear of losing everything have wrapped around your relationship and embedded themselves into every nuance of how you talk to each other.

In my own marriage, the conversation we came back to again and again was about who said what and why. "I told you I was difficult to live with, that I wasn't suited to be a parent, and you said it was okay. You convinced me it would be okay. You convinced me to have kids," Allen would say. I would usually respond something along the lines of, "Grow the fuck up! I didn't make you do anything. And you can't just say you're difficult and that's the end of it." This is an example of the "what actually happened" part of the conversation, where we're trying to get to the truth of something but we often can't see around the idea of blame. Because someone always needs to be blamed. And in the version of truth we commit ourselves to, it's usually the other person. Allen blamed me for convincing him to have kids, and I blamed him for having a bad attitude. The authors talk about how it's so much more productive if we can focus on *contribution* versus *blame*. Blame looks backward and is punitive, whereas contribution is about how to move forward. "As a rule, when things go wrong in human relationships, everyone has contributed in some important way," they say. Focusing on contribution means looking at a situation and seeing how the choices and actions of each person (including things like their temperament and mind-set) were contributing factors—even if they are not all equally contributing factors. Ultimately, contribution is a system that two (or more) people create together, but it can be hard to see our role in the system, especially in the middle of conversations that are charged with blame. This was definitely true of my marriage. I alternated between blaming Allen and blaming myself, and I suspect he did the same. When I was in the mode of blaming him, I found as many reasons to blame him as possible, and the more I blamed him, the more wronged I felt, and the more I needed comfort from someone outside my marriage. When I was in the mode of blaming myself, I turned it inward to shame. How could I possibly be this person? These bad feelings about myself usually led me on a circle back to blaming Allen—*I wouldn't act this way if he were someone different*, I would think. *Everything would be better in our marriage if he just had a better attitude.* The biggest mistake I made was thinking that he didn't love me enough, or love the kids enough, to change his attitude. When I forced myself to go back through everything and "map the contribution system"—as the authors say—starting with how we met, how I presented myself and how he presented himself, and how we built our marriage, I was able to see our individual contributions a bit differently. I *did* convince him to have children, knowing it wasn't something he was naturally inclined to do. I *did* tell him it would be okay and we would figure it out. I did contribute to everything we were dealing with—as did he. These realizations didn't make all the frustration dissipate, but this ability to see things differently did help me get out of the blame cycle. So the first part of the conversation to mine in the spirit of honesty is the idea of contribution—yours and your partner's.

The authors also explain how unspoken feelings underlie every difficult conversation. We know from our discussion of prosocial honesty that we need to pay close attention to feelings and emotions (*Be mindful of emotions*) when giving feedback or making some other decision about how honest to be. When it comes to our most intimate relationships, this is exponentially more important—and yet, it is exponentially harder to uncover those buried feelings. I knew that feelings were a challenge for Allen, especially given the way he grew up. He wasn't a person very in touch with his feelings, and they would tend to leak out when he was least expecting it (definitely when I was least expecting it). However, I didn't always account for my own unexpressed feelings, either. People often tell me that I'm a good listener. I'm naturally curious and I like to hear people's stories. I have learned, as a journalist, how to be quiet and gently encourage someone to keep talking. The phrase I hear most often when interviewing someone is, "I usually don't tell people as much as I'm telling you." I assumed this was just the essence of my character, and followed me into every relationship. In the case of my relationship with Allen, I came to realize that I had stopped being that person. My own feelings and expectations of marriage drove so many of our conversations, but I wasn't necessarily aware. "Good listening requires an open and honest curiosity about the other person, and a willingness and ability to keep the spotlight on them. Buried emotions draw the spotlight back to us," the authors write. I made so many of our issues about Allen—and it was about him—but it was also about my unexpressed feelings. In my new commitment to vulnerability and revealing truths about myself as a means of connecting with others, I assumed I was getting at the reaches of those deepest feelings. But in fact, I was missing a whole range of feelings around my ideas of what marriage was. I wanted to be adored. I wanted to be fulfilled. I wanted to be the person who motivated great change in my partner. I was blind to how much I wanted, and how resentful I was that I couldn't get it from Allen. These were mostly unrealistic things. Every conversation about Allen's failings (and there were many conversations of this nature) was also a conversation about my disappointment and unmet expectations.

The authors talk about how you have to "negotiate" with your feelings, because they are dynamic—formed based upon your thoughts, which can change as you take in new information or rethink old information. There is a notion in popular relationship psychology that when you tell your partner how you feel, he or she is supposed to listen and not offer judgment or advice, because you're not looking for that. You're just looking to be heard and to express a feeling. While this has merit, because it *is* vitally important to be able to say how you feel without your partner constantly swooping in and trying to pick it apart, it's also ineffective when it comes to our tired scripts about feelings. When you are hurt or scared or sad and you need a safe space to vent or to express a raw emotion without being judged, you do need your partner to simply listen to you, validate you, commiserate with you, and perhaps comfort you. That isn't the same as stating overall feelings about the relationship as a whole. These statements tend to have words like "always" and "never" attached to them. One of the things my husband would say is, "I feel like I have absolutely no power in this relationship, like I never have a say in anything and I have no control over anything. It's how I feel, right or wrong, I'm just telling you how I feel." I believed it was how he felt, but from my point of view, it was quite skewed, because, in fact, he tried to control everything and constantly wanted a say in everything. But saying to him, "You're wrong, asshole!" wasn't productive. Neither was trying to "fix" it. So when he would express his feelings, I would just throw up my hands and say, "Okay, it's how you feel." But it didn't really do either one of us any good. The same is true when I would say, "I feel like you never offer me any emotional support." He had learned the same rule I had about letting your partner tell you how they feel, so would similarly throw up his hands in frustration.

It's really a bullshit thing we've been told to do around feelings. Because in fact, feelings can be *flat out wrong.* By like, a lot. You don't just get a pass on something because you label it a feeling. That's hardly the end of the discussion or exploration. You have to negotiate with those feelings. Negotiating means examining our own story, our own contribution, and our own unexpressed feelings one or ten layers down from the feelings we are actually expressing, and asking our partner to do the same. That we need to negotiate with our feelings doesn't mean we are bad people. That we have developed a feeling about something based on a certain pattern of thinking doesn't mean that we are stupid, selfish, irresponsible, indulgent, unkind, or uncaring. Calling bullshit on our feelings doesn't mean we're unworthy or shitty to our core. We get confused, though, because of the third hidden conversation: the identity conversation.

Recall in the workplace honesty chapter, we talked about how we tend to claim an identity that's either personal, relational, or collective, and how those identities can influence our decisions around honesty—specifically, they can lead us to lie to protect our own ego, to protect someone else, or to protect the group we belong to (*Think about who you are being*). Those are excellent insights about identity, but there is still one more way we can slice identity, as it relates to the way we interact with others. Challenging our feelings can mean challenging how we see ourselves, that is, our identity. For example, I needed to see myself as a self-directed, even-keeled, low-maintenance person with a live-and-let-live attitude who only wanted to love and be loved, and Allen needed to see himself as someone who was independent and non-traditional, but was somehow coerced into marriage and parenthood and therefore, not as much could be expected of him because he was emotionally limited. We were each quite committed to these roles. "A difficult conversation can cause you to relinquish a cherished aspect of how you see yourself," the authors write. First, you have to be aware of the identity you're trying to protect, and then you have to—this is my new favorite word—*complexify* it. Instead of reducing your identity to this or that, you make it about the "and." I am this *and* I am that. I built my identity around things I was sure I *wasn't*. Hence, it was hard for me to let go of this idea that I *wasn't* a person who would coerce someone into doing something and that I *wasn't* a person who expected too much. I would double down on these identities when they felt threatened, and Allen was doing the same. I had to get to the "and"—I am a thoughtful person with a realistic outlook on life who doesn't want to manipulate others, *and*

I have high expectations of marriage, *and* I can be very persuasive in the pictures I paint. Related to that, a big part of me keeping my continued feelings for the other man secret had to do with how I saw myself. I was a person who was faithful, who did right by others, who tried her hardest, who was extremely empathetic. Admitting the truth of everything challenged those identities—because people who are faithful, try hard, do right by others, and practice empathy generally do not make out with someone who isn't their spouse behind their spouse's back. Once I came clean to Allen about everything, I realized all of the "ands" I had been overlooking in that arena, too. When you make room for multiple identities standing together, it's a smoother path to honesty.

There are all kinds of theories about how to make marriage better—that you need to learn how to fight more fairly, how to communicate more (or perhaps how to communicate less), how to listen better, or how to respect each other more. I've read books about marriage that espouse these various theories, and Allen and I also saw a marriage counselor for a while (who we really liked, though I think we spent more time amusing him than actually confronting some of our problems because I was afraid to talk about what was really going on). When it comes to trying to navigate honesty, none of those things have been as helpful as the notions of *mining all parts of the conversation*—specifically (for me) mapping the contribution system, negotiating with feelings, and complexifying identity.

At the same time that I believe that better conversations can help you increase the honesty inside of your marriage, I also believe that there is honesty in silence, too. Sometimes you can only feel the emotional weight of a situation by standing in the space of what isn't being said. I think back to when Georgia's class had a special concert on Veterans Day. It's a tradition at my kids' elementary school that the second grade prepares a short performance for parents on or around Veterans Day. Each child also invites a special veteran in their life to attend, if they are able. After the children sing half a dozen patriotic songs, including the theme song for each branch of the service, all of the veterans are invited to the front of the room, where they take turns saying their name, branch of service, and years served. Many of the veterans are aunts and uncles or friends of the family. They are relatively young, and have recently served, or served during the Gulf Wars. But Georgia and her peers belong to a generation whose grandfathers served in Vietnam, and on that particular day, these men comprised about a quarter of the veterans there. I didn't pay much attention at first. It wasn't until the veterans began to say their names and when they served that I slowly became aware of the difference in posture and tone of voice between the younger veterans and the Vietnam veterans. The Vietnam vets tended to say their years in a resigned, quiet way, "Army, 1968–70." They knew once they said the years, everyone would know that they were sent to kill, for a war the country had stopped believing in. I'm not saying there wasn't pride. I'm not saying that every Vietnam veteran feels shame. It isn't my place to try to guess at the complexity of feelings those men in their late sixties and early seventies felt as they stood there. But as I sat there crying, I felt the room absorb it all. There was a sense of heaviness and regret and knowing that we had done so much wrong and treated these men so poorly, and this moment— though lovely and with the best of intentions—was only somehow highlighting what couldn't be changed. To try to use words to make it right or soothe or ameliorate would have been too small, too trite. To say it aloud would have broken the intensity of the silent knowing. Silences don't deceive or relieve the tension the way words do. A silence can't sidestep or make a cost/benefit calculation. You can ignore the silence and close your heart to it if you want. But it is there whether you like it or not, raw and real and honest.

There are silences inside of relationships, too, and sometimes I think honoring those silences is as important as mining the conversation. When things in our marriage were at their worst, Allen and I would sit at the dinner table with the kids flanking us, and not speak— or at least not to each other. It was a sad, discontented silence, not an angry silence. I hated it, but words alone couldn't fix it. Some silences you can't fake your way out of with the same old tired phrases and sentiments. You can only absorb and occupy them.

There are also contented silences and spaces of meaningful quietude you find on the other side of conflict and confusion. So many evenings now, Allen and I sit at the dinner table, our children chatting away, and feel the silence of a solid partnership. Even if one of us is in a mood, or the day hasn't gone well, or there is a deep sense of frustration about one of the children related to some piece of shitty behavior they are up to (which is like, *a lot*), it is a silence that conveys, "I have your back," and there is nothing we have to say.

What About Those Broken Promises?

Broken promises are one of the biggest transgressions within romantic relationships. In other words, people regularly make promises to their boyfriend/girlfriend/partner/spouse that they wind up breaking—which really pisses off their romantic partner. Wake Forest University psychology professor Lara Kammrath and her graduate student, Johanna Peetz, wanted to look at why people break promises in interpersonal relationships (Kammrath is now at Wake Forest, but she conducted the research while at Wilfrid Laurier University; Peetz is now an associate professor of psychology at Carleton University). "Very often, it's not on purpose that someone breaks a promise, but rather, it's because they were flaky or just forgot. But the other person may take it as a lack of love, and sometimes perceives it as a betrayal," Kammrath explains. The person on the other end of a broken promise may even see their partner's broken promise as a kind of deception, as in, "You said you would be there by six thirty, and you weren't there until eight. You *lied* to me!"

Kammrath and Peetz wanted to see what kinds of interventions might fix this problem, and help a flaky partner better keep their promises. They found something interesting. People who had more self-regulation (what we might call self-discipline or follow-through) tended to keep their promises more. That's not surprising. So what might help people with lousy follow-through? The researchers wondered if simply reminding a flaky person how much they loved their partner would help that person keep their promises better. That turned out to be the worst strategy, Kammrath says. It made the promise-breaker feel in the moment like they would do *anything* to keep their promises. In fact, being reminded of how much they loved their partner made people with poor self-regulation over-promise. Can't you just hear it? *I love you so much! Of course I promise to finish building the fence/send out the invitations/clean the cat litter! I'll even service the car, too!* And then . . . their natural personality kicks in, and they wound up breaking the promises. But since they had promised *even more* in their heightened state of wanting to make their partner happy, they failed *even more*. "That extra charge of emotion is temporary. It doesn't tend to help people with follow-through on promises," Kammrath says. But it does piss off the partner *even more*.

So what's to be done? Kammrath and Peetz write: "Given that breaking a promise can have negative effects on relationships, it might be a good idea for highly motivated people to make special efforts to keep their enthusiasm in check when promising." It may make you feel worse in the moment, but if follow-through isn't your specialty, it's probably more honest to promise less to the one you love.

Finding the Slack in the System

In my role as a freelance writer, I work with several clients, and was frustrated with my biggest one—a company that represented 30 percent of my income—for more than a year. They provided me with steady work, and because I was supporting my family, that was a nice thing. But their policies were hard to stomach. They micromanaged, made everything more complicated than it needed to be, and generally regarded their writers as employees, not as freelancers. Every time they would announce a new policy, I would feel low-level rage. I tried making gentle suggestions to the people in charge, but nothing ever changed—or if it did, the "good" change they instituted just wound up causing even more stress. I was too afraid to express my true frustration, because I knew that if I did, there was a good chance they would get rid of me (they had a history of doing that to people who didn't toe the line). I complained about them to other writers, to the point that I was becoming someone I didn't like. At the end of summer of 2018, I decided I would give it another year, hoping that in that time, I would build up enough work from other clients to walk away. But then, one afternoon a few weeks after that—as I was in the middle of writing this book, in fact—they sent out an email about yet another stupid new policy, and I suddenly knew it was time to leave. I sent an email to the head of the company that afternoon and told her that I could no longer write for them because I was a freelancer, not an employee, and their culture simply didn't match mine. I felt liberated and joyous. While it was scary to know that I now had to replace the income (I'd only been able to replace about 10 percent of it to that point), I didn't care. That feeling of knowing it was time to walk away gave me the ability to be completely honest. We've all had experiences like this—when we've reached the place where we know exactly what there is to lose, but we can no longer hide the way we feel. It's the place from which all the legendary "I quit!" stories originate.

But is there another way to get to that place? Do you always have to be ready to walk away before you can release the honesty? My work example hardly aligns neatly with the example of being honest in marriage. What it does align with, though, is the idea that fear can keep us holding back. Being afraid of everything there is to lose keeps us tightly tethered. However, perhaps some degree of that is a healthy fear. After all, do we stay faithful to our significant other because we truly do not want to be intimate with anyone else *ever*, or because we are afraid of what we have to lose if we were to stray? I avoided taking my emotional affair into more of a physical affair not because I adore everything about monogamy, but rather, because I was afraid of the ramifications. I was right to be afraid and to use that to keep me in check.

What I'm particularly interested in is whether or not we can lib-erate some of those decisions from our fear of *losing everything*. Can we see these decisions in a different way? Is it always a fear of losing something that keeps us holding back a truth, or can it be a kind-ness—or even an opportunity to shape a truth in a better way than the outright one? Put another way: Does every truth need to be shared in marriage? How can we share the necessary ones, while reframing the other ones we're not going to share, in essence, finding the slack in the system, so that our notion of honesty isn't stretched and stressed to the point of bursting spectacularly—most likely inside of one of those "difficult conversations" we just analyzed?

To find out, I go back to the research on prosocial lying, and the idea that we should let insight guide our decisions around how much honesty to reveal in any given situation. Telling someone their work is fantastic because we don't want to hurt their feelings is not the right call if we have the insight to know that our feedback could substantially help them. Intention matters, but you need your heart and your brain to work together to figure out how to sidestep and/or tell a prosocial lie of omission or commission (*Intention matters. So does refinement*). Workplace and social situations aren't marriage, though. You're not building a life with the co-worker who invites you to the home jewelry party you don't want to attend or the student who is fragile and could really use a break, but unfortunately is not a very good writer. Side steps are glorious when you get to leave somewhere at five o'clock; they're a bit trickier when you wake up next to the person every day.

Anne Gordon, associate professor of psychology at Bowling Green State University, worked on a study with one of her graduate students, Mary Kaplar, where they looked at the difference between how some-one in a romantic relationship viewed lying to their partner, versus how they viewed being the one who was lied to. They had under-graduates write two narratives—one was a narrative of a time when they told a lie to a romantic partner, and the other one was a narrative of when they were lied to. When Kaplar and Gordon analyzed these narratives, they found that the lie tellers were far more likely to claim altruistic motives (which I'm calling prosocial motives) than the lie receivers. "We have a tendency to think our own lies are little white lies, but when tables are turned, we do not like being lied to," Gordon tells me. People talk about the lies they tell their partner far differently than they talk about the lies their partner told them. In fact, the narratives of the lie tellers had a total of two hundred and six references to what motivated their lies, whereas the lie-receiver narratives only had twenty-six references of motivation. In their stories of lie telling, people talked about feeling guilty for the lie, describing themselves as honest, but caught in a bad situation. They focused on the ending— usually a happy ending—as a justification. They also tended to blame the lie receiver—explaining that their partner somehow provoked the lie. But flip that around, and in their stories of being lie receivers, they talked about their anger at being lied to, and said that they were confused and hurt by the lie. We may lie to our loved one because we love them, but our partner is not feeling the love. *At all.*

And yet, there are times where telling the full truth to the man or woman you love seems like a disservice. As Perel writes, "Respect is not necessarily about telling all, but about considering what it will be like for the other to receive the knowledge." For example, let's look at a woman having flirtatious banter with a man who isn't her husband. Let's say he's another dad from her kids' school, and that this banter happens three times, in the somewhat controlled environment of working the school concession stand during a soccer game. Each time, she leaves feeling sexually charged and goes home and has fantastic sex with her husband. She feels a bit conflicted. She isn't planning on doing anything with the sexy dad from the concession stand. It's innocent, she tells herself. And yet, part of her feels guilty. After the third time, her husband says, "Wow, we've had great sex lately. I love it, and am not complaining. But I'm a little curious: Is there a reason why?" He doesn't say it in an accusing way, but rather, more of a playful way.

What does honesty mean in that situation? We can look at it through many different lenses. Does she have insight into what her husband needs from her? Does she know his preferences? For example, if she knows that he sometimes lacks confidence, telling him that she is turned on by someone else seems the wrong call—like it might assuage her guilt, but would only make him feel bad. A side step of "I've just been turned on more lately, for reasons I don't completely understand" would make more sense. On the other hand, if he hasn't done such a fantastic job paying attention to her sexually or she hasn't created the space to see herself as sexually vibrant, then perhaps this is an opportunity to have a conversation about what kinds of things turn her on—namely, how remembering she is a sexual creature really ignites her passion, and how sometimes, it takes talking to someone else to remember that. The truth could either be an amazing opportunity to start a conversation that could ultimately strengthen their marriage and turn that sexual spark into a full-on inferno, or it could be a hurtful, probably unnecessary confession that won't help anything and very well may kill the renewed sexual spark they've both been enjoying so much. No matter what our eighteenth-century German friend Immanuel Kant says about it never being okay to lie (he never married, by the way), there is no objective right answer as to what she should say. You may read this and think it's clear what she should do—or what the husband should do if it were reversed and he was getting turned on by another woman grabbing hot dogs off the concession grill (innuendo fully intended!)—but here's the deal: *You're not in it.* None of us are in it, except the two people in the couple. What the partner facing the dilemma needs to ask him- or herself is: Do I have a purpose for being honest?

Honesty on Purpose

Shortly after Allen and I began our reconciliation, I wrote in my honesty journal: "I don't have to tell everyone, especially Allen, everything. That's not what honesty is about. It's not confessional or saying it to say it because it's too hard to hold in and you just want someone to share the burden. It should have a reason. It should be sacred in some situations.

Strategic, even. But not in a bad, self-serving way." I realize the notion of "strategic honesty" sounds like a slippery slope, and I agree. There are plenty of situations where we can objectively say what the right answer is. Returning incorrect change is part of a social contract that we're going to do our best to operate honestly, for the good of all. Ditto for résumés, affidavits, testimonies, public records, accounting ledgers, news bulletins, and any number of places where society will fucking crack in half if people aren't honest. But the contract of marriage is not about the good of all; it's an intimate system between two people, where the decisions behind honesty are both sacred—and, yes, strategic.

So this is what I say: *When you love someone, honesty is about sharing with a loving purpose.* This is principle number nine, and though it can be applicable in other situations, it is particularly applicable inside of marriage and/or committed relationships. The first part, "When you love someone," is a qualifier, because the stakes are higher (i.e., there is more to lose). The second part, "honesty is about sharing," is important, because it's not about "confessing"—it's about sharing, which implies a sense of mutual respect and goodwill. The third part, "a loving purpose," is the special sauce. A loving purpose doesn't mean your partner will love what you have to say. It means that the truth you are sharing is coming from a place of love, and that there is a purpose for why you share. When I decided to be honest with Allen about my emotional affair, my main motivation wasn't guilt. Sure, I had some guilt, but that wasn't enough of a reason to share. It needed to have a purpose. My purpose initially—the first time I told him, back in 2013—was that I couldn't seem to articulate what was wrong with our marriage, from my perspective, and the only way I could make him take it seriously was to be honest that I had developed feelings for someone else. Then, four years later, my purpose in telling him was that I needed to bring this thing to the light so that we could have the real and difficult conversations that we had been avoiding. I didn't know the outcome, but I knew the loving purpose. I wanted to open up the conversation, and burst the bubble of shame and secrecy so that we could deal with the situation together. I still think about loving purpose when I share things with Allen. So if I've made plans to see the other man for lunch (we're still friends, though it's vastly different now), or I have a meeting that involves him, I always share it with Allen. It's not guilt that motivates me to share, because I don't feel guilty. My loving purpose is to keep things in the light, because we can all see them there.

Recently, I asked the other man why he never told his wife about his feelings for me. We had talked about this before, but in light of writing this chapter, I wanted to ask again, to see what I may have missed. Like me, he felt guilty, didn't like holding on to the secret, and felt like the connection he had formed with me was indicative of how much he wanted things in the marriage to change. He tried to make that change in other ways, though. He thought about telling his wife many times, he told me. There could have been a loving purpose, but there was such fragility in his marriage, and he feared that if he told her, it would be the end. The fear of the outcome—of everything he had to lose—kept him silent. It wasn't about keeping things from her because he's a person who likes to keep secrets; it was about fear of losing his family. "Every time I looked into my kids' eyes, I couldn't do it," he said.

Can we liberate our honesty decisions from our fear of losing everything? I don't know. I think focusing on sharing with a loving purpose can help. When we look at it that way, honesty is such a wonderful opportunity. Could you not just say to your loved one: *Hey, I'm turned on by the hottie I serve hot dogs with at the soccer field. I want to jump your fucking bones after I see him/her, because I remember how it feels to be mysterious to someone. Let's figure out how we can get a little bit more of that feeling in our marriage, because I love you and it's worth it?* This seems like a loving purpose indeed. But it also depends on having someone to receive our loving purpose, and that can be a real X factor. Does each person have enough sexual confidence and ownership of their own pleasure either to say this or to hear this? Is each partner able to handle the reality that their lover is turned on by lots of other people? If you never talk this way to each other, can you suddenly start? I don't know, because I'm not in your relationship. To be sure, there are so many other factors inside of marriage—our expectations, our notions of who we are, our tendency to blame, our reliance on old scripts—that it's a rather complicated soup that can't be boiled down into a tidy principle about honesty. It doesn't mean we shouldn't keep trying, though.

Honesty imbued my marriage with a new kind of lightness—and I mean "light" in two ways. Being honest with Allen brought aspects of our relationship into the light, and it also lightened the mood of our marriage. Even when Allen is gripped by anxiety or I see him tilting toward old ways of thinking, I am less likely to catastrophize, to think his temperament has much to do with me, to presume I can "fix" it, or to get defensive, preachy, coachy, or frustrated. *Judi, this is marriage*, I say to myself. *This is how it goes. Stay in the light and just see what happens tomorrow.* Tomorrow might be better. It might be even worse. But on the whole, our relationship is no longer tied to the ups and downs that follow the days. Still, I sometimes think about some other life I could be living. I realize now that I'm not the only married person to do this, and that it's not a sign of a bad marriage. In fact, my favorite passage in former First Lady Michelle Obama's book *Becoming* is when she reveals something her mother once told her.

> [She] would tell me that every year when spring came and the air warmed up in Chicago, she entertained thoughts about leaving my father. I don't know if these thoughts were actually serious or not. I don't know if she considered the idea for an hour, or for a day, or for most of the season, but for her it was an active fantasy, something that felt healthy and maybe even energizing to ponder, almost as a ritual. I understand now that even a happy marriage can be a vexation, that it's a contract best renewed and renewed again, even quietly and privately—even alone.

Mrs. Obama goes on to talk about how she doesn't know what alternative life her mother may have been dreaming about, about what possibilities her mother may have entertained while cleaning the windows each spring after a long Chicago winter, but that, as a married woman herself in a relationship that's had its ups and downs, she gets how that pondering works, how that daydreaming serves a very distinct purpose. She writes: "Maybe you spend the whole day considering new ways to live before finally you fit every window back into its frame and empty your bucket of Pine-Sol into the sink. And maybe now all your certainty returns, because yes, truly, it's spring and once again you've made the choice to stay." To me, there is no clearer description of honesty in marriage than that. It's a continual choice, but it's not a choice you can truly make unless you've carefully considered the seemingly more exciting and better alternatives. We just don't seem to have the vocabulary to talk about that honestly, though. We fear the idea of betrayal so much that we fall silent, and it does us a disservice. At least, it did me a disservice.

Perel writes in *State of Affairs* that so many couples say to her something along the lines of, "Why did we have to go through an affair to have honest conversations with each other?" I wonder the same thing. Why did it almost have to fall apart for me to understand the way honesty worked inside my marriage? I think it's because marriage is a strange bird. As a system, it's unrealistic and mostly unnatural. It's difficult and it sets people up to fail. It only works about half the time, and would be a terrible bet at a Vegas casino. Being married has brought some of the worst aspects of my personality to the forefront, and made me sink to my knees in sobs on the bathroom floor more than once. I so often think, *What on earth made me decide on this person, forever? How ludicrous!* It's so utterly preposterous sometimes.

And yet, I haven't come across a system that would work better for me.

If we operated from that kind of raw honesty, maybe the whole thing would go a little bit smoother.

Reviewing the Honesty Principles

Mine all parts of the conversation.

- Instead of looking for who to blame, map the contribution system inside your relationship—what did you contribute to the situation, and what did your partner contribute? (*When things go wrong in human relationships, generally all people involved have contributed in some way.*)

- Your feelings (and your partner's feelings) are not static; they are ever-changing, and based on your thoughts and perceptions. Find the next level under the feelings you are expressing and negotiate with those deeper ideas. (*We don't get to label something a feeling and then call it off limits.*)

- Complexify your identity inside of your marriage. Opt for "and" instead of "or." (*I had to let go of cherished aspects of how I saw myself.*)

When you love someone, honesty is about sharing with a loving purpose.

- A loving purpose doesn't mean your partner will love what you have to say. It means that the truth you are sharing is coming from a place of love, and that there is a purpose for why you share. (*I didn't tell Allen out of guilt, I told him because I wanted to force the conversation.*)

- Share your truths with the intent of opening up a conversation, not shutting it down or shaming the other person. (*Does the wife need to share with her husband that she was turned on by the other sexy dad?*)

CHAPTER 8

Honesty and Parenting

"**W**HAT ARE YOU DOING?" I asked my son, Maxx, one December evening in 2016. He was holding the iPad in such a way that I could tell he didn't want me to see what he was doing. He eyed me cautiously. "I'm looking up if Santa is real or not," he said. He was eight years old at the time, and desperate to know the deal with Santa Claus.

I took the iPad from his hands. "Maxx," I said, "why do you want to know so much?"

"Because I feel like you're lying to me," he said, trying to blink away the threat of tears.

Fuck.

He had been asking me for weeks if Santa was real, and I kept brushing it off. What was I supposed to say? "No, Santa is completely made up and your dad and I have been keeping up this strange charade that the entire culture seems to sanction because it's 'fun,' and 'magic' and somehow related to the 'joy of Christmas'—so basically yes, we have been lying to both you and your sister." Wasn't I supposed to just go along with the story? Wasn't it a fun story? Wasn't this one of the best parts of Christmas for children?

But the way Maxx looked at me . . . He was genuinely distraught. He'd always been a logic-minded kid, not much for magic and myths. He demanded proof of God in kindergarten. Instead, I tried to explain my secular humanist—there is probably some higher power but I really don't know, so just be a good person and don't worry— view, borrowing from a John Lennon lyric, and saying, "God is a concept." Maxx replied, "So you're saying his name is God Concept?" I tried to further explain it wasn't a "he" and was more like a story about how we should love each other. He walked away frustrated and decided the whole thing was bogus. I had already screwed up God and set the stage for him to get recruited into some fundamentalist sect that promised answers and emphasized how parents lied. And now, he was asking me to tell him the truth about Santa. How could I lie to my child? But wasn't telling him the truth "ruining" Christmas?

"Let's go get ready for bed, and I'll tell you," I said to him, to get him away from Georgia, two years younger and still full of magical belief. As he got his pajamas on, I told him the truth—that dad and I (and all the moms and dads) were Santa and always had been. That it's supposed to be a fun story for kids, not a story that stresses them out. And that we were never trying to "lie" about it, but rather, just to carry on a tradition we had enjoyed as kids. For a minute, I saw that look again—the one he does when he's trying to blink back embarrassed tears. Had I made a mistake? "Are you glad I told you?" I asked, trying not to sound desperate, but blinking back tears myself.

"Yes!" he said, brightening again. I breathed a sigh of relief. We talked a little bit about how Dad and I had carried it off so well all these years, and he loved getting the "insider scoop." "Just one more thing," I said to him as I turned to leave. "You can tell Georgia if you want—I know I can't stop you from saying whatever you're going to say to her. But I will deny that we ever had this conversation. I will flat out lie," I told him.

"You won't," he said, not believing I could be convincing.

"Try me," I said.

"Georgia!" he called down the steps. "Mom just told me Santa isn't real!"

"Huh?" I said, cool as anything, as Georgia came to the bottom of the steps. "You're crazy. I just told you all about how real Santa is!" My performance was spot-on. Maxx looked at me with those big eyes again and I winked. He couldn't believe I could be such a convincing liar.

Neither could I.

Two years later—as I was working on this book, in fact—I would have nearly the same discussion with Georgia. The day after Christmas in 2018, when she was eight years old, she said, "Okay, I really need to know now. Is Santa real or not?" She had casually asked the question a few times that holiday season, but in a way that suggested she didn't really want to know—often saying "never mind, I believe!" before I could even formulate a response (I think because she was afraid she wouldn't get any presents if she said she didn't believe). But now, with Santa—and her load of presents—behind us for the year, she wasn't messing around anymore with her question. She wanted to know, because, just like Maxx, it had started to feel like a strange lie she wasn't in on, and she didn't like not knowing. I took the same gentle approach in breaking the news to her, and she had nearly the same reaction: slight disappointment, but immense relief to know the truth. In the weeks before Christmas, I had really wanted her to figure it out on her own, because it felt so strange to keep holding to the story (probably because I was working on this book). I didn't want to spoil it for her as long as the belief was still important to her. But when it felt like a liability rather than a piece of fun magic, I knew it was time to be honest.

Honesty and Magic

In my research on honesty and parenting, I have discovered there are two kinds of parents: those who have really strong feelings about the Santa story, and those who muddle through and really don't care that much. I was always the latter. Santa was fun, but mostly inconsequential to my childhood. I had six siblings. Someone told me the deal pretty early, but I don't remember who or when or even caring much. For me, the magic of the holiday was how the living room looked when all the lights were out and only the tree was lit. It was about cookies and everyone being together and that amazing Barbie Dreamhouse that I got when I was about eight or nine. My husband, who is logic-minded just like his son, never believed as a kid because it didn't make sense to him. But he still didn't have strong feelings about it. Santa? Sure. Whatever. That was our approach. When our kids were little, like three and four years old, it was just a cute story, full of mystery and magic. But by the time they were eight years old, upholding and defending the story just started to feel . . . weird. And, you know, like a lie.

It's such a strange lie, too: An old man knows everything about you and all the children in the world—whether you're "good" or "bad"—and he sneaks into your house while everyone is sleeping (maybe he even peeks into your room and sees you in your bed) and leaves things in your living room. You can send him letters, but you can't ever talk to him or see him. He can only see you. When you read it in black and white, it's unbelievably creepy. Yet we've built a culture around it. There are numerous op-ed pieces written about whether or not parents should perpetuate the Santa myth, and they all make good points. Santa isn't real, and if you purposely and habitually tell your child he is, and go out of your way to keep up the façade, it is dishonest. That is intolerable to some parents, which I get. I also get that it's a special story, and it gives many children seventeen kinds of delight because it's mysterious and magical and special, and it's fun to be part of that with your child. Philosopher Thomas Carson—the one who helped us define all of the terms associated with honesty—never liked the idea of lying to his children about Santa (they're grown now). "My wife loved everything about Christmas and Santa, though, and I wasn't going to cross her. I just didn't say much about Santa," he tells me. One of his problems with the story is that it correlates being "good" with getting more presents. So what are poor children to think? That they are bad? How awful is that? "Parents also use it as a threat or manipulation to get kids to behave. There is an insincerity about it," he says. On that point, I definitely agree—though I have been guilty of that manipulation, especially when my kids were toddlers (which is when you reach for anything you can to make it through the day).

While I think the Santa dilemma is a good way to kick off the discussion about what it means to be honest with children, I think it's also fairly easy to dispense with, because it falls into the realm of other-worldly belief. Otherworldly belief gets its own principle, and it's quite simple: *You don't need to pit honesty and otherworldly belief against each other.* What else besides Santa, the Easter Bunny, and the Tooth Fairy counts as otherworldly belief? Religion for sure, whether it's the kind I grew up with—the brick-and-mortar, heaven-and-hell, these-are-the-rules-to-follow-and-the-things-to-believe kind that involves miracles and virgin births and Jesus (or an equivalent prophet)—or the kind I follow now, which is actually just a loose spirituality that calls upon the universe and the power of love. All of the less serious shit counts, too: magic, fairies, and the idea that animals can talk. Lore and traditions are also part of this principle. Life with children would be far less textured if we had to focus on the limited scope of what we actually know to be factually true about the world. Otherworldly belief doesn't just make life fun; it also makes it rich, and it gives children stories bigger than themselves to help make sense of the world and understand the power of imagination. Make-believe is such an important part of the creative process for kids. My son was done with make-believe pretty early on, but my daughter, at eight, still loves dramatic play. These days, her dramatic play usually involves pretending to be a YouTuber and talking to her mirror (her pretend camera). She loves talking about her "fans," and I love indulging her in her scenarios. Before pretend YouTube fans, it was pretend fairy warriors that defended against evil. She would ask me, with a dreamy look in her eye: "Mom, are fairies real?" My answer was always, "Well, I like to think they are." In those instances, she wasn't asking me for a logical answer. She was asking me to join her in belief.

The honesty part comes when your kid wants to step outside the otherworldly belief and have a discussion about facts—as my kids eventually did with Santa. Then, I do believe it's important to engage at the level of reality they are asking for. It's also about recognizing what lights your kid up versus what shames them. My kids were starting to feel embarrassed and uncomfortable for not being able to discern the truth about Santa, and I clearly didn't want that. I know parents think that when kids stop believing in Santa, it represents the "end of innocence." But I think innocence ends the minute they feel shame, the minute they tap into that emotion human beings are hardwired to feel. A compassionate, honest word from us can go a long way in assuaging that, even if it means we have to recognize they aren't babies anymore. I think too many parents hold on to the Santa lie because it's too painful for them to admit their kids are growing up.

Santa and other mythical creatures represent a phase of childhood, and while it's tricky to know what to do, it's temporary. But when children are asking about religion—a thing that befuddles a good many adults—the waters get a bit muddier. I am a fan of saying, "I am not sure what is fact and what is belief," or "I don't know any of these things to be facts, but I like to believe them anyway." I'm a little bit into crystals and the powers they hold. In particular, I have two polished stones—a piece of selenite and a piece of blue aragonite—that I often hold and play with while I'm working. Georgia is fascinated by them. She wants to know their powers and if they really "work." "Well, I just like holding them, and if it feels like they help, then that's enough for me," I say to her. I say a similar thing to Maxx when he asks where his grandpas are. "I don't believe in God or heaven," Maxx said to me recently. He wanted to know if I believed. I told him that I wasn't sure—some days I did believe and other days I didn't. "But I do talk to my dad and to my brother Paul. I feel like they help me," I told him. I *do* believe this. Otherworldly beliefs don't necessarily need worldly evidence. Why not be honest about the fact that you don't have any, but you still believe anyway? Or that you don't believe. Or that you change your mind daily. Or that it's all up for grabs. I think one of the best things we can model for our children is uncertainty and constant questioning. I've-been-there-done-that with nuns and priests and their practice of telling me what to believe about the state of my soul, and it's one thing I have purposely decided not to pass on to my children. I have many honest conversations with them about that (to the point that they sometimes roll their eyes and say, "We get it, Mom! It's up to us to decide what we believe about the God thing!"). There are entire books devoted to talking to children about religion, and this is not one of them. The only clear thing I have learned around this area since I started focusing on honesty is to pay attention to these conversations and engage thoughtfully with the questions they ask, instead of just answering them in rote ways, especially if the rote answers stopped working for you a long time ago.

Now, let's talk about sex.

Pimps, Orgasms, and *Oh My God, Why Are You Asking That?*

Part of the reason I started my honesty journal is because I suspected I was glazing over answers to my kids' questions—not intentionally trying to deceive them (except, apparently, when it came to Santa Claus), but not thinking hard enough about whether I was giving a truthful, but age-appropriate, response. I made this decision to focus on being more honest just in time, because Maxx—who is ten as I write this—is a precocious, curious kid who does not like being talked down to or lied to. And he has a lot of questions, especially about sex. I wrote in my *Times* article that when he asked me what a pimp was, I went ahead and told him the truth (after first explaining what a prostitute was). Getting an honest answer from me spurred him to ask even more questions. I liked that he was coming to me with questions, so I eventually told both of my kids, "When you ask me something, I will do my best to answer honestly. I may not share private information, but I will try to explain things in a way you can understand." We had already given him the book *It's So Amazing* to read, which goes through human reproductive parts and what they do, how kid bodies change into adult bodies, and what sex is and how babies usually get made. He knew the basics, but telling him I would be honest with him really opened the floodgates, and let me tell you, the water has continued to flow. And flow.

For example, in the past year, I have gotten the following questions: Do all women have orgasms? Do women need to have an orgasm to get pregnant? What is squirting? Does "giving head" mean a blow job? Can blow job also mean giving oral sex to a woman? Why do people want to have sex anyway? If orgasm and ejaculation aren't the same thing for a man, how does a man know which it is? What does the word *cunt* mean? Why would anyone rape someone? Do kids get raped?

And these are just questions I can think of off the top of my head as I sit here and type. I have answered every single one of these cringe-worthy questions honestly (though I did have to defer the orgasm/ejaculation one to my husband). Not one time did I *want* to answer the question. I wanted to run and hide. I would often buy time by saying, "First, tell me where you heard that and what you think," just to gauge where he was with it. A good bit of these things he has heard either on Instagram (where he is involved—with my supervision—in a large freestyle trampoline community) or from hanging around teenage boys at some of the freestyle flipping events he goes to (while most of the talk is focused around the ideal spring setup on a trampoline or how to get more rotation on your quadruple back flip, he does sometimes meander into inappropriate teenage conversations). It is incredibly uncomfortable to explain squirting ("something a girl might do when she has an orgasm, just like a man ejaculates"), but I knew that if I didn't, he would simply look it up on the iPad. I'd rather him come to me when he has a question, not ask Siri. (If you're wondering why I even let him use Instagram at all, that's a fair question. The answer is that it's how he connects to this community of extreme athletes he belongs to—kids who live all over the world. His account, which is on the family iPad, technically belongs to me, and I monitor it as closely as I can. Yes, I have serious doubts about it. Keep reading.) As for Georgia, I've also had the basic talk with her about how babies are made and what all the parts are called (and I passed *It's So Amazing* on to her). So far, she asks far less questions than my son.

Sex educator Amy Lang, author of *Birds + Bees + Your Kids,* affirms my decision to answer everything honestly. "Set yourself up as the go-to person to talk about sex," Lang says. She advises that you have the first sex talk with your kid by the time he or she is five years old, meaning you give them a basic explanation of what all the parts are and the usual way that babies get made—saying the actual words, like egg, penis, vagina, vulva, sperm, and clitoris. The talk should include high-level information about boundaries ("Right now, it's not okay for you to touch someone else's private parts or for them to touch yours") and a rough outline of your values on sex ("Sex is a great thing that grown-ups enjoy and it's how we're all here, but it's not for kids"). By third grade, she says, you should talk to them about puberty, and how their body is going to change. And then by middle school, you should make sure they have the facts about the whole range of sexual acts (including oral sex and anal sex), orgasms, sexually transmitted infections (STIs) and how to protect against them, relationships and consent, and more of your values. "You don't have to be a full-on sex educator," she says. Still, more information is better than less information. "Most of what comes out of our mouths is not enough information," she says. Kids don't need tons of extraneous details, but their questions are a good chance to open up a wider conversation about values, so that they start to learn about healthy relationships early on. So when my kid asks me if giving head is the same thing as oral sex, I can say, "Yes, and . . . oral sex is a way that people like to be sexual without worrying about getting pregnant. It's part of a healthy sex life. But it's definitely not for kids. It's for later."

"You are a trustworthy resource, so you want to show up in a trustworthy way," Lang says. One of her best tips is to use third person if your kid asks any specifics about you, which they tend to do more when they're little, since older kids are thoroughly grossed out by thoughts of their parents having sex. For example, if your little one asks, "Do you like sex, Mom?" give a third person answer like, "Most people who are healthy do like sex." While I've focused this discussion on answering kids' sex questions honestly, the reality is that you shouldn't wait to be asked to be honest and open with your kids about sex. Right now, the public school system waits until middle school, which is far too late. In fact, in countries where they have sex education as early as kindergarten—like the Netherlands—the rate of teenage pregnancy and STIs is lower than here, and though Dutch teenagers don't wait any longer to have sex than American teenagers, Dutch teenagers (boys *and* girls) report having more positive first experiences. Much has been written about the Dutch approach to sex education (search author Bonnie Rough), and the lack of shaming around sex in general. I love the idea of less shame, but I'm still pretty damn Midwestern, and liberated or not, it is difficult for me to explain an orgasm to a ten-year-old ("Like a sneeze, but better"). I grew up in a house where we absolutely did not talk about sex. My dad, rest his soul, was stoic and Puritanical in many ways. My mom was less so and would have answered my questions, but I was too embarrassed. That, combined with growing up Catholic and getting the message over and over that sex was linked to sin, made me downright stupid about how the whole thing worked and what it meant. This is probably why it took me a while to figure out my views on sex, and to fully enjoy it and see myself in a sexual way. I'll go through some uncomfortable honesty to have it be different for my kids.

Kids Know When Puppets Are Lying

As parents, deception lurks in many places. We tell lies of omission and half-truths to our kids, as well as utter a good many unexamined statements. We palter, change the topic as a means of avoidance, and frequently tell them both prosocial lies and self-interested lies. We also routinely conceal information from children and keep secrets. Not to mention the times we just "fake it 'til we make it"—pretending to be enthused about something we have absolutely no interest in for the benefit of someone else.

I was only half-aware of the honesty choices I was making with my kids before I started paying attention. For example, I rarely noticed when I was lying in front of them for the sake of politeness or to spare feelings, and I didn't consider how that must have felt contradictory, since I often said things like, "Your dad and I value honesty," or "We are raising you to be honest." Hence, I want to return to an idea I brought up early in the book—that we learn conflicting messages about honesty as children, which winds up causing confusion, guilt, and shame. Face it: The way our parents talked to us was probably dysfunctional, and the way we talk to our kids about honesty probably is, too. "Despite the stories we tell children, the fact is that there is honesty we punish and deception we encourage," says Robert Feldman, author of *Liar in Your Life*. You want an honest kid, but you want a polite kid. And those two are often at odds with one another. Not only do most of us act inconsistently when it comes to deception, we don't even know how to talk about it in a coherent way.

There are really two issues here: (1) why we should strive to be more honest with kids about a whole range of things we don't want to be honest about, and (2) why we need to have better conversations about honesty with kids, since they are watching everything we do.

First, why should we strive to be more honest with kids? Or rather, why pay attention to our honesty choices with our kids—following the principles I've set out thus far—in our attempt to be more aware and engaged people? There are some easily discernible reasons, like being honest with kids about sex can decrease their chances of teen pregnancy and STIs, and set them up for healthy sexual relationships later in life. There is also emerging research about how kids are affected by their parents' fibs. An experiment at the University of California–San Diego found that preschoolers and young elementary schoolchildren who had been lied to by the experimenter were more likely both to cheat (they peeked at something when they weren't supposed to) and then to lie about whether or not they peeked. Basically, kids who were lied to tended to lie more themselves. In a news release, the study authors say, "The actions of parents suggest that they do not believe that the lies they tell their children will impact the child's own honesty. The current study casts doubt on that belief."

Another study out of the Massachusetts Institute of Technology found that kids (ages six and seven) are pretty smart about when you're concealing relevant information. Using toys, experimenters manipulated conditions so that some kids weren't told everything about what a toy could do (but the kids were led to believe that they were being told everything). Once those kids realized the experimenter wasn't telling them everything, they explored and worked to fill in the gaps themselves—and then were less likely to trust the experimenter when she gave them another toy to explore. The researchers point out that children don't need every detail of everything—like what kind of batteries the toys take—but they do have a sense of when they are being purposely misled about information that would have been helpful to have. The experiment was with toys and puppets who gave instructions, so who knows if it completely generalizes to parents. Still, the bottom line is that kids may start believing you less if you lie to them, whether by commission or omission.

It's so basic, I almost feel silly typing it, but yet, we kind of forget: If you want to raise honest children, who also see you as a trustworthy source for information, you need to practice being thoughtfully honest yourself. By *thoughtfully honest*, I mean using the honesty principles to help you wade through situations. It's both the small utterances you say without thinking and the clutch times, when you know what you're about to say is going to matter a lot. Since starting my honesty journey, I've focused on curbing my use of unexamined statements—those statements we dash off without deeply engaging with what we're saying. Not only are these low-level lies, they also shut down the opportunity to have a meaningful conversation with our kids. For example, Maxx or Georgia may ask, "Are you and Dad ever going to get divorced?" My knee jerk reaction used to be, "Don't worry about that" or "Of course not." Now, I say something more like, "Well, marriage can be kind of hard even when people really love each other, and it doesn't always work out. But your dad and I love each other and are committed to always trying hard to make ours work, because we want to all be together as a family." I'm slipping in a subtle message about my values: First, that I believe marriage can be hard and we should never judge people who are divorced, and second, that Dad and I love each other and value the hard work of family life. I can't give them a definitive answer about if their dad and I will ever divorce. I don't think we will. But I also don't think it's that helpful of an answer, if my goal is to share my values with my kids. Now, if they were absolutely freaking out and losing sleep over their worry that we're going to divorce, I would address it in a slightly different way. I realize that sometimes kids need pure reassurance, not a subtle message about values. But to discern the difference, we have to be paying attention, not resorting to the same scripts.

It's also challenging when children hear about scandals and tragedies, or when they start to ask questions about politics. One thing I value about how I grew up is that we had an open forum at the dinner table to talk about things like history and politics and current events. My parents were informed because they read constantly, watched the news, and listened to a diversity of voices. They expressed their opinions freely, but they didn't tell us we had to share those opinions. I'm trying to do the same thing with my kids at the dinner table. When my kids were really little, I wasn't sure what was appropriate and what wasn't. Now, I think nearly any topic is appropriate, as long as I give the context and explain it in a way they can understand. I decided a while back that I wasn't going to avoid thorny conversations and questions, whether it's about why Donald Trump wants to build a wall, or the Me Too movement, or a video Maxx has just seen on Instagram of a black person being called the "N" word. I don't necessarily feel qualified to talk about things like sexual consent, xenophobia, or racism. What if I get it wrong? But what do we think will come from hiding behind the things we don't feel qualified to discuss? When it comes to equality and justice issues, one of the things I'm committed to is educating myself, so that I have more thoughtful answers for my kids. For me, this has meant seeking out resources written by black educators and racial justice activists, like Beverly Daniel Tatum's *Why Are all the Black Kids Sitting Together in the Cafeteria?* (the twentieth-anniversary edition, which has been updated) and Layla F. Saad's *Me and White Supremacy Workbook*. There is far too much misinformation and far too many offensive Instagram memes at kids' disposal for today's parents to be abdicating on the difficult stuff. Just as with information about sex, I want to be the go-to person for my kids on a wide variety of issues. I have to be willing to engage on those issues, though, even if it means I get it wrong before I get it right, or have to endure being uncomfortable.

Three Steps to Having Better
Conversations About Honesty

Victoria Talwar, a psychologist at McGill University in Canada, studies lying in children. In her lab, they've done numerous experiments with children and deception, as a way to understand how kids develop both socially and cognitively. She and her team studied this by having kids, ages six to twelve, watch videos where puppets were either lying or telling the truth. Scenarios ranged from the puppets lying for their own benefit (blaming others), to lying to protect someone, to telling the truth in a way that harmed someone. After they watched the videos, the kids were asked what they thought. While all the kids had no problem distinguishing lies from truth, the younger kids tended to think the truth was always the right thing, whereas the older kids understood more nuance. In particular, the older kids didn't like it when the puppet tattled, and they were more conflicted when lying meant another person faced bad consequences. "Children get a lot of messages from their parents saying that lying is always bad, but at the same time they see their parents telling 'white' lies to make life easier. Depending on their age, this is likely to be a bit confusing for children," Talwar explains in a news release about the study.

The older children get, the more they become focused on consequences, and the more shades of gray they see. They also get more adept at lying, as Robert Feldman found in his research, which included having children and adolescents purposely tell lies to mislead. First graders were unconvincing liars, seventh graders were pretty decent, but college students were experts. Parents may think children grow out of lying, he says, but the opposite is true. "Children grow *into* lying, learning to become more thoughtful and more nimble liars as they make their way into young adulthood," Feldman writes. And they learn, in large part, by watching adults. Kids are a little bit like Siri: always listening in the background, waiting for your cue. They hear the little lies you tell, whether you're talking on the phone with a relative and lying about why you aren't attending a family function, telling the clerk at a retailer who always asks for an email address that you don't have an email, or gushing with the neighbor about their new car, when only minutes before, you were ranting to your spouse about why anyone would ever buy a Buick.

Instead of an honesty principle, I've got three steps to help with this—three things that I have been trying to do myself.

Step one is to pay attention and try to stop doing that mindless lying shit. Try to avoid it whether kids are around or not. I'm trying myself, but it's hard. Even with focused attention, I'm still going to let loose with unexamined statements and fibs to the neighbor. It does get easier once you pay attention to it (remember, keeping an honesty journal tends to expose you to a thought or behavior at least five times in one day—which is five times more than you would have thought about it before). I'm learning to simply smile and say less, and get more comfortable with direct but kind phrases like, "No, thank you," and "Not for me, thank you." (*Say what you mean, but don't be a jerk.*) I've learned that I don't have to fill in gaps in conversations with praise that isn't sincere, force reactions that aren't authentic, or make up stories to get out of doing things. Practice your simple, truthful, direct, and kind statements.

Step two is to tell your kids they can call you out on deception they witness. Have a discussion with your kids about how you are trying to be more honest, and you know there are times where you should be honest, but you tell a fib, and that if they see you doing that, once *they're in private with you again* (that's key), they can point it out or ask you why you told the fib. There may be times when you've told a prosocial lie of kindness, like my lie to the swimmer in my lane. If your kid catches you in that kind of prosocial deception, my suggestion is that instead of getting defensive, you walk it through with them—why you chose to tell the prosocial lie, and ask what they think about it or if they would have done it differently. In fact, that would be a wonderful conversation to have. Most likely, though, they're going to catch you in lies that involve them.

For example, Georgia and I were at the farmers' market a few weeks ago, and we bought a few things—honey, olive oil, scones— which is more than I had intended to buy, seeing as how I didn't actually need honey, olive oil, or scones. The last booth was the alpaca craft booth, otherwise known as The Most Expensive Shit on the Planet. Alpaca wool is lovely and soft and props to the alpaca farmers for doing such a weird and cool thing, but there was no way I was buying a twenty-dollar keychain for my daughter's backpack that looked like a puffball. "Puh-lee-hee-heease!" she begged, clutching the puffball like her entire lifetime of joy depended on it.

"No. I'm out of money. We need to go," I said gently.

But she knew the drill about Mommy trying really hard not to lie. "Are you really out of money?" she said, though to her credit, she said it quietly enough so that the vendor, who was otherwise occupied with another customer, didn't hear.

I sighed and patted her hair. "No, you're right. I wasn't being truthful. I actually do have a few dollars left, and they probably take credit cards anyway. But I don't want to spend this much money on this right now," I said.

"Okay," she said. She still wanted it and looked longingly at it as we made our way to the car, but that I answered her honestly counted for something. Now, another time, she may have thrown a fit even after I was honest. She's still a kid and does kid-like things like throwing fits when she doesn't get her way. But the exchange—her calling me out on the fib and me coming clean in a respectful way—was helpful for both of us.

Step three is look for the open spaces in the conversations around honesty. We lie for a range of reasons, including fear, empathy, self-preservation, and avoidance of shame. So often, there is a subtle lesson to pull out inside of that deception. When you engage with the deception, you can find the lesson—and when you engage with the deception in front of your kid, it's a chance to share the lesson and to connect with them.

My least favorite part of the yearly well visit with my kids is when the pediatrician asks the series of questions about at-home behaviors. We're good on the eating meals at home and eating fruits and veggies. We're good on the getting exercise every day. We suck on the screens, though. The question is usually something like, "Do your kids watch screens more than [some ridiculously small amount of time] a day?" I made the mistake of lying when Maxx was eight (because by then, we had definitely blown the guidelines). Of course, he corrected me and told the doctor that he watched the iPad and TV far more than an hour (or whatever) a day. I glared at him and he just smiled. The next year, on the way to the doctor for his well checkup, Maxx said something like, "I'm going to be honest if the doctor asks about screens. You always lie." Hello, punch in the freakin' gut. My first response was rising anger . . . but then, I remembered my honesty work. Instead of getting mad, I realized this was an opportunity. "You're right," I said. "I do tend to lie about it. I shouldn't. But do you know why I lie?"

"Because it's bad that I use the iPad so much."

"It's not *bad*. It's just that doctors think kids watch screens too much, and they're right. But I don't always follow what they say. We shouldn't lie to doctors about things to do with health, though."

"But you do," he said.

"I do," I said. "Because a little part of me feels ashamed that I should be a better mom. I often feel like people are saying I'm not a good mom if I do certain things or don't do certain things. I feel judged. Do you ever feel that way?"

"Yeah, about my behavior. I'm bad sometimes and I know it."

What a golden moment to talk about the difference between *how we act* and *who we are*, about guilt versus shame, about how it feels to be judged by other people, and the way that makes us feel and how we react. I can't remember every word I said to Maxx, because we've actually had several of these conversations around his ADHD, and how we separate his behavior from the core of who he is. But I remember the spirit of that moment in the car and the conversation with him where I was able to show him that I feel judged, too—that I struggle with these same things. That's a great lesson, and a place I never would have expected a conversation about lying to the doctor to go.

When you open up to your kids about your own struggles, especially around honesty, you show them that honesty is a dynamic concept that takes vulnerability, courage, and discernment. It's not a mindless, permanently fixed "policy." I believe seeing honesty as dynamic and keeping a running dialogue with children about it is a better approach than repeating the same tired adages that your behavior—and their behavior—will oftentimes belie.

Digging into Family Secrets

Every family has their secrets, some less benign than others. Kids hear whispers and rumblings, inheriting stories with missing details and admonishments not to ask too many questions. But what happens when they grow up and they want to know the whole truth? This is something I've thought quite a bit about, not because I have any particular gnawing family secret, but because I know so many families do, like the family of my brother-in-law Mike. Mike has been married to my sister Laura for more than thirty years, and he's like a brother to me. He has an interesting history, and is the only person I know with three birth certificates. After his birth father, Steve, left when Mike was a few months old (his parents were teenagers), Mike's grandfather adopted him. Then, Mike's mother married and Mike's stepfather adopted him—but he died after about a year. Mike never had any relationship with his birth father, though he knew his name and that he still lived locally. Mike never seemed to have any curiosity about him. I would often ask Laura why Mike didn't go digging around and try to meet the guy. She thought it mostly had to do with Mike's mother telling him that his birth father and his family were "terrible people." If he asked too many questions, it would upset his mom, and he didn't like doing that. Plus, the guy left. If he didn't want anything to do with Mike, then Mike decided that he didn't want anything to do with him.

Then, when Mike was around fifty, his mother died, and he found himself wondering about this guy named Steve who he shared genetic material with. Steve wasn't hard to track down (he did, in fact, live locally), although he had already died, too. Mike found out that his birth father had gone on to marry after leaving his mom, and had three other children. Mike met the grown children—his half siblings—one evening, and he enjoyed it so much. Can you imagine? Meeting three siblings you never knew? We were all excited for Mike. But the next week, Steve's widow told Mike that her husband was not his father—that Mike's mother was "running around" on Steve and merely told him that Mike was his child. The half siblings ghosted Mike and wouldn't talk to him anymore. This was crushing to Mike. It's crushing now to me, even thinking about it. Though Mike believes his mother and thinks the wife is trying to protect her deceased husband's reputation, now he's left with more questions and more frustration than he started with. "I wish I had just left it alone," he tells me. He knows that the Kettelers are his family. But still, that little piece of who he is and where he came from is just left hanging out there.

With easy access to home DNA tests, like those provided by Ancestry.com, a lot of family secrets aren't staying secret anymore. People who thought they were full siblings are finding out they are actually half siblings, and that the person they thought was their biological father is actually not. People are learning about siblings, cousins, and nieces and nephews they had no idea existed. The secrets of one generation are being uncovered by the next, and with the DNA test trend only increasing, a lot more secrets will continue to be exposed. A February 2019 piece in *The Wall Street Journal* about the effect DNA tests are having on families reported that by 2021, more than 100 million people will have their DNA tested. The *Journal* piece featured two sisters who learned, via an at-home DNA kit, that both their mother and their father had affairs. The one sister learned that the man she thought was her biological father was actually not, and the other sister learned she had a half brother. It caused pain and rifts in the family, as well as joy and a sense of finally understanding certain things. Some members of the family wanted to know the truth, while others shied away from it because they were already happy with the narrative they had.

Peter Rober, clinical psychologist and professor at University of Leuven in Belgium, has done work on family secrets, including writing an autoethnography called "Silence and Memories of War: An Autoethnographic Exploration of Family Secrecy," where he digs into his own family secrets. Rober's maternal grandfather was held by the Germans during World War II, and he rarely spoke of it, other than to say it was similar to "Boy Scout camp." After his grandfather died, Rober started researching what the prisoner of war camps were like. He quickly realized that his grandfather's experience was nothing like a Boy Scout camp. So why didn't his grandfather tell the truth about the brutality of his experience—even when a young Rober asked him directly? Because silence was a way to protect the people his grandfather loved, and knowing the truth can be a burden. "Why break the silence and take the risk of being overwhelmed by painful memories that threatened the well-being of everyone in the family?" Rober says, noting that although there is a bias against secrets, secrecy can often be a gift. While his mother initially listened to what Rober had uncovered about the brutality of the camps, within a few months, she was back to the story of it being like Boy Scout camp. The truth of what her father had experienced was too painful to believe, so she reverted to the story she had always believed. There is a similar story line on the popular network television show *This Is Us*. One of the main characters, Jack, fought in the Vietnam War, and kept his experiences there mostly hidden from his children—telling them he was "just a mechanic." It was too painful for him and he didn't want his children to feel that burden. Of course, now that Jack is gone and it's too late to ask him, one of Jack's children is on a mission to uncover the story, because he realizes there is more to it than he told them. Even with my proclivity for wanting to share and speak about my experiences, as a parent, I intuitively get that impulse to want to shield my kids. But as a daughter, I also intuitively get wanting to know the story.

Rober acknowledges that we're all wired differently—curiosity to uncover the truth, to get to the "full" story is a very powerful motivator for many people. Although the idea that there is a "full" story is often misleading. Oftentimes, it's more about opening up the conversation to be able to talk about things the children (or other family members) have been dissuaded from talking about. "Maybe it is not only about knowledge being withheld but also about being deprived of a space in which to say what is on your mind, what bothers you, or what puzzles you," Rober writes in a piece on family secrets in the *Journal of Marital and Family Therapy*. This is true of my friend Annie, whose mother was a hoarder (they removed twenty-three tons of trash from the home—filling one and a half semitrucks—when her mother died a few years ago). Annie grew up with deep shame around her mother's hoarding and never told anyone what was going on at home. "It was a secret drilled into us as kids, to not talk about it," she says. Annie refuses to be silent about it as an adult, though. It is very important for her to speak the truth and be open about it, because the secrecy was both dangerous and destructive.

Kelly Kautz, a writing colleague of mine, is trying to open up the conversation in her family in another way. She is currently researching *The Skeleton Club*, a book that tries to answer the question of whether or not her great-grandmother was involved in a Satanic cult that drugged and sexually abused children and sacrificed animals and humans. Kautz's mother began to recall memories when she went to therapy after having dreams about being abused and witnessing murders. "According to my mother, her grandmother was a sociopath who murdered people and buried some of them in her cellar," Kautz tells me. Kautz's mother had told her stories about the great-grandmother, but it wasn't until Kautz had children of her own that she wanted to know the truth. "I want to know where I come from, and where my boys come from," she says. However, the odds of corroborating what her mother says about the great-grandmother being involved in a Satanic cult are against Kautz. The FBI investigated more than twelve thousand claims of occult sexual abuse during the Satanic Panic of the 1990s, and wasn't able to prove any of them. Not only does this give Kautz pause, at times, the whole thing feels like a lose-lose situation. "If I prove my mom's memory true, then I'm uncovering these awful things that can't be brought to justice now because everyone responsible is dead, but if I prove it false, then I'm saying this thing she has built her life around isn't accurate," she says. And yet, Kautz's drive to know is so strong. I feel that if I were in her position, mine would be as well.

Peter Rober, who often counsels families with secrets, understands this dilemma well, having lived it personally. Since Rober published his autoethnography, some of his colleagues have said they have family silences, too, and want to research them. They ask him for advice. He doesn't always encourage the digging. "It's hard to do it," he says. There can be something to gain for the children, especially if a topic has been off limits and the children want to be able to have conversations about it. But exposing secrets for the mere purpose of exposing secrets may not be as satisfying as family members think it is. They are often left with pain that has nowhere to go, and with questions that no one is around to answer.

It does make me wonder, as a parent, what I might want to keep secret from my children because I thought it would be too painful for them. It's hard for me to say, because I wasn't a soldier or a prisoner of war, and I don't have an experience of extreme brutality or a similar upsetting situation in my past. I do have experiences of shame, though, and things that are potentially embarrassing for my children to know. In writing this book, I've thought a lot about the fact that they may read it someday, and learn what transpired between their dad and me, and that I dabbled in unfaithfulness. They may piece together that this all must have happened during that really hard summer when Mom seemed to be crying a lot, and that one time when she came to dinner in tears and Dad said it was allergies, but they knew it wasn't because the energy in the house was so weird. They'll know things about my sex life and that I used to fake orgasms (sorry about that, kids). They'll know some of my deepest shames. While I don't find the need to actively go tell them all these things, especially while they are ten and eight, I am not very bothered by the thought of them knowing as young adults or adults. In fact, I like the idea of them knowing my struggles. I want them to respect me, but I don't ever want them to think that I haven't dealt with my share of pain. I want them to know that I used the pain to try to make sense of my life and the world, and I want them to mine their own pain to learn from it. In one of Oprah's Super Soul Sessions, writer Glennon Doyle talks about how she tells her children that instead of running away from their pain or trying to mute it with drugs and alcohol the way she did, they should run *toward* their pain. She tells them, "That pain was meant for you." In a related blog post, she describes pain as a traveling professor. I love that idea, because I do think that our struggles are our best teacher. Is some people's pain far greater and more devastating than others? Yes, of course. And while you may have guilt that your pain seems not as significant as others, or bitterness that your pain seems so much greater than others, neither of those feelings will get you any closer to making sense of it. I'm of the mind-set to do your best to use your pain and share what you've learned with your children, because not only can it be your lifeline, it might be theirs at some point.

Parenting Shame

To be a parent today is to face a constant hailstorm of attempted shame. People try to shame us on a daily basis—mostly other parents, but also childless people and sometimes our own family members. In turn, we do it to others, often without truly thinking about what we're saying and how we're reacting. I recently saw a post on Facebook (or as I like to call it, Shamebook) from a woman who I consider a friend, albeit a casual one I only see every once in a while because she lives across the country. But I know her to be smart and funny and generally supportive of others. She was responding to the inflammatory viral video from January 2019 of the Covington Catholic High School boys and the incident in Washington, D.C., with the Native American elder. (Cov Cath is the brother school to Notre Dame Academy, my high school, and two of my brothers went there.) I have many thoughts on this video, but for our purposes, what matters is that the son of one of my close relatives goes to this school and was there (though he was not visible in the video). This relative is someone I love deeply, and know to be a good parent with solid values. My friend's post started, "I'm not one to shame other parents. But seriously, shame on these parents!" I understood her frustration (I had my own, too), but I also knew she was completely unaware of the actor-observer bias at work. Here was an educated person who threw all critical thinking out the window to ride the shame train. And for what? To make herself feel better about her own parenting. Even more disturbing is that I wondered if I would have jumped on the shame train, too, if the incident hadn't involved my community and my family. I took a beat and refrained from saying anything because I knew someone involved. But if I hadn't? It may have been me. It's so easy to fall into castigating other parents, especially around highly charged issues.

It isn't just Facebook. Shame flows freely at family gatherings, in the grocery store, in parking lots, on airplanes, at work, and when we're out with friends. We shame and are shamed for being too free-range . . . or too helicopter-ish. For letting our kids have too much sugar . . . or for being too strict about sweets. For letting our kids play football . . . or for not letting them play football. For not having enough limits on screen time . . . or for having too many limits on screen time. For deciding to medicate . . . or deciding not to medicate. For staying home with kids . . . or not staying home with kids. For being unable to control restless kids in a restaurant . . . or for giving an iPad to restless kids in a restaurant. Women are shamed harder on most of these things—shame that starts during pregnancy (try ordering a latte, "yes, with caffeine, thank you very much," when your baby bump is quite apparent)—but men do not escape it. My husband faces his share of attempted parent shame, too, often in the areas of discipline (too much or not enough) or his decision to quit his job and stay home with the kids (Have you ever listened to the way men talk about providing for their families?).

A few years ago, I wrote a *New York Times* piece about how Maxx loved to jump on the trampoline, how it was something we had connected around, and how we did flips together (he has since taken trampolining to an extreme place, but at the time, it was still new). Some commenters tried to shame me for letting my kid do something so dangerous. The physicality of it frightened them, and I was cautioned to be more aware of safety. Several months later, I wrote another piece—in the very same parenting section of the *Times*—about navigating Instagram with Maxx (who was then nine years old). I was positively eviscerated in the comments for letting my kid become a zombie in front of the screen. People called me a child abuser and told me I was setting him up for a lifetime of addiction. They told me I was a horrible parent (more than one comment used those exact words) and pleaded with me—pleaded with me!—to "force" my kid to go outside and get fresh air. You know, to do something like jump on a trampoline. KJ Dell'Antonia, author of *How to Be a Happier Parent: Raising a Family, Having a Life and Loving (Almost) Every Minute*, and former editor of the popular parenting column Motherlode at *The New York Times*, had the job of moderating the comments on that column for years (she and I never worked on a piece together at the *Times*). "What I learned was that the most negative commenters—the shamers—they were the ones who were ashamed. I read them over and over again for years, the same people, saying much the same things," Dell'Antonia tells me when I ask her what it was like to have to walk through that muck every week. "I guarantee one frequent commenter had worries about her own weight, because any time weight came up, there she was, shaming writers and kids and choices. Other commenters needed support for their choices around breastfeeding, or discipline, and they expressed that need by shaming the writer's different call and hoping, I think, that their own vehemence would convince themselves."

Modern parenting often feels like a shame show of such epic proportions that you cannot fucking win. You. Can. Not. Kim Brooks makes this point in her book, *Small Animals: Parenthood in the Age of Fear*. She focuses heavily on mother shaming and the horrifying phenomenon of people calling the police on parents (nearly always mothers) for daring to take their eyes off their children for a moment. Brooks was charged with child endangerment when someone called the police on her for allowing her four-year-old to stay alone in a locked car with a car alarm set (with perfect temperature conditions) playing on an iPad while she went into Target for approximately seven minutes—several of those minutes where she could see the car. She had to hire a lawyer, and appear in court. Ultimately, she wound up with community service, but other mothers have faced worse consequences (particularly women of color), like having their child taken to foster care for a few weeks while social services "investigated" such crimes as letting a nine-year-old walk to the neighborhood park alone, where several dozen of her friends were playing. This fearmongering around child safety makes me incredibly angry, but that's not exactly the point here. The point is that casting shame on each other—because parent-on-parent shame is the most unrelenting kind of shame—impedes our ability to have honest and fruitful discussions about things. We are always either on offense or defense, whether our strategy is to throw the first punch to let people know we're not messing around, or to use self-deprecating humor or sarcasm, or to fight back with scathing personal attacks that imbue as much "otherness" on fellow parents as possible, so that we can see them as almost belonging to a separate species, like "oh, the vegans," or "those parents who are lazy and just don't want to parent." Offense and defense are about scoring points for yourself, as you prevent the other team from scoring points. It works really well in sports, but not so well in parenting, where the entire point system seems to me to be based on shame. We're volleying and kicking and blocking and tackling so much that we often can't figure out how to utter an honest word. Our constant fear of being attacked, coupled with our need to attack, makes it very hard to open up and have real discussions.

I can't believe this is the only way.

LET'S BREAK IT DOWN into two interrelated buckets: experiencing shame because of others' comments/glances/rolled eyes, and attempting to shame other parents via our own comments/glances/rolled eyes. "I feel like other people can't necessarily shame you," Dell'Antonia says. While someone else's comment to us can certainly make us feel anger, it usually only makes us feel shame if we are already doubting ourselves. "What I learned at the *Times* as a regular target myself was that after a while, if a comment bothered me (other than just for being offensive), it tended to be a sign that I myself was worried about what I was doing. I needed to do a little work there, either to feel confident about my choices or change them—because if I cared what an anonymous commenter thought, I was in big trouble," she says. The first part then, is being honest with yourself about your own insecurities, because that is where the shame will poke through.

Which brings me around to the second bucket: our need to shame others. As Dell'Antonia points out, our need to disparage, cast judgment, and endlessly express our opinion in public ways mostly comes from our own shame and insecurity. I'm not sure which one needs to come first: stopping the flow of shame inward or cutting off the flow of shame outward. I do know that they are interrelated. When you let go of your own need to shame, others' shame starts to lose its power. The shame doesn't disappear, but it doesn't gut you quite as deeply. It takes practice to go to another place besides shame. This is what I continue to work on, noticing why I go to shame and judgment of others (especially other parents). When I see a type A mom that overschedules the hell out of their kid and talks about ensuring they get into a good college, I want to bring out the shame and lord my superiority as a free range mom who doesn't believe in overscheduling or putting so much pressure on kids. But . . . why? What does this accomplish? What does it serve to get into a battle on social media about this? Why do I want another parent to feel like they are screwing up? Why do I care at all? I only care because of my own insecurity and my own need to reinforce my decisions. There is a lot more adrenaline in firing off a nasty comment or casting a disapproving glance. It feels way more powerful in the moment. To let go of the need to shame is to let go of a feeling of power. But it was never real power anyway, just a mirage.

Is there any hope for the masses of parents to stop all this business and just be more honest? Dell'Antonia doesn't have the perfect answer any more than I do (and I feel like if someone had it, it would be her!), but she has a thought. "Maybe we need to take our self-honesty more public," she says. This reminds me of one of my favorite examples of public self-honesty regarding a parent working through her shame. From the stage of *The Moth*—a live storytelling show—comedian Bethany Van Delft tells the story of having her daughter, Lulu, who has Down syndrome. Van Delft talks about how she went from feeling a joyous rush of love to the most profound despair in the moments after Lulu was born and she realized she had Down syndrome. For months, Van Delft swung between depression and navigating the world, robot-like, just trying to do everything she could to care for Lulu and involve her in early interventions. She felt anger, sadness, embarrassment, confusion, guilt—and shame. So much shame. Shame that she wanted a baby after the age of forty. Shame that she felt like she had misled all the people who gave her cute baby clothes because they thought everything was "normal." Shame that she felt the way she felt about Lulu having Down syndrome. For months, Van Delft told no one these feelings. Speaking them aloud was too terrifying—what would people think of her? To admit her disappointment and sense of failure that the child she had was not the child she expected? Too risky. Most of her friends ghosted her, but she finally opened up to one friend, who didn't judge her or try to talk her out of her feelings. She just listened. Van Delft said that speaking the truth of everything she was feeling, "lifted a weight off my soul." After that, she began to be able to see Lulu through fresh eyes, as a happy little girl who loved to laugh and make other people laugh. She also began to see that all parents tend to worry that they aren't suited to raise the children they have, for a variety of different reasons, and that she had far more of a kinship with other parents than she ever realized.

I love Van Delft's bravery in sharing the story, and speaking from an honest place about her disappointment and fear in having a child who would have different needs than typically developing children. Parents of children with special needs not only have to navigate a more complicated world, there also isn't much space for them to speak honestly about their sorrows and fears—without feeling shame. There isn't a lot of space for parents in general to speak honestly about their children. We're allowed to talk about some of our fears and worries, that is, the acceptable ones—like will our kid make friends and will they excel in school? But the deep, shameful stuff—like when we feel disappointment in them, dislike of them, regret over having them, and anger that we are in the situation we are in—is much harder to share.

What if we did share it, though? What if we all thought about what shameful but heartfelt parenting story we could tell from *The Moth* stage—not because we're actually going to perform, but because sharing it with someone, maybe just one person, could lighten our burden? What would your honest story be? What would happen if you shared it now, either in a public way (like on social media) or in a private way, with someone you sensed might need to hear it? What would happen if you stepped off the parent shame train, confronted your deepest fears and insecurities around parenting, and spoke honestly about them? Let me tell you one of my big insecurities right now: ruining my kids' brains by letting them watch YouTube and use screens so much, especially my son (who is now almost eleven and uses Instagram daily). Through it, he is able to connect with his fellow extreme athletes who do elite trampoline tricks like him. It's a wonderful tool for meeting athletes all over the world who share his passion for this niche sport, which is the reason I agreed to let him use it. He also sees highly sexualized women wearing thong bikinis. He hears the word *cunt* and listens to misogynist lyrics, without understanding what he's even hearing. He gets direct messages from shady people and winds up getting added into chat groups of boys discussing highly inappropriate things. He sees troubling images of sex and violence. He sees people using racial slurs. I monitor and delete and block—he does, too—and I keep the lines of communication open, but I often wonder if all those *Times* commenters were right and I made a colossal mistake in opening this door so early. It scares me and I second-guess myself every day—which is why the shame found me to begin with. My husband and I weren't completely united on the decision, but my husband went along with it. When he gives me the "I told you so" look when Maxx tells us about something disturbing he saw, I feel deep, deep shame that I have screwed up and the damage will never be repaired. On one hand, I feel like I'm doing something right that he is telling me. But on the other, I'm certain that I'm doing something very wrong that he has disturbing things to tell in the first place.

We are all scared about something, all worried about our colossal mistakes, all desperate to defend them in the same breath we're shamed by them. I'm not saying we all face the same challenges or have the same fears. After all, it's naïve of me—from my comfortable suburban bubble—to think I have any idea of the challenges faced by a single mother in a neighborhood riddled with drugs, who is only trying to keep her kid focused on school and staying out of trouble. Or immigrant parents, who are desperately seeking asylum to keep their kids safe. What an idiot I am if I think we are all in this boat together, with economic disparity and racial injustice as it is. It's not about unity (though of course the idealist in me longs for it). It's about your personal choice—the only thing you control—to opt for honesty over shame. That's all you've got. A series of moments when you can share an honest truth or dole out a dose of shame.

Which will it be?

Reviewing the Honesty Principles

You don't need to pit honesty and otherworldly belief against each other.

- Otherworldly belief gives children stories bigger than themselves to help make sense of the world and understand the power of imagination. (*Are your children asking you the truth about otherworldly belief because they logically want to know, or because they want you to join them in belief?*)

- "Facts," "evidence," and "truth," don't need to fit neatly into otherworldly belief—but be honest about which is which when your kid asks. (*"I don't know any of these things to be facts, but I like to believe them anyway."*)

CHAPTER 9

Self-Honesty and the Stories We Tell

*Nothing ever goes away until it has taught us
what we need to know.*
—Pema Chödrön

Before Jeannette Walls, author of *The Glass Castle*, was a best-selling memoirist whose story was made into a Hollywood movie starring Brie Larson and Woody Harrelson, she was a poor West Virginia girl whose family led an unconventional and nomadic lifestyle. She grew up hungry, without plumbing or decent education, and without many of her basic needs met. Her parents were unstable and had periods of extreme neglect of their children, which was only fueled by her father's alcoholism. At seventeen, she fled West Virginia and moved to New York City to be with her sister, Lori, who had already escaped the dysfunction of their home (they then sent for their brother, Brian, and later for the youngest, Maureen). There, in New York, she finished high school and put herself through Barnard College.

Walls aspired to do what she had always labeled "serious journalism," but an editor at *New York Magazine* told her that her "serious" pieces were boring, and put her on the movers and shakers beat. At first, the stories seemed frivolous. But as she covered the beat more and more—working her way up at *New York Magazine*—she began to appreciate the hunt for "truth" among celebrities who were trying to hide their squabbles and shove things under the rug. She found herself enjoying the challenge of covering that world, and threats of getting sued stoked her "inner yard dog" who was always gearing up for a fight. All in all, things were going pretty great in her life. She had a covetable job. She was married to a successful businessman. She had a Park Avenue address. On paper, she had made it. And then . . . she started thinking about what truth really meant. "The longer I covered the celebrity beat, the more I realized the truth couldn't be condensed into a snarky little paragraph," Walls says. Not only that, she worried daily that she was going to be "found out" for who she really was—a poor West Virginia girl pretending to be someone else in the big city. The story of her upbringing, and the shame attached to it, gnawed at her with each passing year. Plus, her parents had followed her to New York City and were squatting in an abandoned building. It was only a matter of time before someone connected her with them. She even saw her mother digging through garbage one day. She still loved her parents, even as she saw their faults. Say what you would about their parenting style, she recognized that they were still living life on their own terms.

Was she?

That's the question that haunted her. Who was she, and why was she so afraid to talk about where she came from? "I knew that journalists had to be anonymous. Once I revealed my past, I knew I was exposing myself. I was saying, 'This is who I am,'" Walls tells me. While she was fearful about sharing her background, the exhaustion of hiding from her past was wearing her down. "A friend told me that secrets are like vampires. They suck life out of you. Once exposed to light, there's a moment of terror, but then they lose their power," Walls says. Her second husband—she and her first husband had divorced by this time—encouraged her to tell the story of her upbringing, and at the age of forty, she began to write. In fact, she wrote a draft in six weeks. That first draft was very different from the book (and movie) *The Glass Castle* as we know it today. That early version included far more about Walls's years in New York City, and far less about her childhood. In fact, it took five years to peel away the layers of honesty. Walls was never intentionally misrepresenting situations and experiences, but she tended to gloss over the ugly truths of her childhood. Her husband, who had become a trusted editor, often came at her with questions. "He said, 'Okay, if your parents weren't buying food, how did you get by?' and I would say, 'I was resourceful.' He challenged me to really say it and spell it out," she says. Every time she had trouble writing a section, it was because she wasn't being honest (I experienced that same thing in writing this book, by the way). For Walls, the process was painful at times, but also wholly liberating. That said, she couldn't have written the memoir in a truthful way when she was in her twenties. She wasn't ready to write it until she was ready to confront the story she had always defined herself by, but had never actually owned. So often, we don't want to own experiences we think make us weak, she says, "but usually the best things we have going for us are the things we think make us weak." People now frequently come up to her in tears and tell her they grew up in similar circumstances, but they've never wanted to tell anyone. "It shocks me the number of people carrying around this fear of being discovered for what they considered to be a sordid past. What I hear in all of their stories isn't weakness, but triumph. They are all stories of triumph."

Not everyone has the desire (or ability) to write a memoir delving into their personal history and uncomfortable childhood secrets. Also, I want to be clear that just because someone wants to keep their story private, it doesn't necessarily mean that they are ashamed, or think of themselves as weak. You can own your story for yourself, without having a need to tell that story in a public way. Of course, for Jeannette Walls, owning her story did ultimately lead to writing a memoir. But her finished book was merely the output. The real work of owning her story began with reflecting and thinking about what she had always told herself about her upbringing, and what she had decided it meant. That's what this final chapter on self-honesty is about: the process of reflecting on and deciding what your stories mean. And by stories, I mean both the stories we tell *to* ourselves and the stories we tell *about* ourselves.

Every day, we shape narratives about our experiences, and share them with others in conversations, emails, text messages, speeches, toasts, and increasingly on social media—through posts, Tweets, videos, Instagram "stories" (my new favorite), chats, reviews, and other forums yet to be known that will likely be invented in the time it takes to print this book. We are inundated with chances to tell our story, whether it's speaking out about something that happened to us to show solidarity (such as with #metoo), recounting an experience with a friend, talking about our childhood with our significant other, or using a personal story to illustrate a point in a professional context (such as public speaking or blogging). These narrative instances may be small, but that doesn't mean they don't have consequence. In fact, looking at our stories the way a memoirist might can give us a window into a space we don't investigate that often—the space between what we tell others about ourselves and the internal experience of what it's like to live our life. There is who you *say* you are to others and who you *feel* you are inside your own head and heart. As in, you *say* you love being a parent, but you wake with dread so many mornings when you know the day has to start all over again. You *say* you are not a racist or sexist and believe in the equality of all people, but you know that you benefit from systems you're not doing anything to change. You *say* you've worked hard for every opportunity in your life, but you shove down the feelings of failure you had after getting bailed out by others multiple times. And on and on. It's the stuff that's both little and big, the stuff of a month or a year, a decade or a life.

The space between what you tell the world and your inner life can wind up growing deeper and deeper, until it is a vast cavern that goes so deep you've lost track what's even in there. I think this has always been true, but what's different now is that we have so many more platforms for connecting with others and talking about ourselves. When we are encouraged every day to share our story on social media, it's easy for that cavern of public stories that don't match our personal reality to make us more and more miserable, and to make us feel like we are living increasingly dishonest lives. Internal voices tug at each other— "You're the liar . . . no, you're the liar!" and we wonder what the truth even is. How do you begin to excavate this cavern, and clear a few tons of crap away? How do you tell more honest stories about yourself, whether you're looking to actually publish an essay, have a vulnerable moment with a friend, or just stop lying on Facebook?

In the words of Steven Pressfield, author of *Do the Work*—one of my favorite books on getting hard shit done—you have to, well, "do the work." That is, *do the work* on yourself. That's what self-honesty is. It necessitates that you stop looking around at everyone else and jumping on shame and indignation bandwagons, and instead, do the work to understand what you're so afraid of, why you're hiding, and the ways in which you're lying to yourself.

The Hard Work of Self-Honesty

Essayist Amy Paturel teaches an intense personal essay writing class, and has worked with more than five hundred writers (including me) who are honing their craft. Her students have gone on to publish in outlets like *The New York Times*, *The Washington Post*, and *Good Housekeeping*. The first assignment she gives writers in her class is to share ten things about themselves that others don't know. The list can be silly or serious—and usually people approach it as a combination of both. "Nine out of ten times, people list things that they're embarrassed about, ashamed of, or that make them feel guilty, and that's why they haven't told anyone before," Paturel tells me. She encourages her students to explore those things on the list they had been avoiding telling other people as potential essay topics—not because they necessarily need to share the exact thing on the list, but because thinking about why they haven't told anyone can get them closer to understanding what they are ashamed of and why. As Paturel has discovered—both as an accomplished essayist herself and a coach for others who want to tackle the genre—uncovering shame, embarrassment, or humiliation is usually the first step in being able to write honestly about a topic. For her own part, Paturel has written about her attempt to help her son ditch his thumb-sucking habit and how it left battle scars for both of them. She has explored why she was once drawn to men who needed saving and also why sex for her (at least pre-marriage) has been complicated. She has coached students through writing about issues ranging from the shame of marrying a sex addict to the shame a mother felt when, in a fit of rage, she ripped her daughter's favorite plush toy to shreds.

In the chapter on social honesty, we learned that shame serves an evolutionary purpose. It's part of the mechanism that helped humans be good cooperators—a fail-safe to keep the system in check if other mechanisms don't work. I find it helpful to remember that shame is integral to my species, especially before I really start poking around in my shame. Because you do have to poke around it. Specifically, you need to know your basic shame triggers. I don't mean the output of the shame, or the specific experiences you're ashamed of; that is, I'm ashamed that I lied on my time sheet when I taught gymnastics at the YMCA in 1987. I mean the trigger that underlies the shame, at the very base. The first work to do in self-honesty is to dig and dig *and dig* until you find the bottom of your shame triggers, or the common denominators that underlie most of your experiences of shame. I don't know how many triggers most people have, but I have identified two main ones that I have. My first shame trigger is around being a good person. By good, I mean decent, moral, kind, and altruistic. I've built my life around thinking I'm a good person, but worried that I'm actually not. That I'm greedy, judgmental, narcissistic, uncaring, and only pretending to be a good person so others will take notice and say, "Wow, she really is such a decent human being." My second shame trigger is around the idea of overreaching and not knowing my place, of thinking I am smarter, more popular, or more important than I actually am. It's the fear that everyone is laughing, saying, "Who does she think she is?"

Here is the fascinating thing I've realized about our shame triggers: They work together with our biases, a push and pull trying to keep us from utter emotional collapse. As we learned early in the book, most of us lie to benefit ourselves in all kinds of subtle ways—but we still consider ourselves honest, because we can justify our actions. You might say we have a bias toward justifying. So when I use my husband's season pass to sneak one of my children's friends into the swim club where we belong, I can justify that I'm not really a bad person—the bad person I so fear I am!—because we've paid nearly $400 to belong to this pool and my husband isn't with us today to use his pass, so I'm just substituting someone. It's not really dishonest, because I'm a generally honest person. I'm using my bias to mitigate my shame.

Another fascinating bias we tend to have is related to self-deception. In her work, Yale University professor Zoe Chance has shown that even when people do well on a test because they were allowed to cheat, they still see themselves as responsible for their success. Chance and her research team had groups of people take a general knowledge test. One group took a practice test with the answer key at the bottom (the intentionally vague directions said participants could check their work, but the work should be their own). Unsurprisingly, that group scored higher than people without the answer key. Participants were then asked to predict how they would do on another similar test. The answer key group—who obviously had cheated—predicted they would do equally well again, even after seeing the second test didn't contain an answer key. Of course, they didn't do nearly as well as they predicted. Yet they still predicted they would do well on a third test (which they were also able to see didn't contain an answer key). And they underperformed their expectations again. It was only by the fourth test that they realized they probably weren't going to do so well without an answer key. Chance writes, "Self-deceivers come to terms with reality only when faced with repeated exposure to counterevidence against their preferred beliefs." In other words, it takes a while, because we really want to believe we're smart.

All psychology studies have a twist, though, don't they? In this one, for the third test, Chance gave some people the answer key again, allowing them to score very highly again. For the fourth test, even knowing it had no answer key, those people still predicted they were going to do well. They had learned nothing from the first two tests—get answer key, do well; don't have answer key, don't do well. They just fell right back into the pattern of self-delusion. Chance's study shows just how strong and illogical our self-serving biases can be. It's almost silly. In the same breath that I'm terrified of looking stupid, I actually believe that I'm smarter than most people. My shame keeps me afraid. My bias keeps me confident and operating in the world.

Shame and biases work together to create a script we share with the world when we talk about ourselves. We shape relevant narratives about ourselves in certain ways—ideally, to avoid shame. For example, with my emotional affair, the story I told myself was that it was mostly about what I wasn't getting from Allen in my marriage. Only bad people cheated, and I couldn't be a bad person. Even in the way I talked about it with girlfriends, I emphasized what was lacking in my marriage. That we shape stories to benefit ourselves is nothing new. But when the narrative becomes entrenched and you let it remain unexamined, year after year, that feeling of inconsistency—that space between what you truly *feel* and what you *say*—can start to take on the texture of a black hole: an all-encompassing mass where no light can escape. We're not trying to create black holes in our psyche. In fact, I think we only lie to ourselves about who we are to stay safe. Sometimes, literally safe. I'm reminded of Australian comedian Hannah Gadsby's story in her 2018 Netflix special, *Nanette*, which is funny, uncomfortable, heartbreaking, and triumphant. Gadsby talks about how she had to lie for so long about who she was because until fairly recently, being gay was a punishable crime in Australia. Attitudes were particularly hateful in her small town in Tasmania. Her life was on the line. Lying about who she was nearly killed her, emotionally speaking, but it also kept her safe, in a way, until she was in a place and space where she could live the truth of who she was, and then tell the world about her experience.

This is all to say that it's complicated, and timing really matters. There is no easy formula, like confront shame + live truth = happy ever after! But complicated doesn't mean we give up. It means we dig back in and figure it out.

IT'S FAR EASIER TO CRITICIZE OTHERS than to confront our own shameful self-truths. I'm not talking about the surface self-truths, like, admitting you have a problem with punctuality. I'm talking about the deepest, most confusing pieces of truth—the things you absolutely, positively do not want to be true about yourself. For example, as a white person, one self-truth I have been working to lay bare is my white fragility. Yes, I can vote for the candidates who espouse progressive values and denounce the people and organizations that say racist, misogynist, and xenophobic things. And yes, I can even admit that I grew up in a bubble of whiteness and wasn't always sure what was a racial stereotype, and that I participated in serious appropriation of Native American culture in high school, when I fell in love with the movie *Dances with Wolves*, and hung dream catchers, Henry Farny prints, and pieces of sage in my bedroom. But as Robin DiAngelo, author of *White Fragility*, has pointed out, nothing makes white people like me—the ones who think we are doing all the "right" things now—more nervous than talking about race. I know that as a middle-class white woman, I can disappear into society and pretend race doesn't matter—pretending that is mostly supported by all the systems I rely on. I can choose to talk about race in a book about honesty, or ignore it altogether, and chances are, very few white people would call me out for not acknowledging it. White privilege is inherently unfair, and I feel guilty when I benefit from something unfair. But do I really? Or do I just say I feel guilty because it makes me feel good, but doesn't actually require me to do anything? I tell myself that I should probably just not talk about it—which only fuels my white fragility even more. I focus on the select aspects of my life that I can use as proof that I'm a "good" white person. Like the fact that I'm educated about the history and reality of racism, wrote a master's thesis about white feminism and female slave narratives, and consistently read a lot of books by people of color. Or that I have family members—spouses of siblings, nieces, nephews, and cousins—who are black, Asian, Indian, and Latino, who have been welcomed into the family and are deeply loved. In fact, with the next generation, the extended Ketteler family has become more diverse than seemed possible, considering we grew up in a neighborhood where black lawn jockeys were still acceptable. I want so badly for these progressive aspects of my life to "make up" for something, to counteract the fact that I spend the majority of my time in white spaces, oblivious to racism. Though I grew up this way in my Northern Kentucky suburb, for a long time, I told myself that I had moved away from this. And maybe I was moving away from it for a time. I think back to graduate school and my first job, where I had a large group of friends who were people of color. They introduced me to new restaurants and types of food, to cultural celebrations I wasn't familiar with, and to a variety of experiences in general. My life felt multi-textured. And then my family started becoming more diverse and Barack Obama got elected, and I thought, "Look how far we have come!"

But here we are now, and the bloodshed of people of color has not stopped. It feels like we've moved backward on racial equality, and I want to blame everyone else except me. The painful self-truth is that my naivety and my choices have made me part of the problem, too. For example, one of my favorite things to say about where I live is, "I love the neighborhood, but I wish it had more diversity." I *do* wish it had more diversity, but the fact remains that I chose this neighborhood—this place of mostly white people. I chose it for the good schools, the affordability, the walkability and proximity to amenities, the tree-lined streets full of small-but-charming 1940s Cape Cods, and the feeling that it would be a safe and happy place to raise a family. With its working-class undertones, I could see that there was some economic diversity, and I *hoped* there was racial and cultural diversity. But I didn't really ask questions, and I didn't *truly* factor whether or not it was racially or ethnically diverse into my decision. Though I recognized the limitations of how I grew up, I still went ahead and chose it again to raise my kids. I chose what was familiar. No matter my rhetoric on racial healing, I am a willing participant in this system I claim to want to dismantle. I chose it. It's not the end of the story, of course, and I continue to work in my own life to be accountable and to be an ally for racial justice, which means learning when to speak up and act, and when to shut up and listen. It's my job and no one else's to do this work and educate myself and my kids. But the first step in doing better is to stop justifying and getting defensive and just admit where I am and how I got here. People in general don't want to tackle the self-truths that paint them in a bad light, and cast them as a contributor to a problem they don't want to take responsibility for. We just don't want to do it, because it risks negating narratives we are very attached to, like "live and let live" or the notion of being self-made.

There is a whole category of self-honesty related to examining your role in a situation you don't like, yet still benefit from. White privilege is a sweeping example of this on the institutional level, but there are many other smaller, more personal examples anyone can find once they start paying attention. I'm referring to those situations you complain about or express frustration at, yet do very little to change—usually because you aren't being honest with yourself that you're complicit in creating the situation. These situations are so common—such as in marriage, at work, in consumer choices, in the division of labor at home, on social media, or inside a friendship or familial relationship—yet we so often don't see them. The boss who doesn't respect you, the spouse who travels for work too much, the sibling who won't do their share, the corporation you are certain is at the root of everything wrong with America. We tell ourselves so many fictitious narratives about our involvement in situations. You can ferret out these situations in two ways. One is to make a list of your deepest frustrations, most embarrassing shortcomings, or the things that most piss you off. The other is to make a list of your greatest accomplishments, most deeply held beliefs, and parts of your life you're most proud of. Basically, look any place you have created a powerful self-narrative that a lot rides on you continuing to believe, and then ask yourself what the consequences of not believing it would be. In fact, when you challenge yourself to *honestly* examine a personal narrative about your life that you have always thought was true, it can have a domino effect. And that's the real opportunity for this work. It might break you first, though.

Let me tell you one final story about how that happened for me.

Rage, and Then Listening

I've mentioned my brother Paul a few times, and that he passed away in 2009. In the first chapter, I told the story of how my siblings and I grew closer after he died, and how his death opened up regret in me that I didn't know him better. The truth is, it opened up more than that. Regret was the tip, but underneath were deep questions about my identity and the kind of person I was. I didn't know that at first, though.

Paul was a lot older than me (fourteen years), and I learned as much about him through others' stories as I did through my own experience. I imagine this is common in families where one sibling is quite a bit younger, and the older sibling isn't around for much of their childhood. I mentioned early on in the book that I have the role of family storyteller. I love this role. But when it came to Paul, I was a bit of a lazy journalist for a long time. Instead of personally investigating things, I relied on previously "published" information. The thing about Paul is that all of the previously published information said essentially the same thing: He was a screwup.

Let's compare my life and Paul's life, side by side.

I was a goody-goody who didn't get into trouble, generally did what I was told, and just quietly rebelled in my head. I maintained a 3.96 GPA in college, and I got multiple degrees. There was no danger of getting pregnant, because I didn't have sex until I was twenty-two. I got married a little later in life after I was more established, and I continued to raise kids and have a successful career. I borrowed money from my parents exactly twice in my adult life (both times when I was in graduate school and couldn't make the rent). I've never been arrested, gotten in serious trouble, smoked a cigarette, or done illegal drugs (yes, really, not even pot). If my parents had any fights about me—my education, my attitude, my friends, or my general life choices—I don't know about them. I was a good kid. I was easy and agreeable.

By contrast, Paul was difficult from the time he was born. He started fights and was mean to his siblings. He stole their things and harassed them. He called my sisters fat and provoked my oldest brother, Herb (who is one of the most non-confrontational people on the planet), into more than one fistfight. He made terrible choices in who he trusted. He drove drunk and got arrested. He was caught with stolen drugs and got arrested. He refused to do any work in tenth grade and dropped out of high school. He was an alcoholic. He had a pain pill addiction, on and off. He worked as a roofer, which beat up his body. But he refused to do any other job, and would simply say, "I'm a roofer," whenever anyone tried to help him think about other options. He was stubborn beyond belief and everything had to be on his terms. He only came around for family gatherings when he wanted. He might show up, he might not. He constantly borrowed money from our parents (I'm talking thousands of dollars over a few decades) and had trouble holding a steady job (because of the seasonal nature of roofing). He fought and screamed his way through one marriage and was in the middle of doing the same thing with a second marriage when he died. He had a son, Tony, who he loved, but was never a role model for.

I could go on.

The story I told myself constantly was that I was such a better kid than Paul. A better sibling than Paul. A more responsible adult than Paul. Definitely a better parent than Paul. Why couldn't he get his life together? What was wrong with him? It was judgment on top of judgment, and at the bottom of it, there was superior me.

Then he went and died when he was forty-nine and I was thirty-five.

I did a strange thing after he died and the initial shock wore off: I started talking to him—usually while running, but also while driving or sitting alone in my office. I was polite at first, because you are supposed to be polite when someone dies, and speak in a hushed, reverent way. But gradually, I got meaner and angrier. "I can't believe you died," turned into "You were a self-centered asshole." Once I unleashed angry Judi, I was done being reverent. "Do you know how awful you made things for Mom and Dad? Do you know how Mom would worry? What the fuck was the matter with you?" I attacked him in my head, a one-sided conversation that I carried on as I ran up and down the hills of my neighborhood. Alone in the car, I had freedom to actually yell at him—scream if I wanted. One particular time, I was driving home from the local Veterans Administration hospital. I had gone there to meet with a VA case manager about veterans' benefits for my dad. He wasn't yet in long-term care, but we knew he needed to be because his daily needs had greatly increased. We didn't know how we were going to convince my mom. She was taking care of him and it was killing her slowly, so we were trying any tactic we could think of—hence, I was seeing if the VA could help at all. I left the VA, got in my car, and fell into a rage. I sobbed as I drove, suddenly knowing exactly whose fault this was: Paul's. I let him have it, sobbing and screaming in my car as I headed north on Interstate 71, "You fucking asshole! You never did anything for them when you were alive. Can you just do something now? Anything?! This is killing Mom! She can't take care of him anymore, but she'll never admit it. She'll never willingly give up. Do you have *any use* whatsoever?"

A few days later, my dad got pneumonia. It was the blessing that led him to be hospitalized, and then move into long-term care—first for rehab, but then to live—so that my mother finally got some respite and my dad got the care he needed.

I seemed to have my dead brother's attention at last.

Since he did me a favor, I figured I owed it to him to listen. And that's when we really began to talk. I didn't expect much of these talks, until one day, I sat down and wrote a short story called "Forty-Five Hundred Dollars" in the voice of Paul. It was about the $4,500 settlement he got at age nineteen from his employer when their poor safety practices led him to fall off a billboard catwalk. Those injuries he sustained set him up for a lifetime of pain pill problems. It probably wasn't a very good story, but it was the first time I even considered that he *had* a story. The first draft came to me quickly, as if Paul was writing it for me. I actually heard his voice in my head (this isn't strange—whenever I am writing a speech for someone, I hear them talking in my head). At first, I was just a transcriber, writing down what I heard, without thinking that much about it. It took several months of leaving it alone and coming back again before I read the story the way a reader might, and really tried to understand this Paul character as a person. I held that Paul up against the Paul of my established scripts. I cracked open mental file folders with headings like "screwup brother" and "the one unlike all the rest," looking with fresh eyes at all my ideas about who I thought he was and how I had measured myself against him. As deep and wide as I looked, all I could see were my judgments of him. My stories that cast him as the family screwup and me as the golden child. I saw for the first time that I had been relying on very selective facts to shape my narrative, muting the facts that didn't help make my case and accentuating the ones that did. Now, in my willingness to look again at the facts, I saw that our temperaments—which had always seemed so opposite—were in fact somewhat similar. Didn't I also want to do everything on my own terms? Wasn't I stubborn, too? Whenever I would hit a tough point in my career and someone would suggest to me something else I might try, I would always respond, "I'm a writer. That's what I am." Why was that any different from Paul's insistence he was a roofer? And while I didn't do drugs or drink excessively, I exercised obsessively and had battled a low-level eating disorder and a bad case of perfectionism. When I really thought about it, I saw that we shared several personality traits; my versions of the traits were simply shaped a hair differently, for reasons partly due to luck and timing. As the youngest, coming of age long after the most tumultuous times in the Ketteler family, I had the undivided attention of my parents, who had far more resources by the time I came along. Plus, I had my three sisters to generally adore me and encourage me in anything I did. But for the slightest variation in genetics and order of birth, everything could have been different. Not to mention the fact that Paul most certainly had undiagnosed ADHD and probably also oppositional defiant disorder—which no one knew anything about. It was a different culture of parenting, and our knowledge base about interventions was slim. There were no 504 plans or IEPs in the school system, and no parenting blogs or podcasts. Not to mention the small-mindedness of the Catholic Church always playing in the background. For example, when my mother sought counseling from a priest after her doctor told her not to have any more children after I was born, the priest's only response was, "The Lord will provide." That was the totality of the support. There was very little evidence-based advice, no matter where they turned, whether it was concerning birth control or an out-of-control child. By contrast, I thought about how much support my husband and I had for Maxx's ADHD—the eight-week class we were able to afford to attend at Cincinnati Children's Hospital (one of the best children's hospitals in the country); the books, blogs, and webinars out there; the great relationship with a recently trained pediatrician who was well educated about helping parents get their kids' ADHD under control. The 1970s, in a family of nine that was barely making it financially, in a community where there were few resources for behavioral issues, was not the time and place to have a child with special needs.

Over the course of the next few years, particularly after my father passed away in 2013, I used my conversations with Paul to build my source material. It was during this time that I wrote a middle-grade novel, based very loosely on my upbringing and family, and cast Paul as a character in the story. I wanted to understand his demons, and to create scenes where I could explore those demons. The character wound up not exactly being Paul (I think this is typical when you write a novel based on your own upbringing—you slowly move further away from your own experience and fully embrace the wonderfulness of fiction), but the exercise of reimagining his story in a fictional way helped me rethink my own.

Basically, I had to hear Paul tell me his story, and then I had to change my own. It took him dying for me to be able to do that. I'd like to think I would have done this same thing had he lived, but I doubt I would have, unless I had started my exploration into honesty while he was still alive. God, I wish I had. But I didn't, because things happen in chains, causes and effects, catalysts and catastrophes. There is no time travel, no physical way to make your molecules reappear at the crucial moment in the past, to tell yourself that you've got it all so fucking wrong. There is only today to examine your narrative, open up the mental file folders, and see the fast and loose game you've been playing with facts.

Before you tell a story to the world about who you are, you first tell a story to yourself about who you are. These identity narratives are often based on your judgments of everyone else around you, and fueled by deep shame and hidden biases. Discerning the content of the story you're telling yourself is tricky business. It's so carefully constructed that if you remove a few blocks, you've got a Jenga tower about to topple. I had to let mine topple, so that I could build it back up with more accurate information. Once I started to be honest about one of my entrenched identity narratives, there was space for so much more: seeing the potential for abundance in my marriage, seeing my relationship with my children differently, understanding more clearly who I was in my career and what transparency looked like there, being more vulnerable with friends and family, taking more responsibility for inequities in society instead of just blaming others, and not getting caught up in hating and judging every single person who voted for Donald Trump.

It's not that my conversations with my dead brother are single-handedly responsible for all of those things, though I do like the visual of him standing there with a cigarette in his mouth, long hair in a ponytail, bandanna around his forehead, saying, "Yep, I pretty much fixed your fucking life, little sis. Happy now?" What these conversations with my brother did is help me see that I had something so fundamentally *wrong*. Or perhaps *incomplete* is the better word. I wasn't seeing that my family was, in fact, several different families at different times, and that the version I grew up in was particular and distinct from the one he grew up in. This mattered, because my sense of where I came from has always been the main ingredient of my identity. I'm a Ketteler. There is a reason that I didn't change my name when I got married, and feminism was only part of that reason. "Ketteler" was shorthand for a long list of values and experiences, and I thought I was certain what it meant. Though I always think of myself as operating at the personal level of identity, in this way, I was operating at the collective level of identity, defining myself in relation to "Ketteler-ness." Researcher Keith

Leavitt talks about how we often double down on an identity when we feel it's threatened, making us more likely to lie to protect it. I was doubling down, but the lie I told was to myself. The moment of realizing this—more a slow reckoning than a distinct flash—was the moment I understood that if I was lying to myself about something so basic, yet so big, I was likely lying to myself about a lot of things and keeping it all in check with the confirmation bias.

Cracking open the mother of all self-lies is what self-honesty work is really about. This work doesn't need to come only on the heels of death, divorce, or drama. It can be fierce in its un-remarkableness. You can discuss it with others, or savor the quietness of it. You can write it, sing it, meditate it, dance it, paint it, hike it, photograph it, carve it, spreadsheet it, or use whatever means helps you make sense of your most complicated shit. I can't actually tell you how to go about this work. I can only say that the work of self-honesty, of confronting the shame and bias, of examining the unexamined narratives you tell yourself on a daily basis—this is where living a more honest life begins and ends. It isn't particularly fun. Don't expect anyone to reward you for it, either, or commend you for your bravery. Tracing your honesty story, including the most shameful lies you've told yourself and others, the cognitive dissonance you walked through and continue to steep yourself in, and the patterns of how you lie and misrepresent is a little bit awful. But you won't see the patterns emerge until you force yourself to look at them. I didn't see my own until I started writing this book. I didn't see how the twin forces of hating others' lies while telling my own shaped so much of my childhood. I didn't see how much cognitive dissonance I internalized during my teen years and early twenties—and how I shoved the cognitive dissonance down long enough to have a truer version of myself emerge in my thirties, only to get stuck right back in the dissonance in my forties, as I embraced vulnerability while simultaneously hiding. I didn't see how flawed my story of where I came from was. *I did not see these things.* And it is so hard to really embrace honesty when you don't see the things you need to see. It is far easier to keep posting on social media the version of your life you want to be true or to attack others. Putting a filter on an Instagram photo or filling posts with emotionally charged comments is way more fun than thinking about shame and bias. But it's hollow and sad, too.

So where does it leave us? I think it leaves us a few millimeters away from where we started, but in honesty work, a few millimeters is sometimes all you need. It's about taking a beat, a breath, a moment to be aware. *First, be aware.* You're getting ready to post a family picture from vacation on Facebook, when you know full well that you had a nasty fight with your husband five minutes after the picture was taken? Be aware. You're sidestepping with your mother-in-law because she pushes your buttons? Be aware. Your kid asks what sexual assault is? Be aware. You tell the same two-sentence narrative about your screwup brother? Be aware. You pay no attention to race because "you don't see color" and insist you're not a racist? Be aware. You're wondering if a secret is yours to tell? Be aware. You're talking to the neighbor and little eyes are watching you? Be aware. You have a chance to offer feedback, but you're worried it might hurt the person? Be aware. You assume that you're protecting your kids by not telling them something? Be aware. All of it, all of it, all of it. *Be aware.* You will not be perfect. You will probably sputter and stammer and say the wrong thing before you say the right thing. You will second-guess yourself. You might offend someone, or have to stand in the space of someone's disappointment or hurt. You will most definitely wrestle with dilemmas. You may be called out. But at least you can pay attention. And until you do that, I suggest you stop pointing out all the liars and the cheats in the world.

If the first principle of the book, *First, be aware*, is the most important, the last principle is the most hopeful. Your bonus eleventh principle: *Today is a new day.*

Yesterday matters. But today is where you are. So start here.

WE HAD A GLORIOUS AUTUMN IN 2018. Because I found myself traveling so much that October, I chased autumn around the country. The first weekend in October, I took Maxx with me to Los Angeles, for a story I was writing for *Los Angeles Magazine* about a trampoline event in Venice. Maxx got to do flips on trampolines set up on Venice Beach and I got to enjoy the awesomeness of being in Southern California in October. There was no fall color, but there was the colorfulness of life, and the whole trip turned out to be a fun adventure for my son and me. The next week, I enjoyed the early fall color across the lower Midwest, as I drove from my home in Cincinnati to a writers' colony in Northwest Arkansas. While there for ten days, I watched the gold splendor slowly spread over the Ozark Mountains, a little more each day. I drove back home during the peak week for that part of the country, the usually boring byways of Interstate 70 transformed to ruby red joy. Two days later, I took Georgia with me to Charlotte, North Carolina, to attend my friend Jodi's wedding. There, I got to see the South's version of autumn, deeper and more burnt sienna than the bright gold of the Ozarks. I returned home just in time to catch the edge of our peak week here in Southwest Ohio. My neighborhood was positively on fire, the ordinariness of suburban streets taking my breath away for seven days straight.

And then . . . it was over, and the cold and dreariness came fast. Mid-November descended, and it wasn't messing around. I sat in my window-filled home office one morning and stared at the last little bits of orange. There was a lot in my head besides the waning of my favorite season. We had just commemorated the one-hundred-year anniversary of the end of the fighting in World War I, and our country was flirting hard with the kind of nationalism that had caused that and so many other wars. I pulled out the copy of my dad's Army discharge papers, searching them for some clue, because he always seemed to know what to say about history and complicated things. But it was the same notes and abbreviations as always, detailing facts about his service. The anniversary of Paul's death—November 17—was a few days away. I wasn't overly sentimental about dates, but that one always got me, mostly for the memory of its unexpectedness. Also, I had been struggling with Maxx, because I was always struggling with Maxx. He was such a fantastic and fun kid, and also such a difficult kid to be around. His unchecked energy and smart mouth was so much for me. There were many times where I could not even be in a room with him, and I felt frustrated and guilty about this.

And there was something else. The other man had met someone. In the year and a half since his divorce, he had dated here and there (which I had encouraged—even giving my opinion on which pictures he should post on various dating apps). He had shared a few amusing stories from his dating adventures, and while it was sometimes awkward to talk about, I didn't dwell. I just wanted him to move on and be happy. We were still friends, but it was vastly different from before and not charged with the same emotion. I'm sure it seems incomprehensible to some readers that I would still maintain a friendship with him, and that my husband wasn't threatened or freaked out by this. It baffles me sometimes, too, but all I can say is that the dynamic between Allen and me had shifted so much (and as I write this, it only continues to deepen and grow stronger). Allen and I were accountable to each other in a way we never had been before. I didn't want a life with the other man; I wanted the life I had (even on the shitty days), and I no longer felt the destructive weight of confusion. I felt clear and I didn't take that clarity for granted. I made sure I expressed it to Allen. But still, I found myself unsettled, because I had a feeling the woman the other man had met was going to be The One. I was truly happy for him, but also jealous—which really irritated me. I wanted to be done with all of that, because it felt like it belonged to another me. A Judi I didn't want to acknowledge because I liked the newer version of me so much better. But old Judi stuck around and popped her head out from time to time, with sly little comments. *She's getting to know him and love him and then you won't be important to him anymore.* I knew these messy, low-level feelings were part of the process of moving on, but that didn't eradicate having to feel them.

Everything pressed on me. Not a crisis. Just disappointment. Frustration. I had worked so hard on myself and confronted every honesty demon I could think to confront, and some days were still going to be hard. Some days were still going to feel like I was nowhere. The only solution on this particular day was to go for a run. I still hadn't fully healed from a tough half-marathon I did the month before (squeezed in between all my travels). The race had been on a slippery paved trail and I had to change my gait to stabilize and not fall (Tip: don't run thirteen miles on a slippery surface). It wound up causing a lot of pain in my hips and knees, and even though the pain was mostly gone, running hadn't been much fun in the weeks since. I suited up anyway, because I have learned from the past twenty-three years of running that once you put on the running clothes, there is no reason not to just go run.

After the first mile, I was feeling loose—far better than I had felt since the half-marathon. My pace was strong, but the muscles of my face were pinched. I was thinking *so hard*. Donald Trump. My kid. The other man. Midlife. Busy holidays ahead. My brother. An honesty journey with no end. I picked up my pace, as I often do when I'm full of pissed-off sadness, and Ron Sexsmith, whose vocals I love but are depressing as hell, shuffled onto my iPod. I had forgotten to choose a playlist, so my iPod was on random shuffle, which pulled from my entire iTunes library, including songs that are not the best for running. *Great, I can't even get my music right*, I thought.

And then, around mile three, a Disney princess song came on. It was about Snow White baking a cake. Georgia used to be obsessed with Disney princesses. I had tried so hard to dissuade her from loving princesses, reading her books about female scientists and writers and artists and revolutionaries. But she loved those fucking princesses. There is a hilarious video from when she was about three that shows me trying to convince her to be literally *anything else* besides a princess for Halloween, and she keeps saying, "I wanna be a pwincess!" She wore a crown every day for an entire year. *Every day*. One crown would break and we'd buy another at Party City or Target.

Instead of hitting the forward button, I let the song play for a minute. It was five thousand kinds of ridiculous. The dwarfs were helping Snow White measure flour to make the cake. I started to laugh. Georgia hated princesses now. All princess-related apparel and accessories had been vanquished and she didn't even want to see pictures of herself wearing a crown. "How stupid," she would say, and I would tell her it was all part of growing up. "You contain multitudes," I would say, wanting extra parent points for quoting Walt Whitman. She would scrunch up her nose and walk away.

I kept running, and the ridiculous Disney princess song played. I laughed and I lightened and I remembered that I, too, contained multitudes.

Honesty Principles

1. First, be aware. (Chapter 3)

2. Not every situation is the same. (Chapter 3)

3. Be mindful of emotions. (Chapter 4)

4. Intention matters. So does refinement. (Chapter 4)

5. Think about who you are being. (Chapter 5)

6. Say what you mean, but don't be a jerk. (Chapter 6)

7. Is it your truth to tell? (Chapter 6)

8. Mine all parts of the conversation. (Chapter 7)

9. When you love someone, honesty is about sharing with a loving purpose. (Chapter 7)

10. You don't need to pit honesty and otherworldly belief against each other. (Chapter 8)

11. Today is a new day. (Chapter 9)

Sources

Introduction: Paying Attention to Honesty

"A 2018 paper found," Ximena Garcia-Rada, Heather E.
Mann, Lars Hornuf, Matthias Sohn, Juan Tafurt, Edwin S.
Iversen Jr., and Dan Ariely (2018), "The Adaptive Liar: An
Interactionist Approach of Multiple Dishonesty Domains,"
CESifo Working Paper No. 7215, Category 13: Behavioural
Economics, cesifo-group.de/DocDL/cesifo1_wp7215.pdf.

Chapter 1: My Strange Relationship with Honesty

Judi Ketteler, "It's the Almost That Defines Your Story,"
October 23, 2013, blog post, judiketteler.com/blog/
its-the-almost-that-defines-your-story.

Judi Ketteler, "Monday Morning, in Front of Third Graders,"
November 22, 2013, blog post, judiketteler.com/blog/
monday-morning-in-front-of-third-graders.

Chapter 2: What Is Honesty, Anyway?

"Trump was peddling a theory," Michael D. Shear and Julie
Hirschfeld Davis, "Sean Spicer Repeats Trump's Unproven
Wiretapping Allegation," *New York Times*, March 31, 2017,
nytimes.com/2017/03/31/us/politics/sean-spicer-trump-
wiretapping.html.

Judi Ketteler, "Uphill Climb: Seven Stories on Seven Hills,"
Cincinnati Magazine, November 8, 2017, cincinnatimagazine.
com/columns/uphill-climb-seven-stories-seven-hills.

"Three Minute Philosophy," Immanuel Kant, YouTube video, youtube.com/watch?v=xwOCmJevigw&t=38s.

Thomas Carson, *Lying and Deception: Theory and Practice* (Oxford University Press, 2010).

"Dentist making a big investment," Dan Ariely, *The (Honest) Truth About Dishonesty* (New York: HarperCollins, 2012), 67.

Chapter 3: Is Honesty Really the Best Policy?

"Fudge factor," Ariely, *The (Honest) Truth About Dishonesty*, 27.

"Participants are given a sheet with a grid of numbers," ibid, 17.

"If people are reminded about the value of honesty," ibid, 39.

"My boyfriend won't have sex with me," Seth Stephens-Davidowitz, *Everybody Lies: Big Data, New Data, and What the Internet Can Tell Us About Who We Really Are* (New York: HarperCollins, 2017), 123.

"Side-by-side comparison of the top words," ibid, 160.

"University of Maryland survey of graduates," ibid, 107.

"25 percent prosocial lies," B. M. DePaulo, D. A. Kashy, S. E. Kirkendol, M. M. Wyer, and J. A. Epstein (1996), "Lying in Everyday Life," *Journal of Personality and Social Psychology*, 70(5): 979.

J. P. Gaspar, E. E. Levine, and M. E. Schweitzer (2015), "Why We Should Lie," *Organizational Dynamics*, 44(4): 306–309.

"Prosocial lying can increase trust," E. E. Levine and M. E. Schweitzer (2015), "Prosocial Lies: When Deception Breeds Trust," *Organizational Behavior and Human Decision Processes*, 126: 88–106.

Yael Melamede, *(Dis) Honesty: The Truth About Lies* (2015), documentary.

"A University of Notre Dame study," Anita Kelly (2012),
    "A Life Without Lies: How Living Honestly Can
    Affect Health," Study presented at the American
    Psychological Association's convention, apa.org/news/press/
    releases/2012/08/lying-less.aspx.

"research that looks at honesty from the communicator's
    perspective," E. E. Levine and T. R. Cohen (2018), "You
    Can Handle the Truth: Mispredicting the Consequences of
    Honest Communication," *Journal of Experimental Psychology:
    General,* 147(9): 1400–1429.

"60 percent of people lied," R. S. Feldman, J. A. Forrest,
    and B. R. Happ (2002), "Self-Presentation and Verbal
    Deception: Do Self-Presenters Lie More?" *Basic and Applied
    Social Psychology,* 24: 163–170.

Judi Ketteler, "How Honesty Could Make You Happier," *New
    York Times,* September 19, 2017, nytimes.com/2017/09/19/
    well/mind/how-honesty-could-make-you-happier.html.

Gretchen Rubin, *The Happiness Project, Or, Why I Spent a Year
    Trying to Sing in the Morning, Clean My Closets, Fight Right,
    Read Aristotle, and Generally Have More Fun* (New York:
    HarperCollins, 2009), 10.

Chapter 4: Honesty in Social Situations

"Heintz and other researchers theorize," C. Heintz, C. M.
    Karabegovic, and A. Molnar (2016), "The Co-evolution of
    Honesty and Strategic Vigilance," *Frontiers in Psychology,*
    7: 1503.

"a group of Jewish diamond merchants," Barak Richman (2006),
    "How Community Institutions Create Economic Advantage:
    Jewish Diamond Merchants in New York," *Law & Social
    Inquiry,* 31(2): 383–420.

"Lupoli and his colleagues tested this," M. J. Lupoli, L. Jampol, and C. Oveis (2017), "Lying Because We Care: Compassion Increases Prosocial Lying," *Journal of Experimental Psychology: General,* 146(7): 1026–1042.

"prosocial lies of omission in health care settings," E. E. Levine, J. Hart, K. Moore, E. Rubin, K. Yadav, and S. Halpern (2018), "The Surprising Costs of Silence: Asymmetric Preferences for Prosocial Lies of Commission and Omission," *Journal of Personality and Social Psychology,* 114(1): 29–51.

"a Massachusetts antiques dealer," John Banks, "'I Cheated,' Says Woodworker Who Fooled the Antiques Experts," *New York Times,* March 11, 2018, nytimes.com/2018/03/11/arts/i-cheated-says-woodworker-who-fooled-the-antiques-experts.html.

"a young woman who made a video letter," Ania Bartkowiak and Mengwen Cao, "Coming Out to My Parents in China by Video," *New York Times,* June 22, 2018, nytimes.com/2018/06/22/lens/coming-out-video-china.html.

Chapter 5: Workplace Honesty

"boil moral character into three basic components," T. R. Cohen and L. Morse (2014), "Moral Character: What It Is and What It Does," *Research in Organizational Behavior,* 34: 43–61.

"Cohen's research looks at two types of behaviors," Taya Cohen and A. Panter, "Character Traits in the Workplace: A Three-Month Diary Study of Moral and Immoral Organizational Behaviors," in *Character: New Directions from Philosophy, Psychology, and Theology* (Oxford University Press, 2015).

"Don't be a cheater," C. J. Bryan, G. S. Adams, and B. Monin (2013), "When Cheating Would Make You a Cheater: Implicating the Self Prevents Unethical Behavior," *Journal of Experimental Psychology: General,* 142(4): 1001–1005.

"Netherlands study," J. L. van Gelder, H. E. Hershfield, and L. F. Nordgren (2013), "Vividness of the Future Self Predicts Delinquency," *Psychological Science*, 24(6): 974–980.

"Leavitt and his colleagues studied Army medics," Keith Leavitt, Scott Reynolds, Christopher Barnes, Pauline Schilpzand, and Sean Hannah (2012), "Different Hats, Different Obligations: Plural Occupational Identities and Situated Moral Judgments," *Academy of Management Journal*, 55(6): 1316–1333.

"the identity you claim related to your job," Keith Leavitt and David Sluss (2015), "Lying for Who We Are: An Identity-Based Model of Workplace Dishonesty," *Academy of Management Review*, 40(4): 587–610.

"humblebragging," Ovul Sezer, Gino Francesca, and Michael I. Norton (2018), "Humblebragging: A Distinct—and Ineffective—Self-Presentation Strategy," *Journal of Personality and Social Psychology*, 114(1): 52–74.

"Honesty/Ethics in Professions," Gallup poll, news.gallup.com/poll/1654/honesty-ethics-professions.aspx (Date accessed, December 31, 2018; link seems to be continually updated with latest poll numbers.)

"people who discovered they've been paltered to," T. Rogers, R. Zeckhauser, F. Gino, M. Schweitzer, and M. Norton (2016), "Artful Paltering: The Risks and Rewards of Using Truthful Statements to Mislead Others," *Journal of Personality and Social Psychology*, 112(3): 456–473.

Chapter 6: Honesty in Friendship

Brené Brown, *Daring Greatly: How the Courage to Be Vulnerable Transforms the Way We Live, Love, Parent, and Lead* (New York: Gotham Books, 2012), 34.

"large cross-cultural study of more than 270,000 adults," William Chopik (2017), "Associations Among Relational Values, Support, Health, and Well-Being Across the Adult Lifespan," *Personal Relationships*, 24(2): 408–422.

Belén López-Pérez, Laura Howells, and Michaela Gummerum (2017), "Cruel to Be Kind: Factors Underlying Altruistic Efforts to Worsen Another Person's Mood," *Psychological Science*, 28(7): 862–871.

"Researchers at Wilfrid Laurier University," C. Friesen and L. K. Kammrath (2011), "What It Pays to Know About a Close Other: The Value of Contextualized 'If-Then' Personality Knowledge in Close Relationships," *Psychological Science*, 22: 567–571.

Deborah Tannen, *You're the Only One I Can Tell: Inside the Language of Women's Friendships* (New York: Ballantine Books, 2017), 54.

Sarah Knight, *The Life-Changing Magic of Not Giving a F*ck* (New York: Little, Brown and Company, 2015).

Chapter 7: Honesty in Marriage

"Visceral, loaded, and polarized," Esther Perel, *The State of Affairs: Rethinking Infidelity* (New York: Harper, 2017), 5.

"When we reduce conversation," ibid, 7.

Susan Dominus, "Is an Open Marriage a Happier Marriage?" *New York Times*, May 11, 2017, nytimes.com/2017/05/11/magazine/is-an-open-marriage-a-happier-marriage.html.

"The human imagination," Perel, *State of Affairs*, 43.

"We ask them to be vulnerable," Brown, *Daring Greatly*, 95.

"In each of these conversations," Douglas Stone, Bruce Patton, and Sheila Heen, *Difficult Conversations: How to Discuss What Matters Most*, 2nd edition (New York: Penguin Books, 2010), 7.

"As a rule," ibid, 7.

"Good listening," ibid, 89.

"A cherished aspect of how you see yourself," ibid, 114.

"why people break promises in interpersonal relationships," J. Peetz and L. K. Kammrath (2011), "Only Because I Love You: Why People Make and Why They Break Promises in Romantic Relationships," *Journal of Personality and Social Psychology*, 100: 887–904.

"Anne Gordon, associate professor of psychology," M. E. Kaplar and A. K. Gordon (2004), "The Enigma of Altruistic Lying: Perspective Differences in What Motivates and Justifies Lie Telling Within Romantic Relationships," *Personal Relationships*, 11: 489–507.

Michelle Obama, *Becoming* (New York: Crown, 2018), 51–52.

"Why did we have to go through an affair," Perel, *State of Affairs*, 16.

Chapter 8: Honesty and Parenting

Bonnie Rough, "The New Birds and Bees: Teaching Kids About Boundaries and Consent," *New York Times*, September 27, 2018, nytimes.com/2018/09/27/well/family/the-new-birds-and-bees-teaching-kids-about-boundaries-and-consent.html.

"Research from the University of California–San Diego," Chelsea Hays and Leslie J. Carver (2014), "Follow the Liar: The Effects of Adult Lies on Children's Honesty," *Developmental Science*, 17(6): 977–983.

"News release about Hays study," sciencedaily.com/
releases/2014/03/140319093802.htm.

"Another study out of the Massachusetts Institute of
Technology," H. Gweon, H. Pelton, J. A. Konopka, and
L. E. Schulz (2014), "Sins of Omission: Children Selectively
Explore When Agents Fail to Tell the Whole Truth,"
Cognition, 132: 335–341.

"Victoria Talwar, a psychologist at McGill University in Canada,"
Victoria Talwar et al. (2016), "Children's Evaluations
of Tattles, Confessions, Prosocial and Antisocial Lies,"
International Review of Pragmatics, 8: 334–352.

"News release about Talwar study," mcgill.ca/newsroom/channels/
news/truth-about-lying-childrens-perceptions-get-more-
nuanced-age-263168.

Robert Feldman, *The Liar in Your Life: The Way to Truthful
Relationships* (New York: Hachette Book Group, 2009), 66.

Amy Dockser Marcus, "Two Sisters Bought DNA Kits. The
Results Blew Apart Their Family," *The Wall Street Journal*,
February 1, 2019, wsj.com/articles/two-sisters-bought-dna-
kits-the-results-blew-apart-their-family-11549037904.

Peter Rober (2017), "Silence and Memories of War: An
Autoethnographic Exploration of Family Secrecy," *Family
Process*, 56(1): 250–261.

Peter Rober, Geertje Walravens, and Leen Versteynen (2012), "In
Search of a Tale They Can Live With: About Loss, Family
Secrets, and Selective Disclosure," *Journal of Marital and
Family Therapy*, 38(3): 529–541.

Glennon Doyle, "First the Pain, Then the Rising," momastery.
com/blog/2017/05/10/first-the-pain-then-the-rising.

———, "Pain Is Not a Mistake," momastery.com/
blog/2015/04/21/pain-mistake.

Judi Ketteler, "Connecting, Midair, with My 8-Year Old Son," *New York Times*, October 6, 2017, nytimes.com/2017/10/06/well/family/connecting-midair-with-my-8-year-old-son.html.

————, "When Is a Child Instagram Ready?" *New York Times*, February 21, 2018, nytimes.com/2018/02/21/well/family/children-technology-instagram-youtube.html.

Kim Brooks, *Small Animals: Parenthood in the Age of Fear* (New York: Flatiron Books, 2018).

Bethany Van Delft, "Light and Hope," for *The Moth*, April 11, 2014, themoth.org/stories/light-and-hope.

Chapter 9: Self-Honesty and the Stories We Tell

Jeannette Walls, *The Glass Castle* (New York: Scribner, 2005).

Zoë Chance, Gino Francesca, Michael I. Norton, and Dan Ariely (2015), "The Slow Decay and Quick Revival of Self-Deception," *Frontiers in Psychology*, 6: 1–6.

Hannah Gadsby, *Nanette*, 2018, Netflix special.

Acknowledgments

THIS BOOK BEGAN WITH AN ARTICLE I wrote for Toby Bilanow at *The New York Times*. Thanks, Toby, for taking a chance on a wacky idea and for always letting my voice come through in the pieces we work on together.

I wouldn't be anywhere without my longtime agent, Joy Tutela, who has been the biggest champion of my writing from the beginning, even when I was only half-formed as a writer. Also, many thanks to the other folks at David Black Literary Agency, including Susan Raihofer and Jenny Herrera.

Special thanks to my editor at Kensington Books, Denise Silvestro. I knew I wanted to work with you from the very first phone call, Denise. Thank you for making this book the best version of what it could be. Thank you to the entire editing and design team at Kensington, and also thanks to Ann Pryor and the awesome publicity team for working so hard to get this book into the world.

Thanks to Kate Hanley and Jodi Helmer for your friendship and support. You two ladies are my people. Amy Paturel, you always have the best feedback. So many other colleagues have a knack for offering an encouraging word at the exact right moment and making me feel like a writing rock star, particularly Jenny Fink, Karen Kroll, Laura Laing, Carla Levy, and Richard Curtis. Meagan Francis, thanks for being there for me during a confusing time in my marriage. Ditto that, Paige Byam Soliday. And P.S., thanks for also teaching me how to write, way back when.

John Fox, my editor at *Cincinnati Magazine*, thank you for letting me "test out" honesty-related ideas in my bi-monthly column (even if you didn't quite know that's what I was doing). And to Roberta Zeff at *The New York Times*, thanks for wading into the "kids on Instagram" waters with me. It definitely provided fodder for this book!

Kelly Kautz, thank you for sharing your story. Dan, Ivy, Sarah, Rachel and Rafeé, and Mike, thank you for letting me use your stories in the book, and thanks for reminiscing with me, Tim. I have chosen to keep some people anonymous because of privacy reasons, but know that I am grateful for your willingness to let me tell certain stories that involve you.

For taking the time to discuss research and sort through concepts, thank you to Thomas Carson, Emma Levine, Yael Melamede, Robert Feldman, Christophe Heintz, Matt Lupoli, Taya Cohen, Keith Leavitt, Ivan Oransky, Todd Rogers, Lara Kammrath, Anne Gordon, Peter Rober, and Zoe Chance. Lizzie Post, Amy Lang, KJ Dell'Antonia, and Jeannette Walls, thank you for being so generous with your time and for being willing to indulge all of my questions about not-easy topics like (respectively) etiquette versus lying, explaining orgasms to tweens, dealing with parent shame, and overcoming fear of telling your story.

I've pulled from the work of many researchers, too numerous to cite here. But I must mention Dan Ariely, Brené Brown, and Esther Perel, because I am indebted to their ideas. And Layla Saad, I found you later than I wish I would have, but I'm so grateful for your voice.

My family is my starting point, and my rallying point. To my sisters Laura Thomason and Nancy Porras, thank you for a lifetime of friendship and for our Sunday afternoon conversations. To my other sister, Claire Ketteler, we've been long distance for so long, but you'll always be my big sister who knows more than me. To my two living brothers, Tony Ketteler and Herb Ketteler . . . let's face it, you didn't actually do anything related to this book, but you're always good to share a laugh with and bring the snacks. To my deceased brother, Paul Ketteler, I see you now, and I love our conversations.

To my mom, Mary Ketteler, you are so funny and so earnest, and you have the best stories. I should have listened to them better when I was younger, but I'm listening now. Thanks for showing me a happy marriage, and for instilling in me what matters. And to my dad, Bert Ketteler, thanks for looking after me from wherever you are. I don't know what I believe, but I like to believe you're in my corner and that you hear what I say.

To my husband, Allen. Thomas Hardy may have brought us together, but we left that gloomy Gus behind a while ago. I'm so glad that we're not most people. Thank you for making the strange journey with me, and for being okay with your starring role in this book.

Finally, to my kids, Maxx and Georgia, who distracted me at every turn and reminded me that life doesn't happen inside a Word document.

About the Author

JUDI KETTELER has written for dozens of publications such as *The New York Times, Better Homes & Gardens, Good Housekeeping, Runner's World, Self, Women's Health*, and many others. She's also an award-winning columnist for *Cincinnati Magazine*, where she writes pieces about the weirdness of midlife.

She is the author of *Sew Retro: A Stylish History of the Sewing Revolution + 25 Vintage-Inspired Projects for the Modern Girl* and *The Spoonflower Handbook: A DIY Guide to Designing Fabric, Wallpaper & Gift Wrap.*

When she's not writing, Judi loves running, yoga, and flea markets. She lives with her husband and two young children in Cincinnati, Ohio.

Learn more about Judi at www.judiketteler.com.